# "Speaking of Inalienable Rights, Amy…"

## Doonesbury books by G. B. Trudeau

Still a Few Bugs in the System
The President Is a Lot Smarter Than You Think
But This War Had Such Promise
Call Me When You Find America
Guilty, Guilty, Guilty!
"What Do We Have for the Witnesses, Johnnie?"
Dare To Be Great, Ms. Caucus
Wouldn't a Gremlin Have Been More Sensible?
"Speaking of Inalienable Rights, Amy . . ."
You're Never Too Old for Nuts and Berries
An Especially Tricky People
As the Kid Goes for Broke
Stalking the Perfect Tan
"Any Grooming Hints for Your Fans, Rollie?"
But the Pension Fund Was Just Sitting There
We're Not Out of the Woods Yet
A Tad Overweight, but Violet Eyes to Die For

**In Large Format**

The Doonesbury Chronicles
Doonesbury's Greatest Hits

a Doonesbury classic by

*GB Trudeau.*

# "Speaking of Inalienable Rights, Amy…"

**Holt, Rinehart and Winston**
New York

Published by Holt, Rinehart and Winston, 383 Madison Avenue,
New York, New York 10017.

Published simultaneously in Canada by Holt, Rinehart and
Winston of Canada, Limited.

Library of Congress Catalog Card Number: 75-29722

ISBN: 0-03-017221-7

Printed in the United States of America


The cartoons in this book have appeared in newspapers
in the United States and abroad under the auspices of
Universal Press Syndicate.

10 9 8 7 6 5

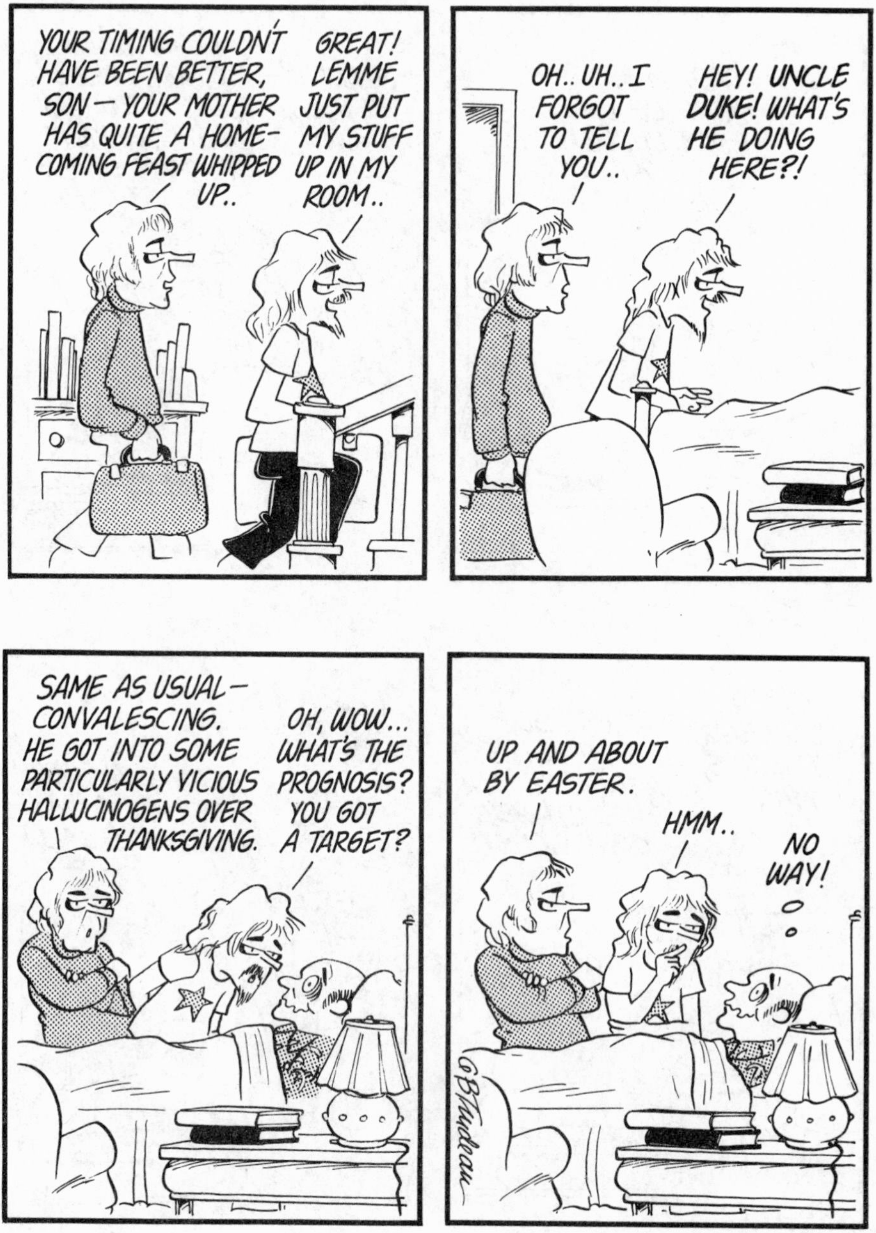
YOUR TIMING COULDN'T HAVE BEEN BETTER, SON— YOUR MOTHER HAS QUITE A HOME-COMING FEAST WHIPPED UP..
GREAT! LEMME JUST PUT MY STUFF UP IN MY ROOM..
OH.. UH.. I FORGOT TO TELL YOU..
HEY! UNCLE DUKE! WHAT'S HE DOING HERE?!
SAME AS USUAL— CONVALESCING. HE GOT INTO SOME PARTICULARLY VICIOUS HALLUCINOGENS OVER THANKSGIVING.
OH, WOW... WHAT'S THE PROGNOSIS? YOU GOT A TARGET?
UP AND ABOUT BY EASTER.
HMM..
NO WAY!
G B Trudeau

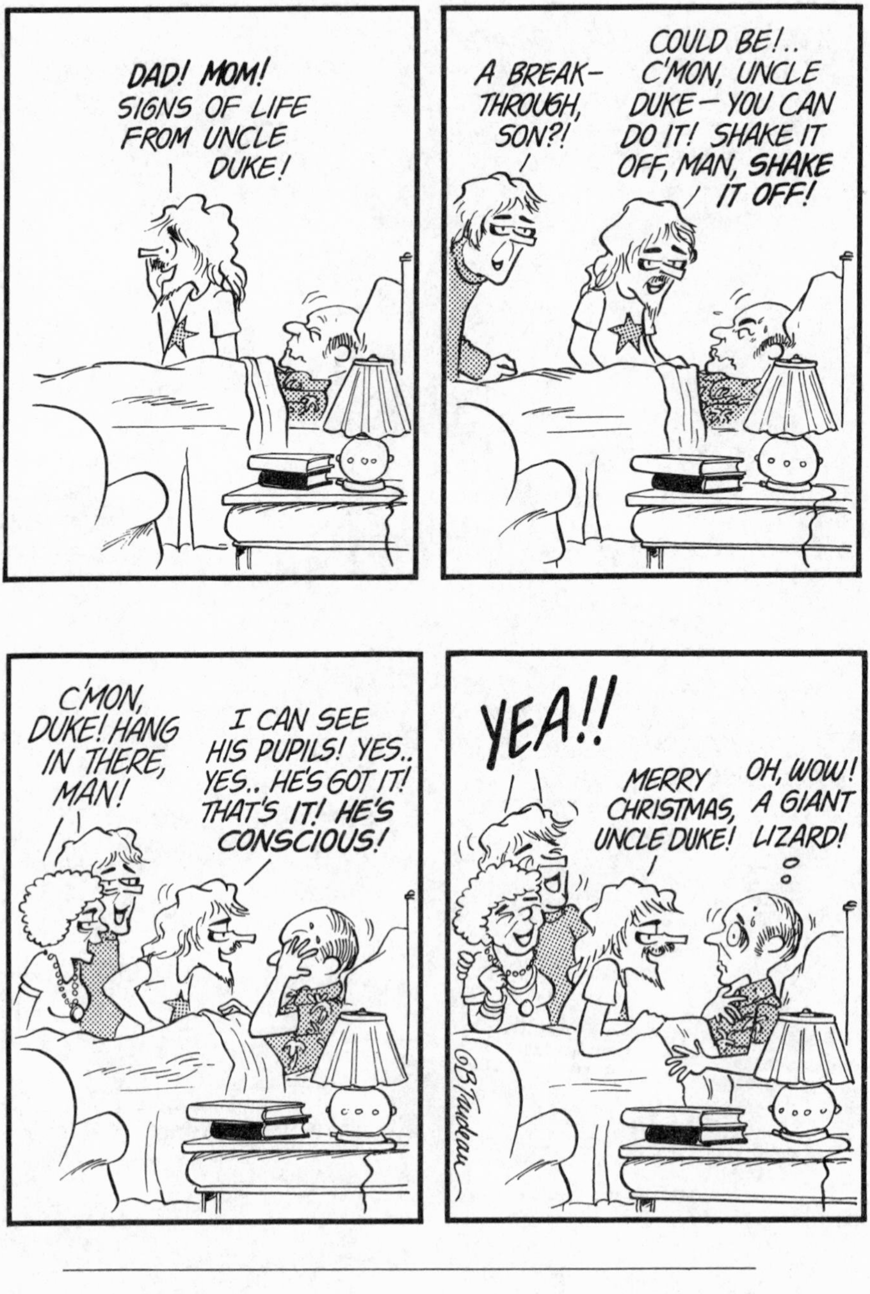
DAD! MOM! SIGNS OF LIFE FROM UNCLE DUKE!
A BREAK-THROUGH, SON?!
COULD BE!.. C'MON, UNCLE DUKE— YOU CAN DO IT! SHAKE IT OFF, MAN, SHAKE IT OFF!
C'MON, DUKE! HANG IN THERE, MAN!
I CAN SEE HIS PUPILS! YES.. YES.. HE'S GOT IT! THAT'S IT! HE'S CONSCIOUS!
YEA!!
MERRY CHRISTMAS, UNCLE DUKE!
OH, WOW! A GIANT LIZARD!
©B Trudeau

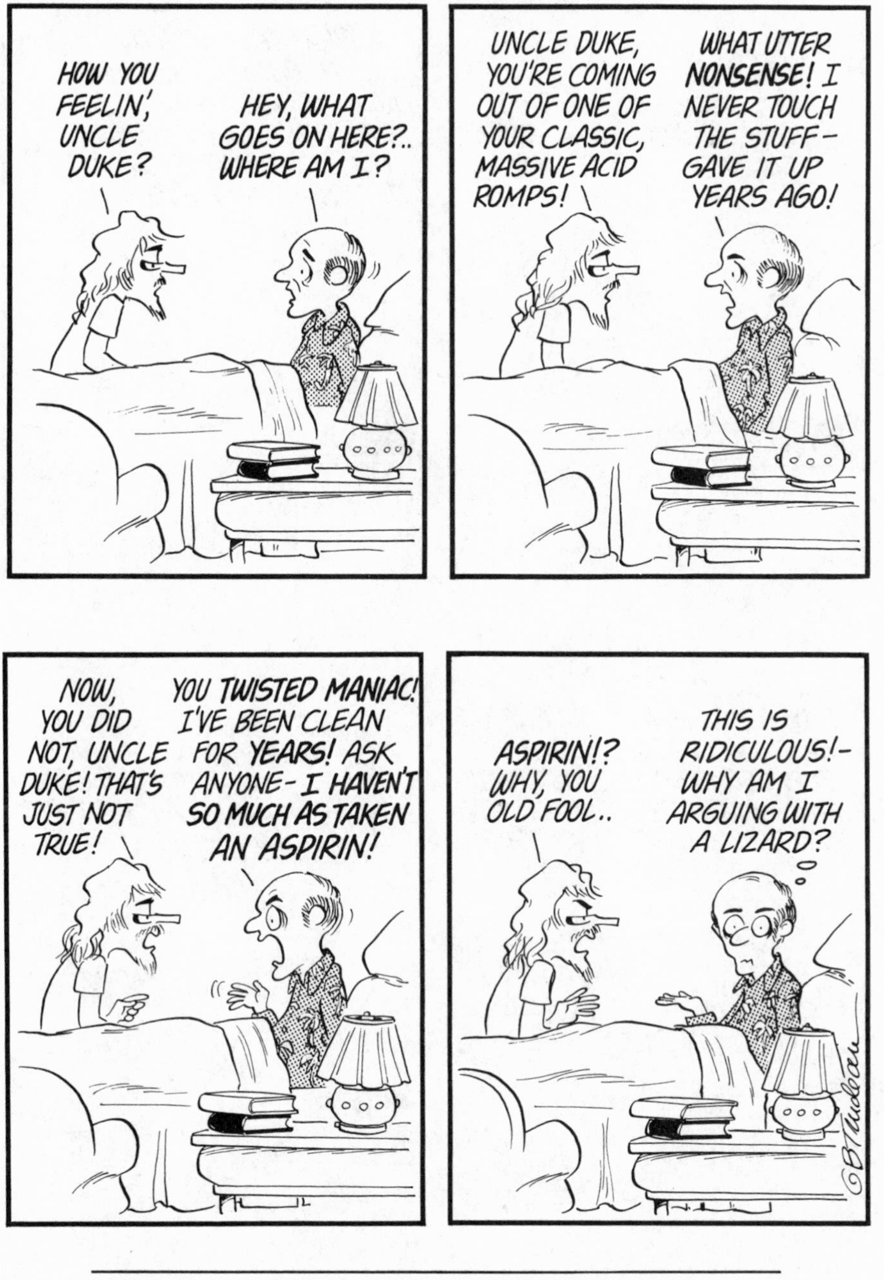
HOW YOU FEELIN', UNCLE DUKE?
HEY, WHAT GOES ON HERE?.. WHERE AM I?
UNCLE DUKE, YOU'RE COMING OUT OF ONE OF YOUR CLASSIC, MASSIVE ACID ROMPS!
WHAT UTTER NONSENSE! I NEVER TOUCH THE STUFF - GAVE IT UP YEARS AGO!
NOW, YOU DID NOT, UNCLE DUKE! THAT'S JUST NOT TRUE!
YOU TWISTED MANIAC! I'VE BEEN CLEAN FOR YEARS! ASK ANYONE - I HAVEN'T SO MUCH AS TAKEN AN ASPIRIN!
ASPIRIN!? WHY, YOU OLD FOOL..
THIS IS RIDICULOUS! - WHY AM I ARGUING WITH A LIZARD?
© B Trudeau

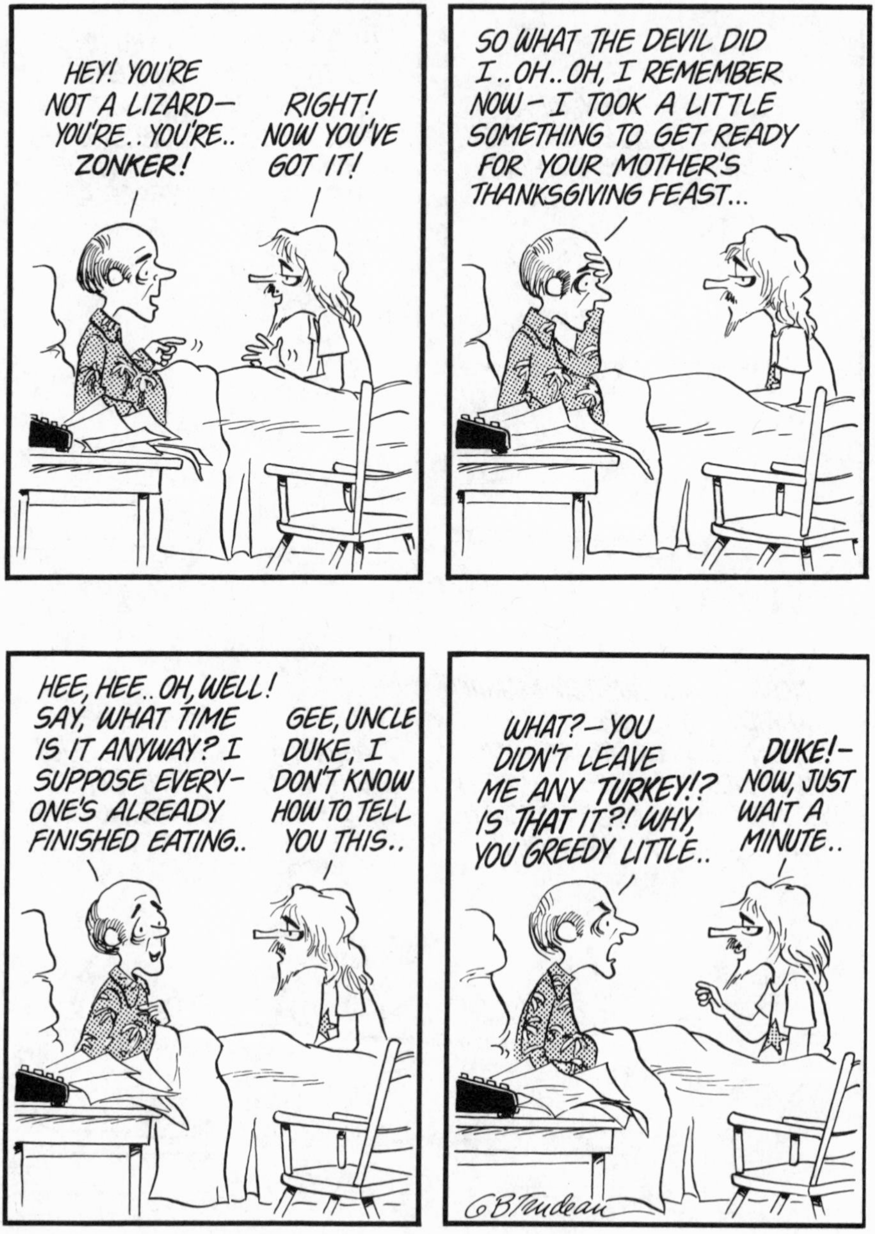
HEY! YOU'RE NOT A LIZARD— YOU'RE.. YOU'RE.. ZONKER!
RIGHT! NOW YOU'VE GOT IT!
SO WHAT THE DEVIL DID I..OH..OH, I REMEMBER NOW – I TOOK A LITTLE SOMETHING TO GET READY FOR YOUR MOTHER'S THANKSGIVING FEAST...
HEE, HEE..OH, WELL! SAY, WHAT TIME IS IT ANYWAY? I SUPPOSE EVERY-ONE'S ALREADY FINISHED EATING..
GEE, UNCLE DUKE, I DON'T KNOW HOW TO TELL YOU THIS..
WHAT?—YOU DIDN'T LEAVE ME ANY TURKEY!? IS THAT IT?! WHY, YOU GREEDY LITTLE..
DUKE!— NOW, JUST WAIT A MINUTE..
GBTrudeau

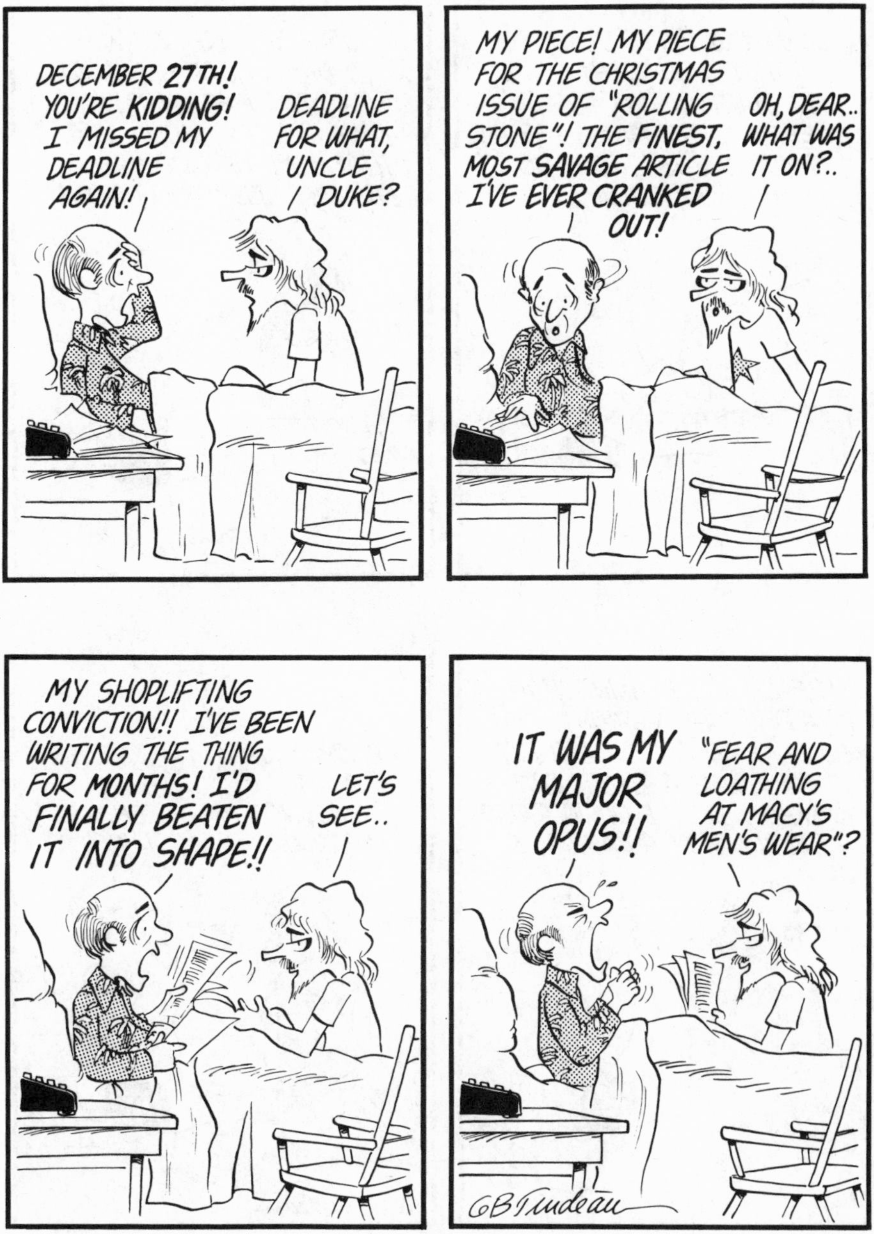
DECEMBER 27TH! YOU'RE KIDDING! I MISSED MY DEADLINE AGAIN!
DEADLINE FOR WHAT, UNCLE DUKE?
MY PIECE! MY PIECE FOR THE CHRISTMAS ISSUE OF "ROLLING STONE"! THE FINEST, MOST SAVAGE ARTICLE I'VE EVER CRANKED OUT!
OH, DEAR.. WHAT WAS IT ON?..
MY SHOPLIFTING CONVICTION!! I'VE BEEN WRITING THE THING FOR MONTHS! I'D FINALLY BEATEN IT INTO SHAPE!!
LET'S SEE..
IT WAS MY MAJOR OPUS!!
"FEAR AND LOATHING AT MACY'S MEN'S WEAR"?
GBTrudeau

YOU KNOW, UNCLE DUKE, I THINK YOU OUGHT TO START GIVING SOME SERIOUS THOUGHT SOME-TIME TO STRAIGHTENING YOURSELF OUT..
RIGHT YOU ARE, ZONK— I DAMN NEAR BLEW OUT ALL MY TUBES ON THAT LAST NUMBER, DIDN'T I?.. THAT KIND OF DERANGED BEHAVIOR JUST CAN'T GO ON!
IN FACT, I'M THINKING THAT IN A FEW DAYS I MIGHT JUST GO BACK TO ASPEN AND TRY TO TURN OVER A NEW LEAF— YOU KNOW, SETTLE DOWN, RAISE A FAMILY, BUY A LABRADOR..
..OPEN UP A LITTLE MASSAGE PARLOR.
OH, DUKE...
GBTrudeau

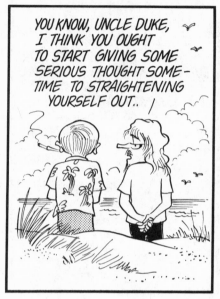

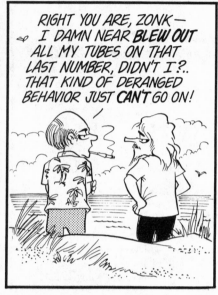

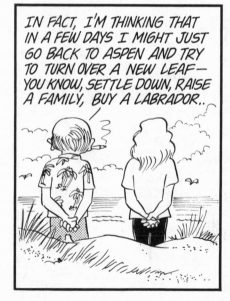

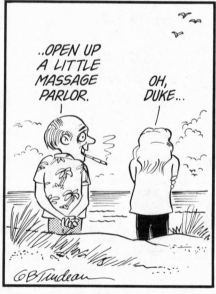

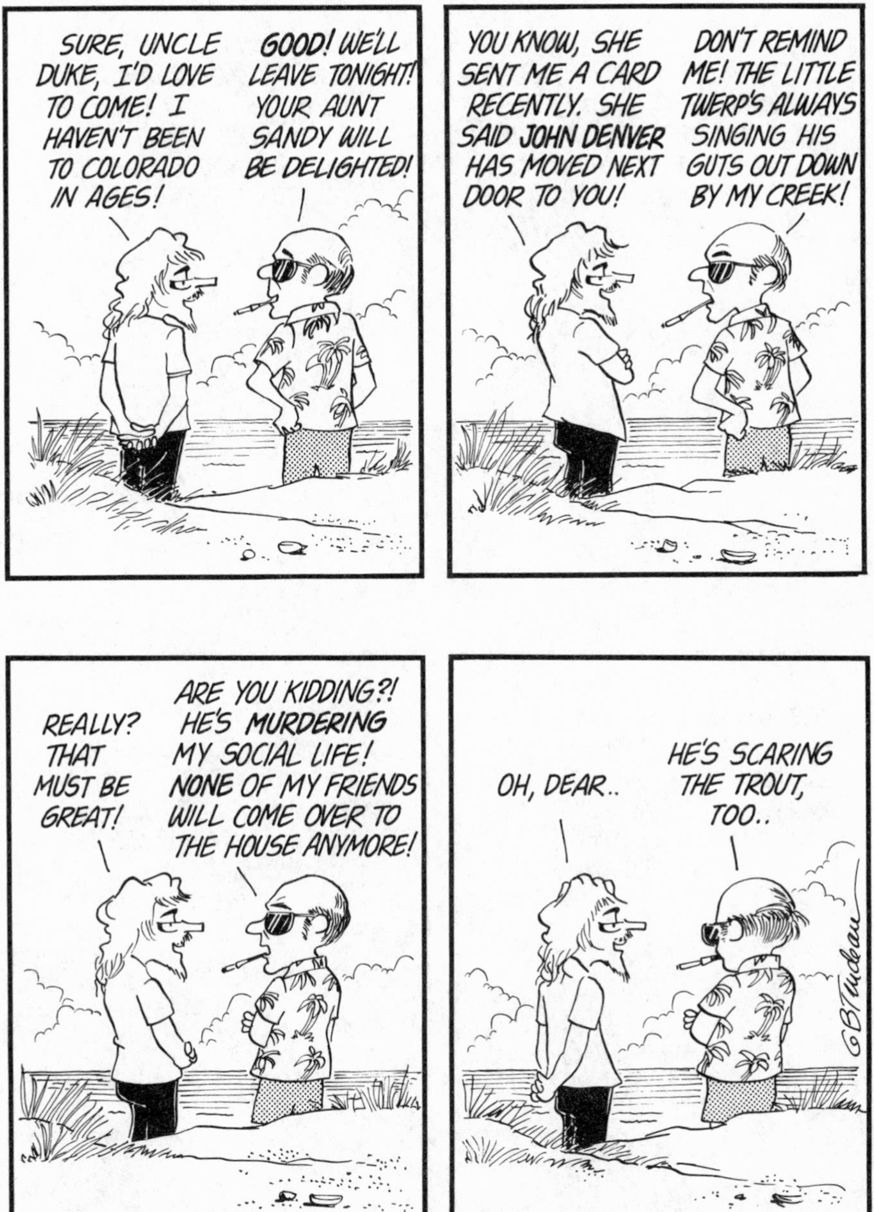
SURE, UNCLE DUKE, I'D LOVE TO COME! I HAVEN'T BEEN TO COLORADO IN AGES!
GOOD! WE'LL LEAVE TONIGHT! YOUR AUNT SANDY WILL BE DELIGHTED!
YOU KNOW, SHE SENT ME A CARD RECENTLY. SHE SAID JOHN DENVER HAS MOVED NEXT DOOR TO YOU!
DON'T REMIND ME! THE LITTLE TWERP'S ALWAYS SINGING HIS GUTS OUT DOWN BY MY CREEK!
REALLY? THAT MUST BE GREAT!
ARE YOU KIDDING?! HE'S MURDERING MY SOCIAL LIFE! NONE OF MY FRIENDS WILL COME OVER TO THE HOUSE ANYMORE!
OH, DEAR..
HE'S SCARING THE TROUT, TOO..
©BTrudeau

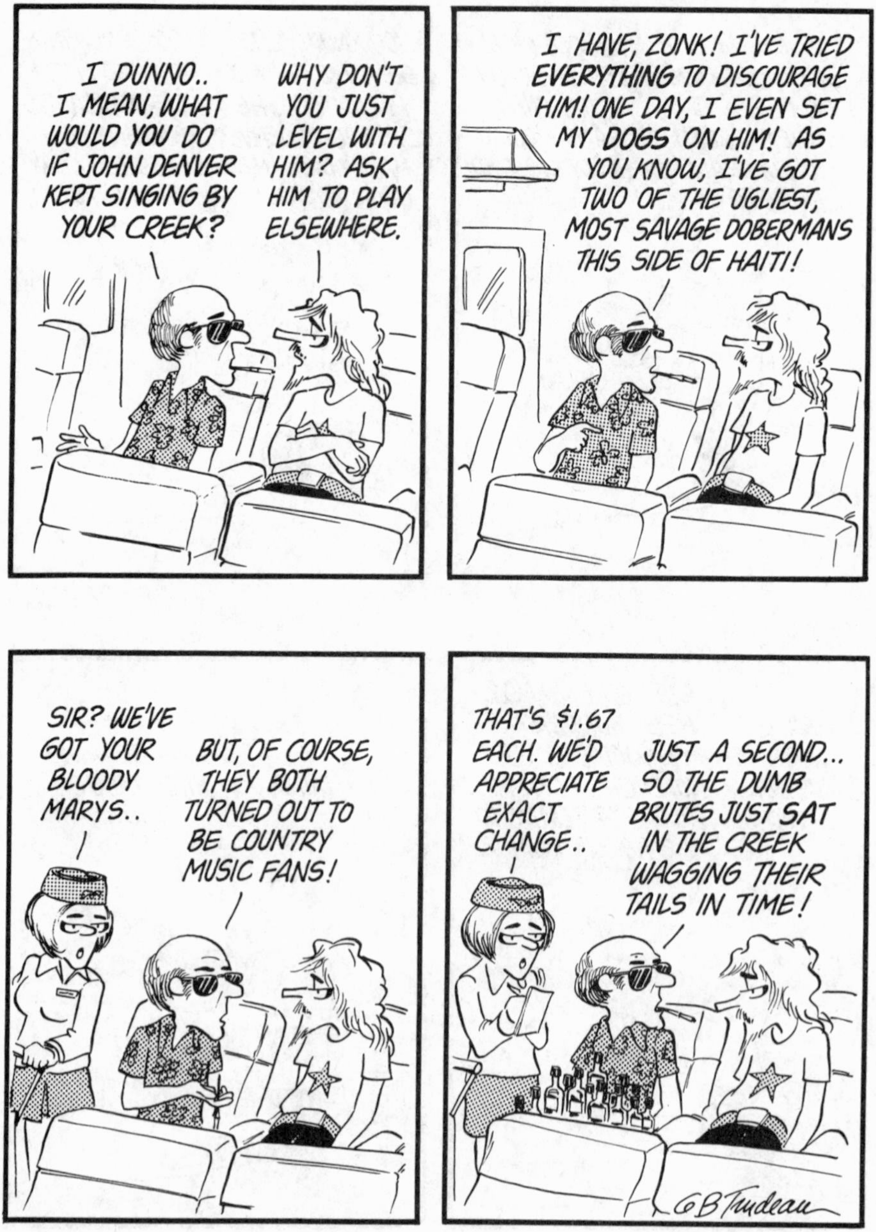
I DUNNO.. I MEAN, WHAT WOULD YOU DO IF JOHN DENVER KEPT SINGING BY YOUR CREEK?
WHY DON'T YOU JUST LEVEL WITH HIM? ASK HIM TO PLAY ELSEWHERE.
I HAVE, ZONK! I'VE TRIED EVERYTHING TO DISCOURAGE HIM! ONE DAY, I EVEN SET MY DOGS ON HIM! AS YOU KNOW, I'VE GOT TWO OF THE UGLIEST, MOST SAVAGE DOBERMANS THIS SIDE OF HAITI!
SIR? WE'VE GOT YOUR BLOODY MARYS..
BUT, OF COURSE, THEY BOTH TURNED OUT TO BE COUNTRY MUSIC FANS!
THAT'S $1.67 EACH. WE'D APPRECIATE EXACT CHANGE..
JUST A SECOND... SO THE DUMB BRUTES JUST SAT IN THE CREEK WAGGING THEIR TAILS IN TIME!
GBTrudeau

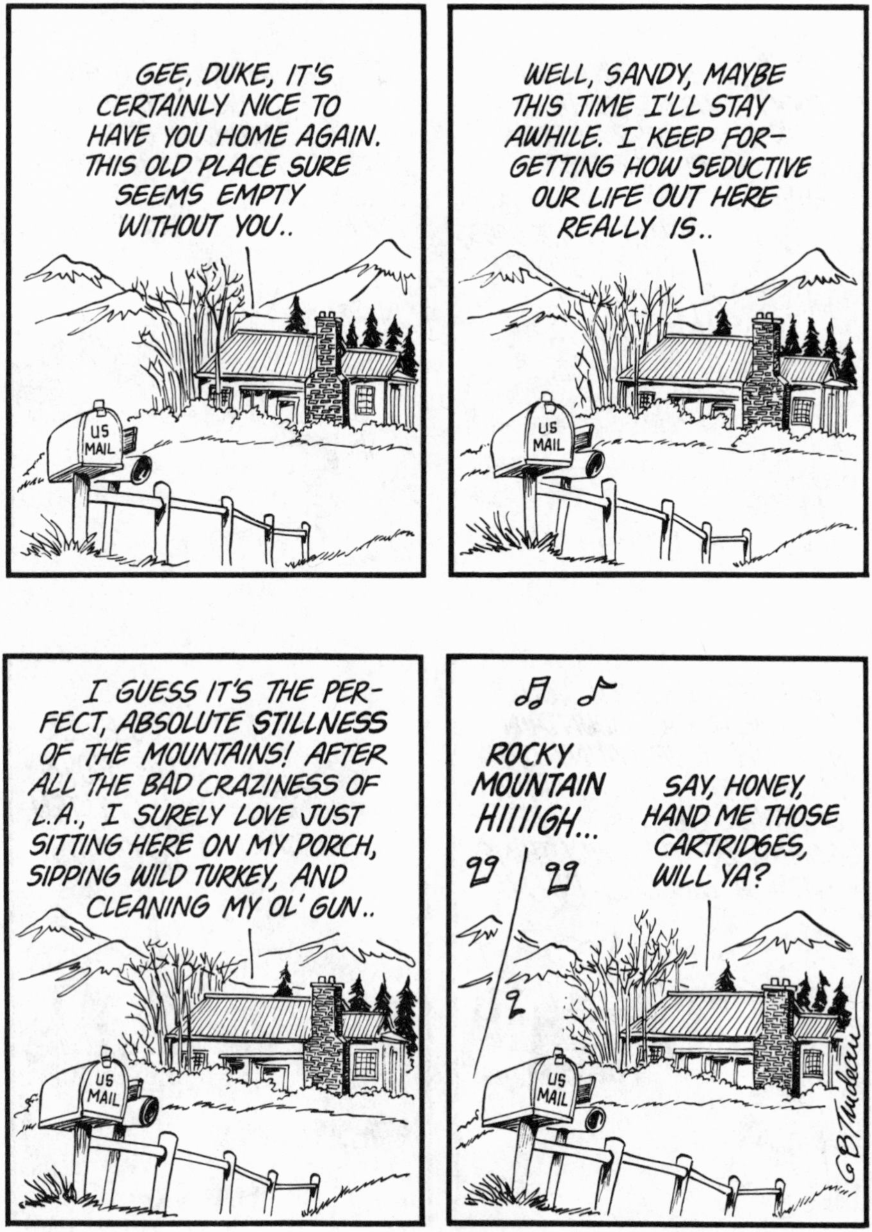
GEE, DUKE, IT'S CERTAINLY NICE TO HAVE YOU HOME AGAIN. THIS OLD PLACE SURE SEEMS EMPTY WITHOUT YOU..
US MAIL
WELL, SANDY, MAYBE THIS TIME I'LL STAY AWHILE. I KEEP FOR-GETTING HOW SEDUCTIVE OUR LIFE OUT HERE REALLY IS..
US MAIL
I GUESS IT'S THE PER-FECT, ABSOLUTE STILLNESS OF THE MOUNTAINS! AFTER ALL THE BAD CRAZINESS OF L.A., I SURELY LOVE JUST SITTING HERE ON MY PORCH, SIPPING WILD TURKEY, AND CLEANING MY OL' GUN..
US MAIL
ROCKY MOUNTAIN HIIIIGH...
SAY, HONEY, HAND ME THOSE CARTRIDGES, WILL YA?
US MAIL
GBTrudeau

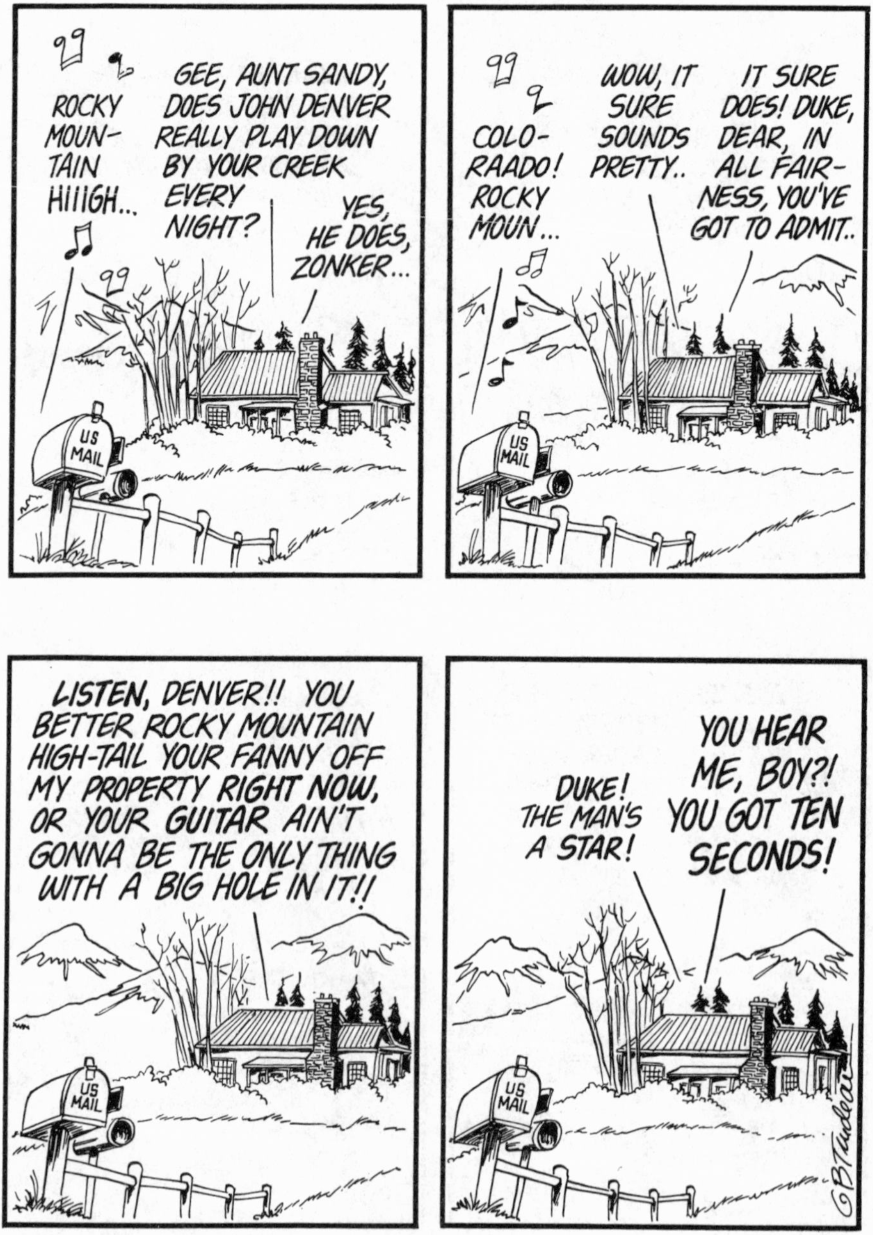
ROCKY MOUNTAIN HIIIGH...
GEE, AUNT SANDY, DOES JOHN DENVER REALLY PLAY DOWN BY YOUR CREEK EVERY NIGHT?
YES, HE DOES, ZONKER...
COLO-RAADO! ROCKY MOUN...
WOW, IT SURE SOUNDS PRETTY..
IT SURE DOES! DUKE, DEAR, IN ALL FAIRNESS, YOU'VE GOT TO ADMIT..
LISTEN, DENVER!! YOU BETTER ROCKY MOUNTAIN HIGH-TAIL YOUR FANNY OFF MY PROPERTY RIGHT NOW, OR YOUR GUITAR AIN'T GONNA BE THE ONLY THING WITH A BIG HOLE IN IT!!
DUKE! THE MAN'S A STAR!
YOU HEAR ME, BOY?! YOU GOT TEN SECONDS!
US MAIL
© GBTrudeau

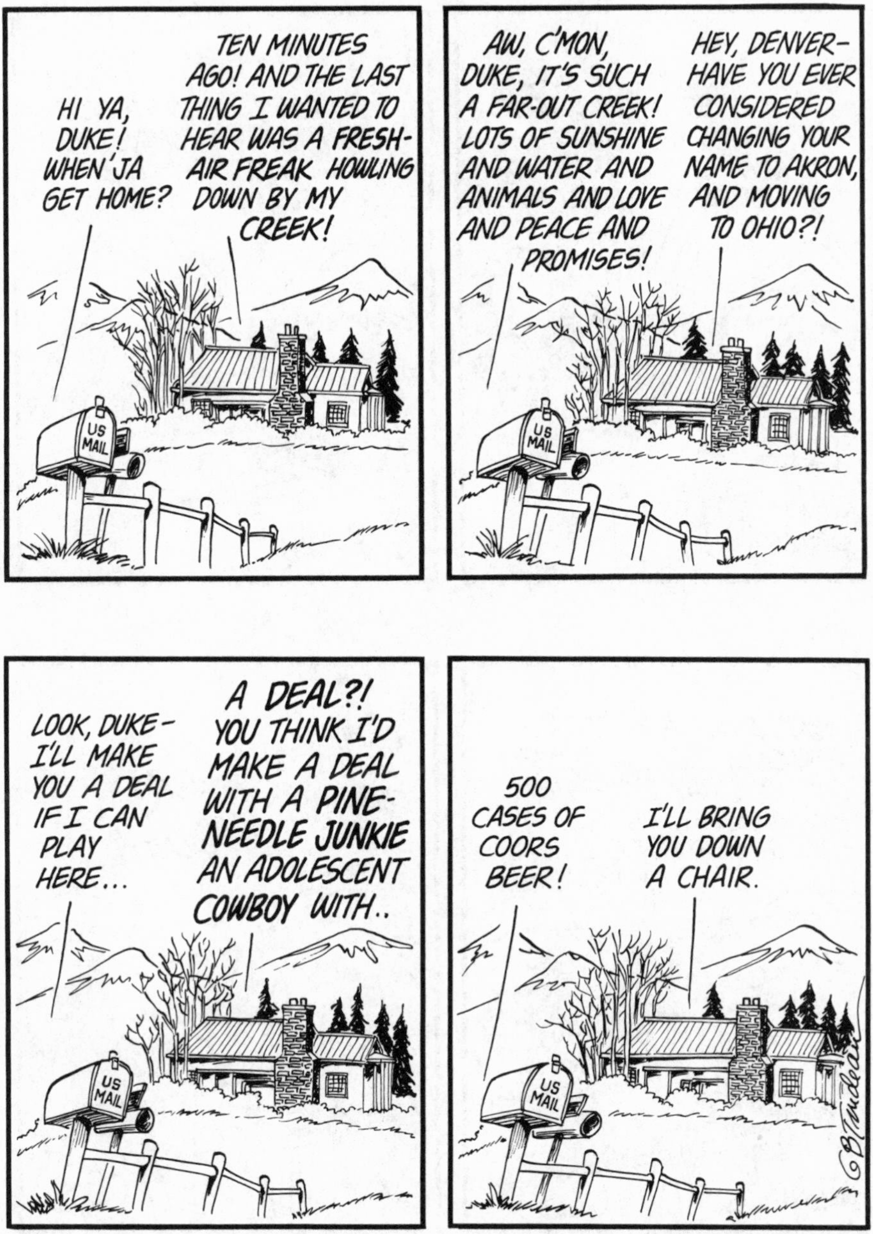
HI YA, DUKE! WHEN'JA GET HOME?
TEN MINUTES AGO! AND THE LAST THING I WANTED TO HEAR WAS A FRESH-AIR FREAK HOWLING DOWN BY MY CREEK!
AW, C'MON, DUKE, IT'S SUCH A FAR-OUT CREEK! LOTS OF SUNSHINE AND WATER AND ANIMALS AND LOVE AND PEACE AND PROMISES!
HEY, DENVER-HAVE YOU EVER CONSIDERED CHANGING YOUR NAME TO AKRON, AND MOVING TO OHIO?!
US MAIL
LOOK, DUKE-I'LL MAKE YOU A DEAL IF I CAN PLAY HERE...
A DEAL?! YOU THINK I'D MAKE A DEAL WITH A PINE-NEEDLE JUNKIE AN ADOLESCENT COWBOY WITH..
500 CASES OF COORS BEER!
I'LL BRING YOU DOWN A CHAIR.
©B Trudeau

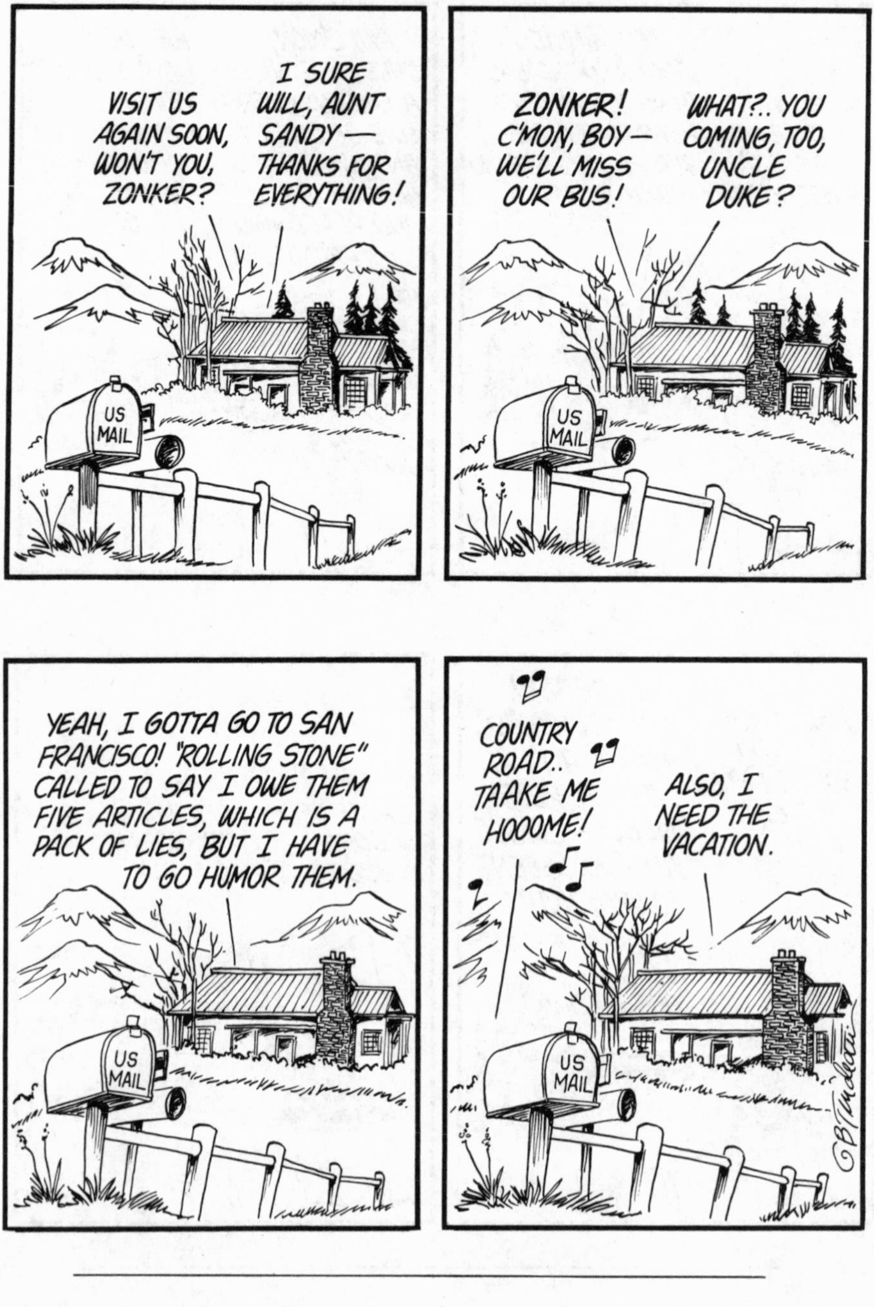
VISIT US AGAIN SOON, WON'T YOU, ZONKER?
I SURE WILL, AUNT SANDY— THANKS FOR EVERYTHING!
US MAIL
ZONKER! C'MON, BOY— WE'LL MISS OUR BUS!
WHAT?.. YOU COMING, TOO, UNCLE DUKE?
US MAIL
YEAH, I GOTTA GO TO SAN FRANCISCO! "ROLLING STONE" CALLED TO SAY I OWE THEM FIVE ARTICLES, WHICH IS A PACK OF LIES, BUT I HAVE TO GO HUMOR THEM.
US MAIL
COUNTRY ROAD.. TAAKE ME HOOOME!
ALSO, I NEED THE VACATION.
US MAIL
©BTrudeau

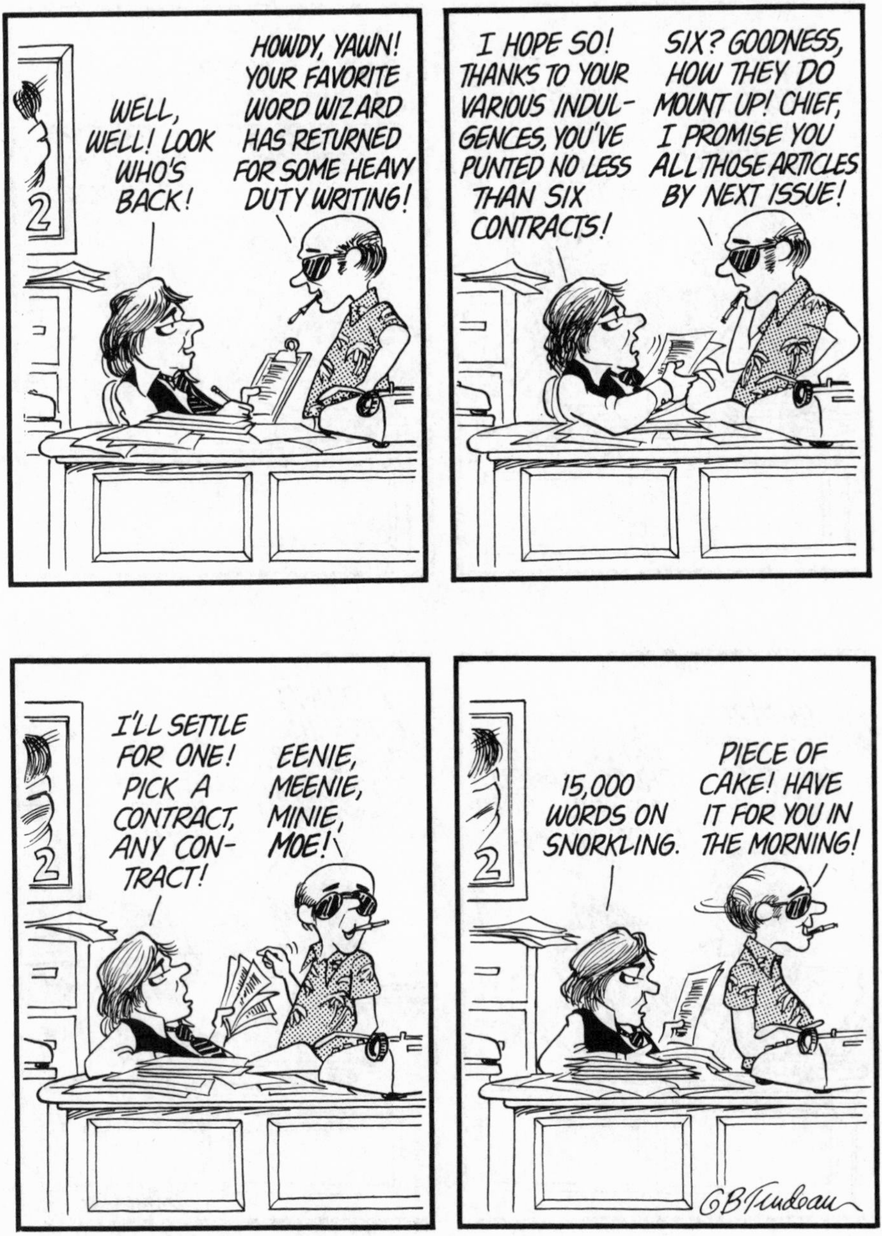
WELL, WELL! LOOK WHO'S BACK!
HOWDY, YAWN! YOUR FAVORITE WORD WIZARD HAS RETURNED FOR SOME HEAVY DUTY WRITING!
I HOPE SO! THANKS TO YOUR VARIOUS INDUL-GENCES, YOU'VE PUNTED NO LESS THAN SIX CONTRACTS!
SIX? GOODNESS, HOW THEY DO MOUNT UP! CHIEF, I PROMISE YOU ALL THOSE ARTICLES BY NEXT ISSUE!
I'LL SETTLE FOR ONE! PICK A CONTRACT, ANY CON-TRACT!
EENIE, MEENIE, MINIE, MOE!
15,000 WORDS ON SNORKLING.
PIECE OF CAKE! HAVE IT FOR YOU IN THE MORNING!
GBTrudeau

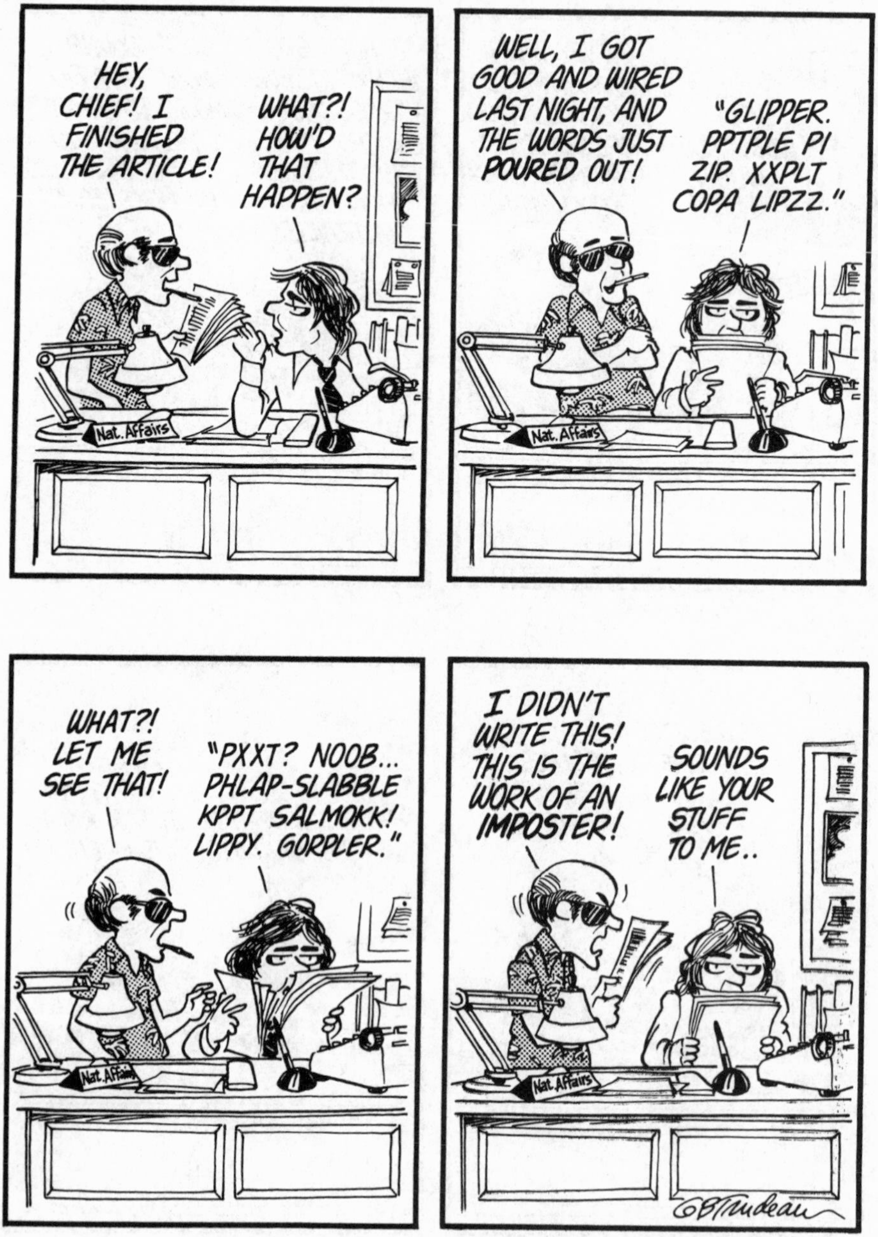
HEY, CHIEF! I FINISHED THE ARTICLE!
WHAT?! HOW'D THAT HAPPEN?
Nat. Affairs
WELL, I GOT GOOD AND WIRED LAST NIGHT, AND THE WORDS JUST POURED OUT!
"GLIPPER. PPTPLE PI ZIP. XXPLT COPA LIPZZ."
Nat. Affairs
WHAT?! LET ME SEE THAT!
"PXXT? NOOB... PHLAP-SLABBLE KPPT SALMOKK! LIPPY. GORPLER."
Nat. Affairs
I DIDN'T WRITE THIS! THIS IS THE WORK OF AN IMPOSTER!
SOUNDS LIKE YOUR STUFF TO ME..
Nat. Affairs
GBTrudeau

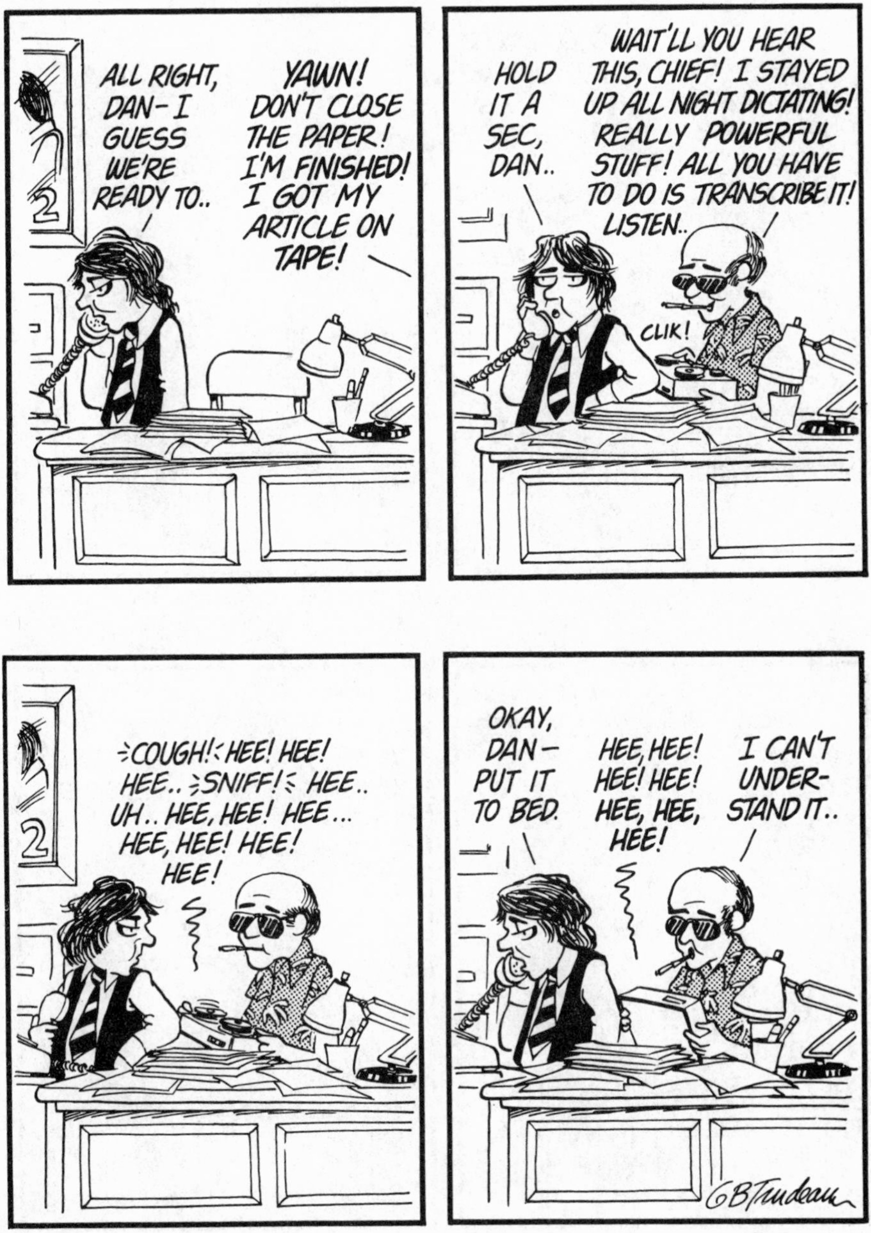
ALL RIGHT, DAN- I GUESS WE'RE READY TO..
YAWN! DON'T CLOSE THE PAPER! I'M FINISHED! I GOT MY ARTICLE ON TAPE!
HOLD IT A SEC, DAN..
WAIT'LL YOU HEAR THIS, CHIEF! I STAYED UP ALL NIGHT DICTATING! REALLY POWERFUL STUFF! ALL YOU HAVE TO DO IS TRANSCRIBE IT! LISTEN..
CLIK!
COUGH! HEE! HEE! HEE.. SNIFF! HEE.. UH.. HEE, HEE! HEE... HEE, HEE! HEE! HEE!
OKAY, DAN- PUT IT TO BED.
HEE, HEE! HEE! HEE! HEE, HEE, HEE!
I CAN'T UNDERSTAND IT..
GBTrudeau

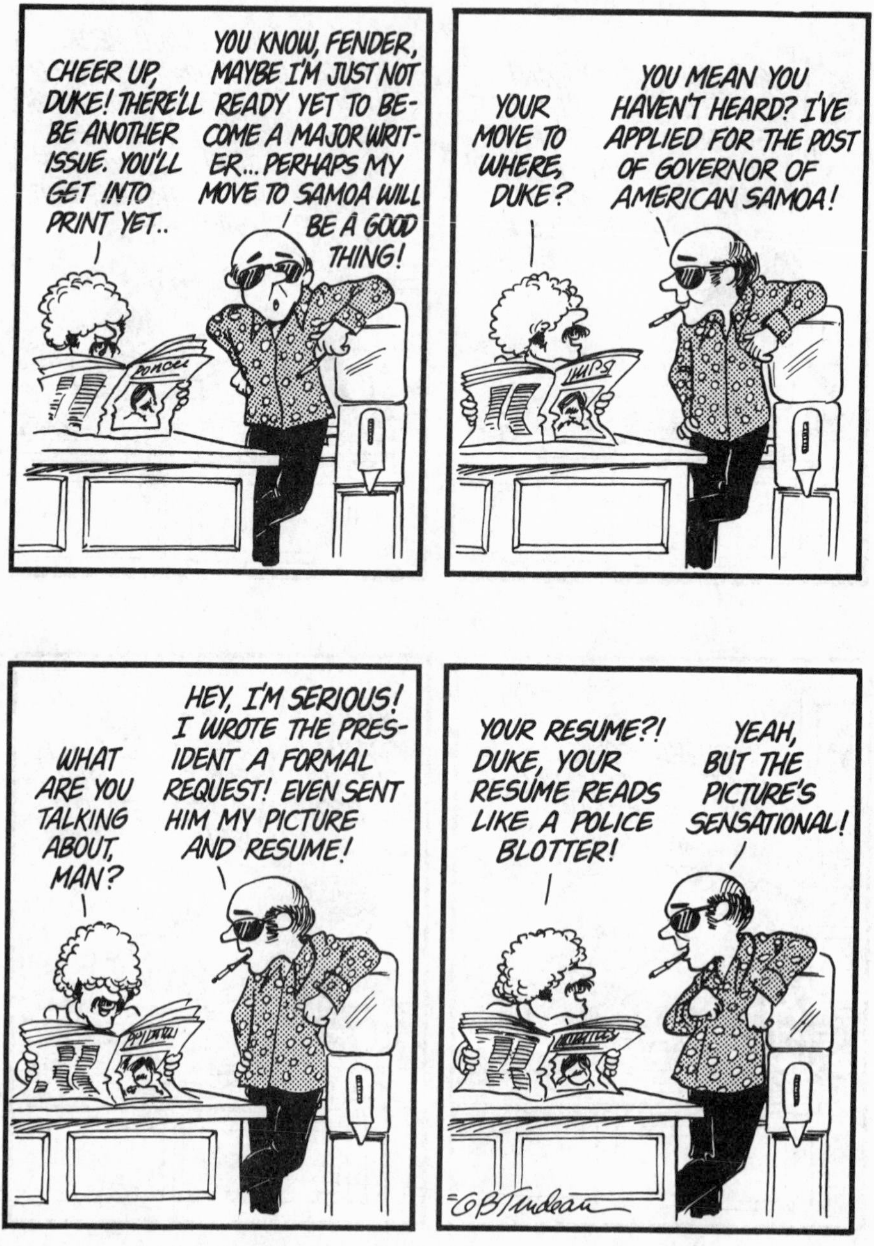
CHEER UP, DUKE! THERE'LL BE ANOTHER ISSUE. YOU'LL GET INTO PRINT YET..
YOU KNOW, FENDER, MAYBE I'M JUST NOT READY YET TO BECOME A MAJOR WRITER... PERHAPS MY MOVE TO SAMOA WILL BE A GOOD THING!
YOUR MOVE TO WHERE, DUKE?
YOU MEAN YOU HAVEN'T HEARD? I'VE APPLIED FOR THE POST OF GOVERNOR OF AMERICAN SAMOA!
WHAT ARE YOU TALKING ABOUT, MAN?
HEY, I'M SERIOUS! I WROTE THE PRESIDENT A FORMAL REQUEST! EVEN SENT HIM MY PICTURE AND RESUME!
YOUR RESUME?! DUKE, YOUR RESUME READS LIKE A POLICE BLOTTER!
YEAH, BUT THE PICTURE'S SENSATIONAL!
GBTrudeau

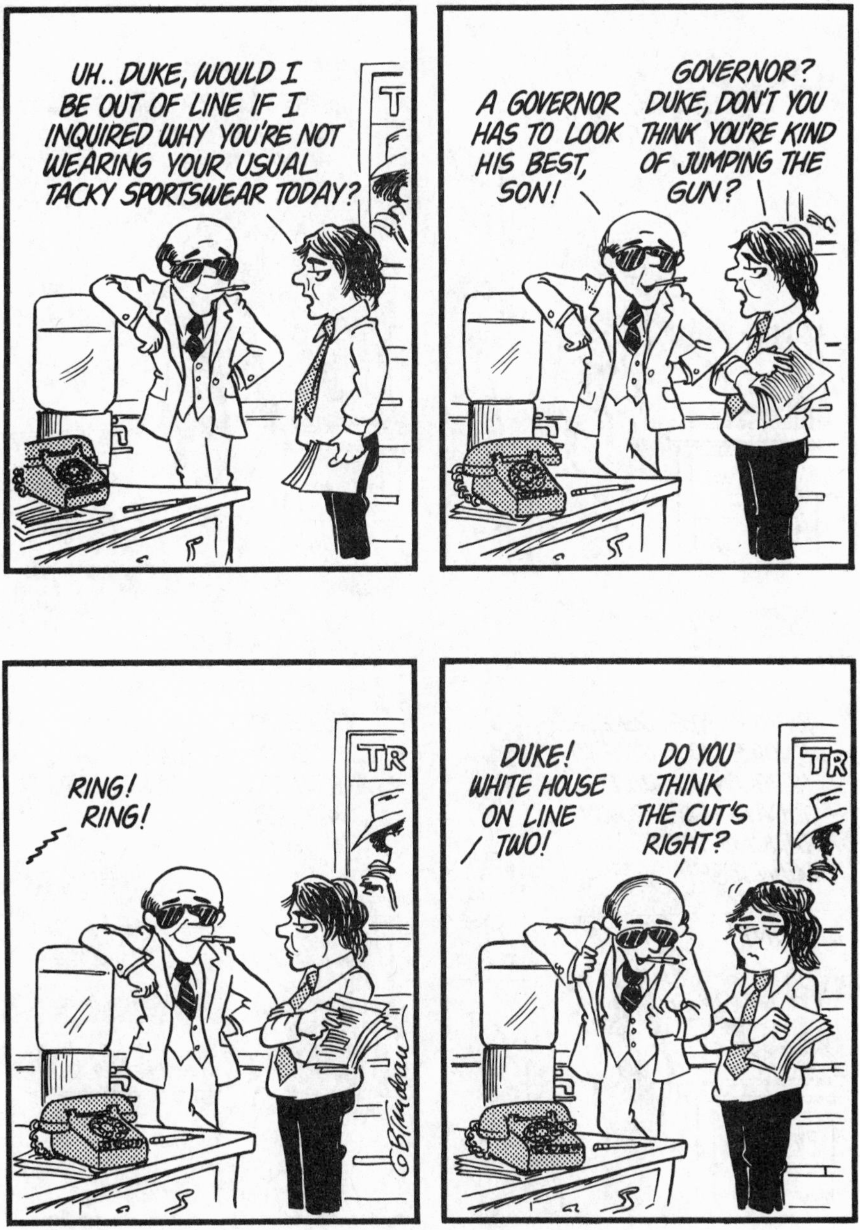
UH.. DUKE, WOULD I BE OUT OF LINE IF I INQUIRED WHY YOU'RE NOT WEARING YOUR USUAL TACKY SPORTSWEAR TODAY?
A GOVERNOR HAS TO LOOK HIS BEST, SON!
GOVERNOR? DUKE, DON'T YOU THINK YOU'RE KIND OF JUMPING THE GUN?
RING! RING!
DUKE! WHITE HOUSE ON LINE TWO!
DO YOU THINK THE CUT'S RIGHT?

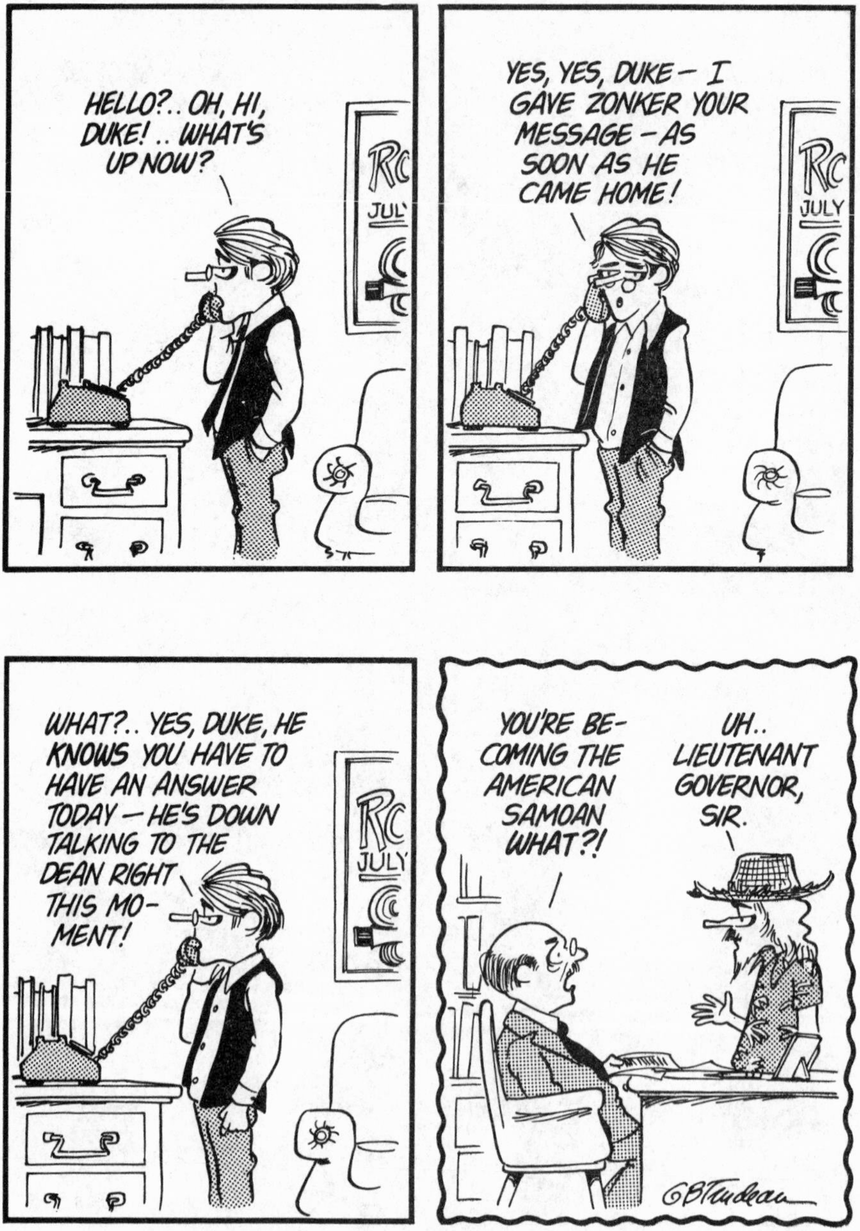
HELLO?.. OH, HI, DUKE! .. WHAT'S UP NOW?
YES, YES, DUKE — I GAVE ZONKER YOUR MESSAGE — AS SOON AS HE CAME HOME!
WHAT?.. YES, DUKE, HE KNOWS YOU HAVE TO HAVE AN ANSWER TODAY — HE'S DOWN TALKING TO THE DEAN RIGHT THIS MO-MENT!
YOU'RE BE-COMING THE AMERICAN SAMOAN WHAT?!
UH.. LIEUTENANT GOVERNOR, SIR.
GBTrudeau

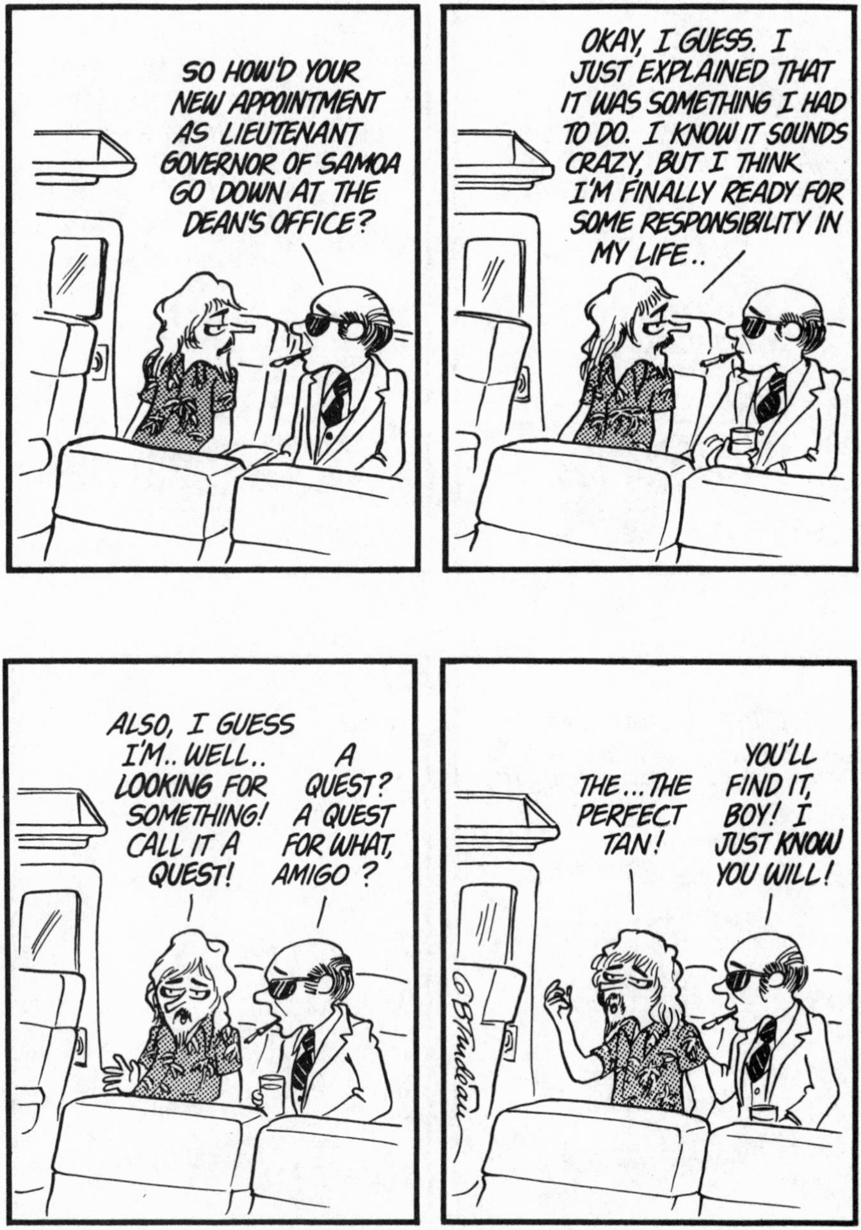
SO HOW'D YOUR NEW APPOINTMENT AS LIEUTENANT GOVERNOR OF SAMOA GO DOWN AT THE DEAN'S OFFICE?
OKAY, I GUESS. I JUST EXPLAINED THAT IT WAS SOMETHING I HAD TO DO. I KNOW IT SOUNDS CRAZY, BUT I THINK I'M FINALLY READY FOR SOME RESPONSIBILITY IN MY LIFE..
ALSO, I GUESS I'M.. WELL.. LOOKING FOR SOMETHING! CALL IT A QUEST!
A QUEST? A QUEST FOR WHAT, AMIGO ?
THE ... THE PERFECT TAN!
YOU'LL FIND IT, BOY! I JUST KNOW YOU WILL!
GBTrudeau

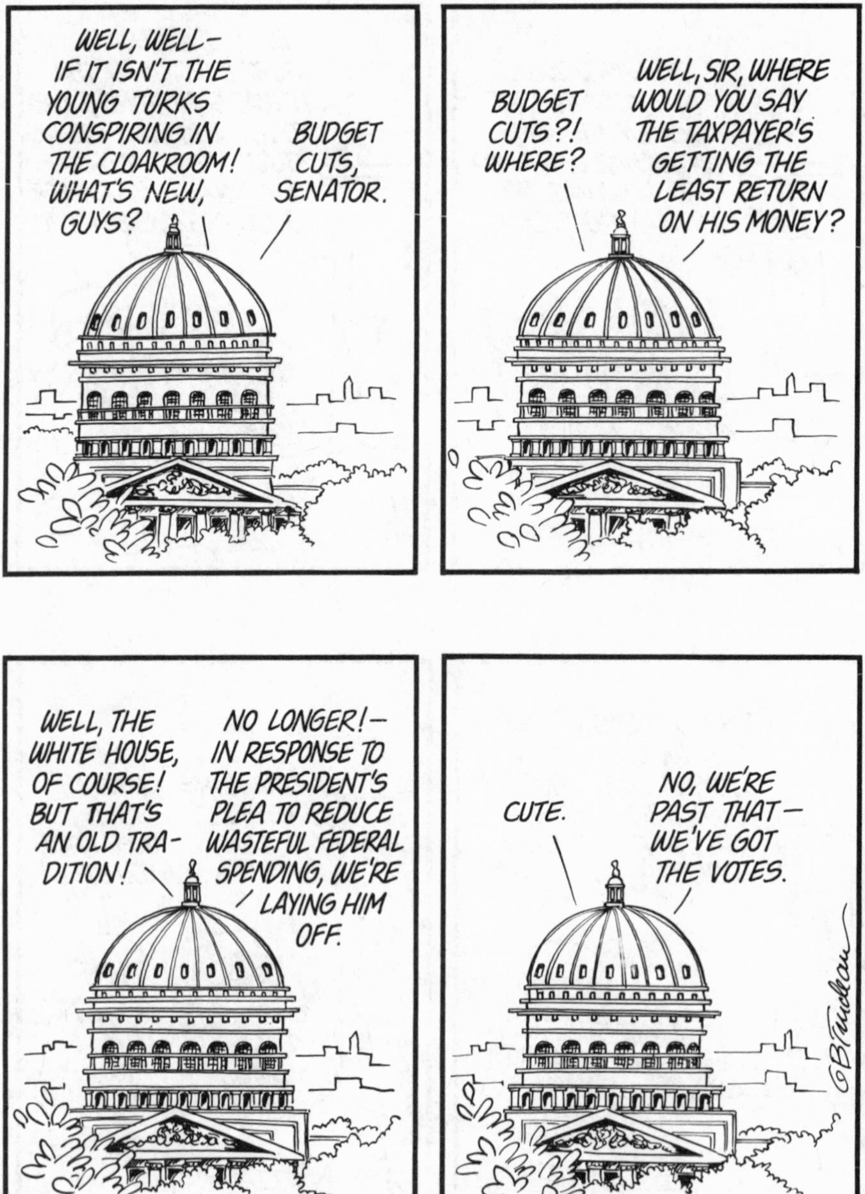
WELL, WELL– IF IT ISN'T THE YOUNG TURKS CONSPIRING IN THE CLOAKROOM! WHAT'S NEW, GUYS?
BUDGET CUTS, SENATOR.
BUDGET CUTS?! WHERE?
WELL, SIR, WHERE WOULD YOU SAY THE TAXPAYER'S GETTING THE LEAST RETURN ON HIS MONEY?
WELL, THE WHITE HOUSE, OF COURSE! BUT THAT'S AN OLD TRA- DITION!
NO LONGER!– IN RESPONSE TO THE PRESIDENT'S PLEA TO REDUCE WASTEFUL FEDERAL SPENDING, WE'RE LAYING HIM OFF.
CUTE.
NO, WE'RE PAST THAT– WE'VE GOT THE VOTES.
©BTrudeau

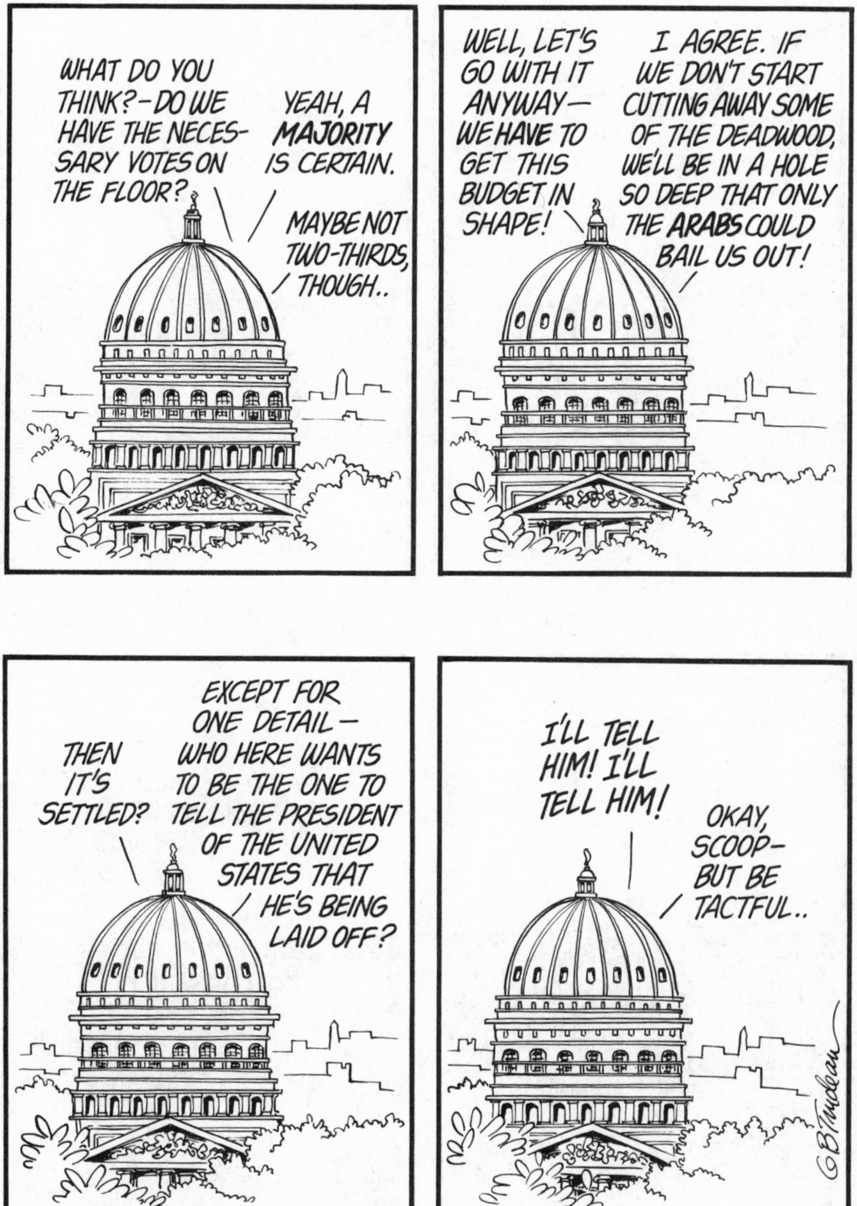
WHAT DO YOU THINK?-DO WE HAVE THE NECES-SARY VOTES ON THE FLOOR?
YEAH, A MAJORITY IS CERTAIN.
MAYBE NOT TWO-THIRDS, THOUGH..
WELL, LET'S GO WITH IT ANYWAY— WE HAVE TO GET THIS BUDGET IN SHAPE!
I AGREE. IF WE DON'T START CUTTING AWAY SOME OF THE DEADWOOD, WE'LL BE IN A HOLE SO DEEP THAT ONLY THE ARABS COULD BAIL US OUT!
THEN IT'S SETTLED?
EXCEPT FOR ONE DETAIL— WHO HERE WANTS TO BE THE ONE TO TELL THE PRESIDENT OF THE UNITED STATES THAT HE'S BEING LAID OFF?
I'LL TELL HIM! I'LL TELL HIM!
OKAY, SCOOP— BUT BE TACTFUL..
© GBTrudeau

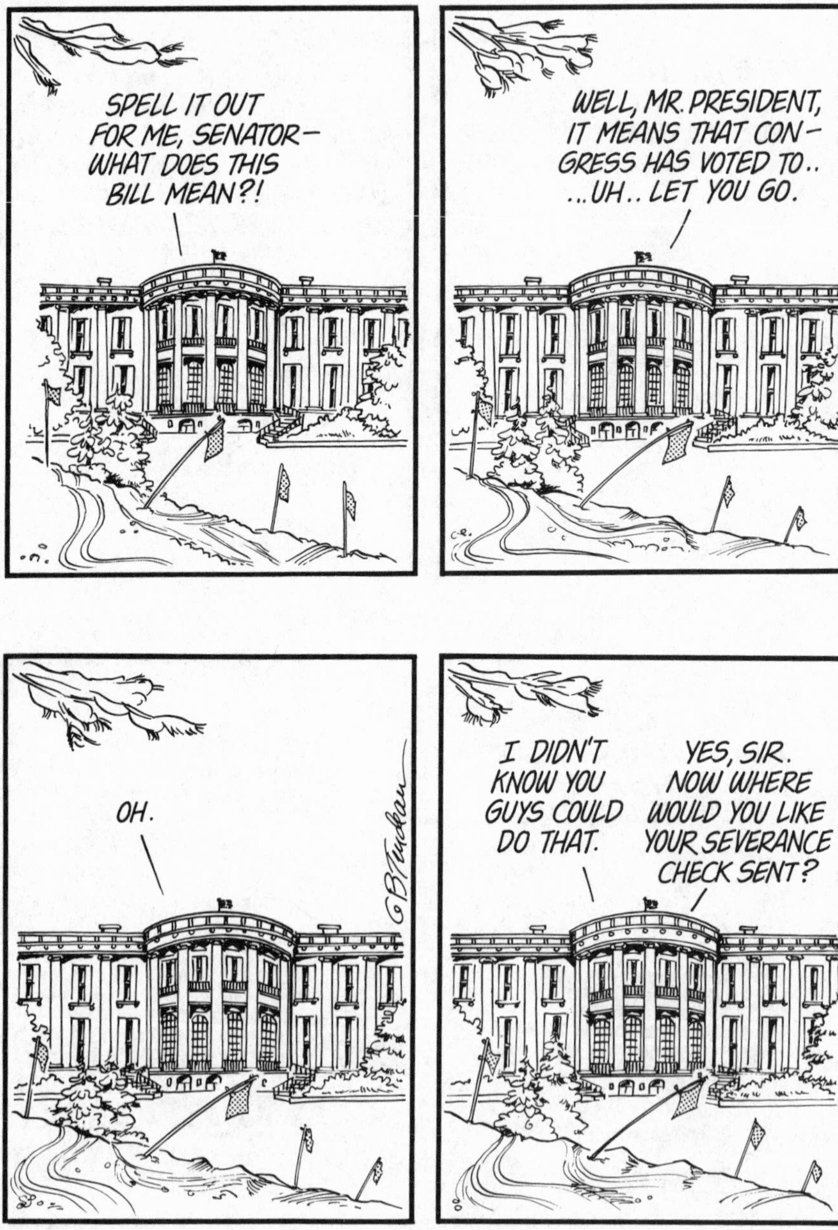
SPELL IT OUT FOR ME, SENATOR— WHAT DOES THIS BILL MEAN?!
WELL, MR. PRESIDENT, IT MEANS THAT CON-GRESS HAS VOTED TO.. ...UH.. LET YOU GO.
OH.
GBTrudeau
I DIDN'T KNOW YOU GUYS COULD DO THAT.
YES, SIR. NOW WHERE WOULD YOU LIKE YOUR SEVERANCE CHECK SENT?

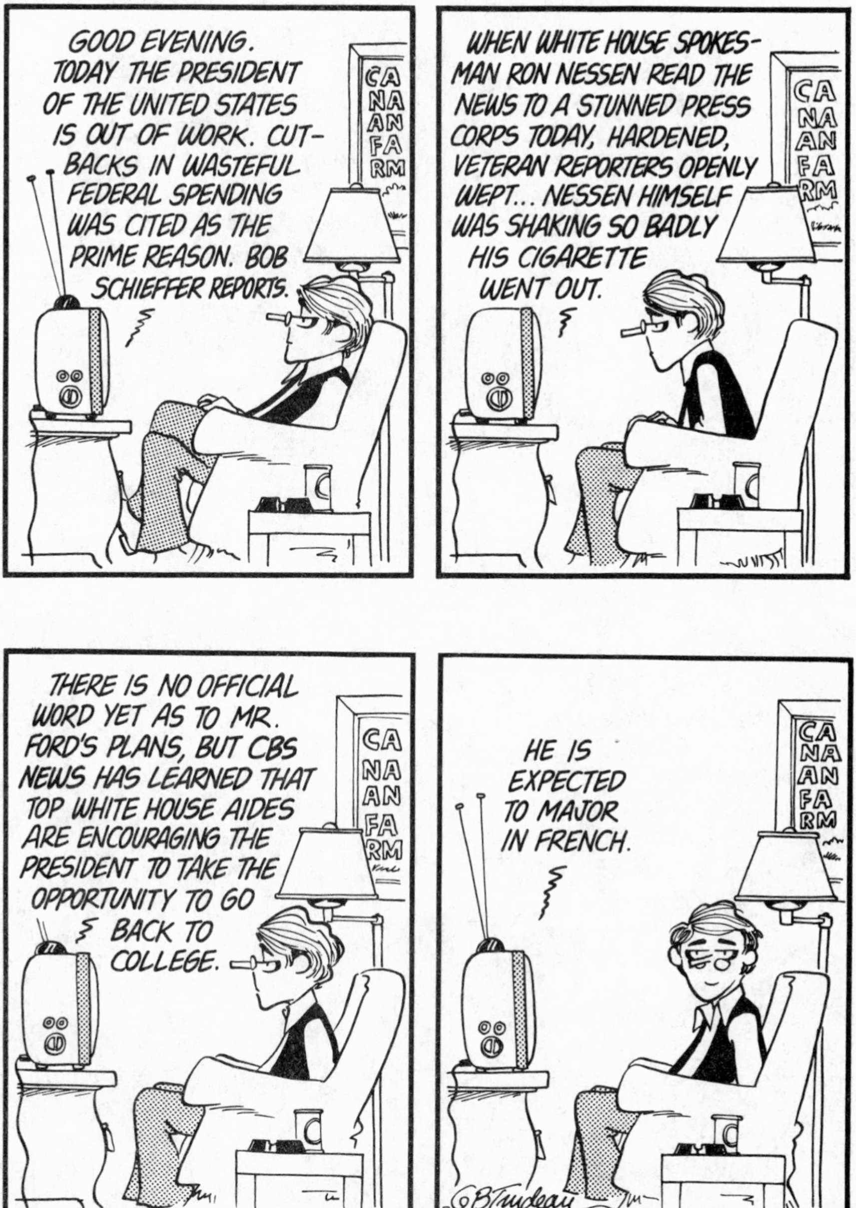
GOOD EVENING. TODAY THE PRESIDENT OF THE UNITED STATES IS OUT OF WORK. CUT-BACKS IN WASTEFUL FEDERAL SPENDING WAS CITED AS THE PRIME REASON. BOB SCHIEFFER REPORTS.
CANAAN FARM
WHEN WHITE HOUSE SPOKES-MAN RON NESSEN READ THE NEWS TO A STUNNED PRESS CORPS TODAY, HARDENED, VETERAN REPORTERS OPENLY WEPT... NESSEN HIMSELF WAS SHAKING SO BADLY HIS CIGARETTE WENT OUT.
CANAAN FARM
THERE IS NO OFFICIAL WORD YET AS TO MR. FORD'S PLANS, BUT CBS NEWS HAS LEARNED THAT TOP WHITE HOUSE AIDES ARE ENCOURAGING THE PRESIDENT TO TAKE THE OPPORTUNITY TO GO BACK TO COLLEGE.
CANAAN FARM
HE IS EXPECTED TO MAJOR IN FRENCH.
CANAAN FARM
GBTrudeau

AS PRESIDENT FORD'S RECENT LAYOFF SO DRAMATICALLY UNDERSCORES, RECESSION EXACTS ITS TOLL FROM EVEN THE NEAR-GREAT. HARD TIMES ON PENNSYLVANIA AVENUE PROVIDE THE GRIST FOR ERIC SEVAREID'S ANALYSIS.
CANAAN FARM
CRIPPLED BY DOUBLE-DIGIT INFLATION AND RELENTLESS RECESSION, ANOTHER FORD FACTORY HAS CLOSED DOWN. BUT UNLIKE ITS DETROIT NAMESAKE, THIS FACTORY PRODUCED HOPE AND INSPIRATION FOR MILLIONS OF AMERICANS, AS OPPOSED TO PICKUP TRUCKS.
YES, AT THIS INSTALLATION, THE EMPLOYEES WERE THE ENGINEERS OF PUBLIC POLICY, THE MACHINISTS OF STATE INITIATIVES, AND THE FOREMAN WAS A WELL-MEANING MANAGER ON WHOSE PUNCH CLOCK TIME HAD FINALLY RUN OUT.
TO CARRY THE ANALOGY FURTHER..
GBTrudeau

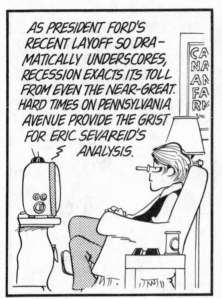

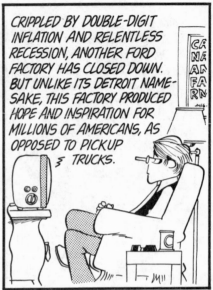

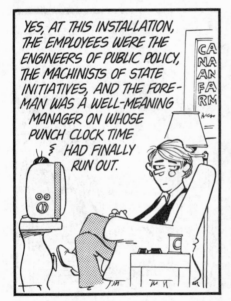

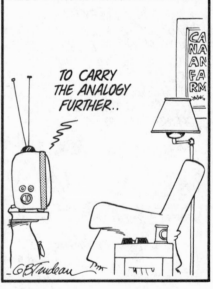

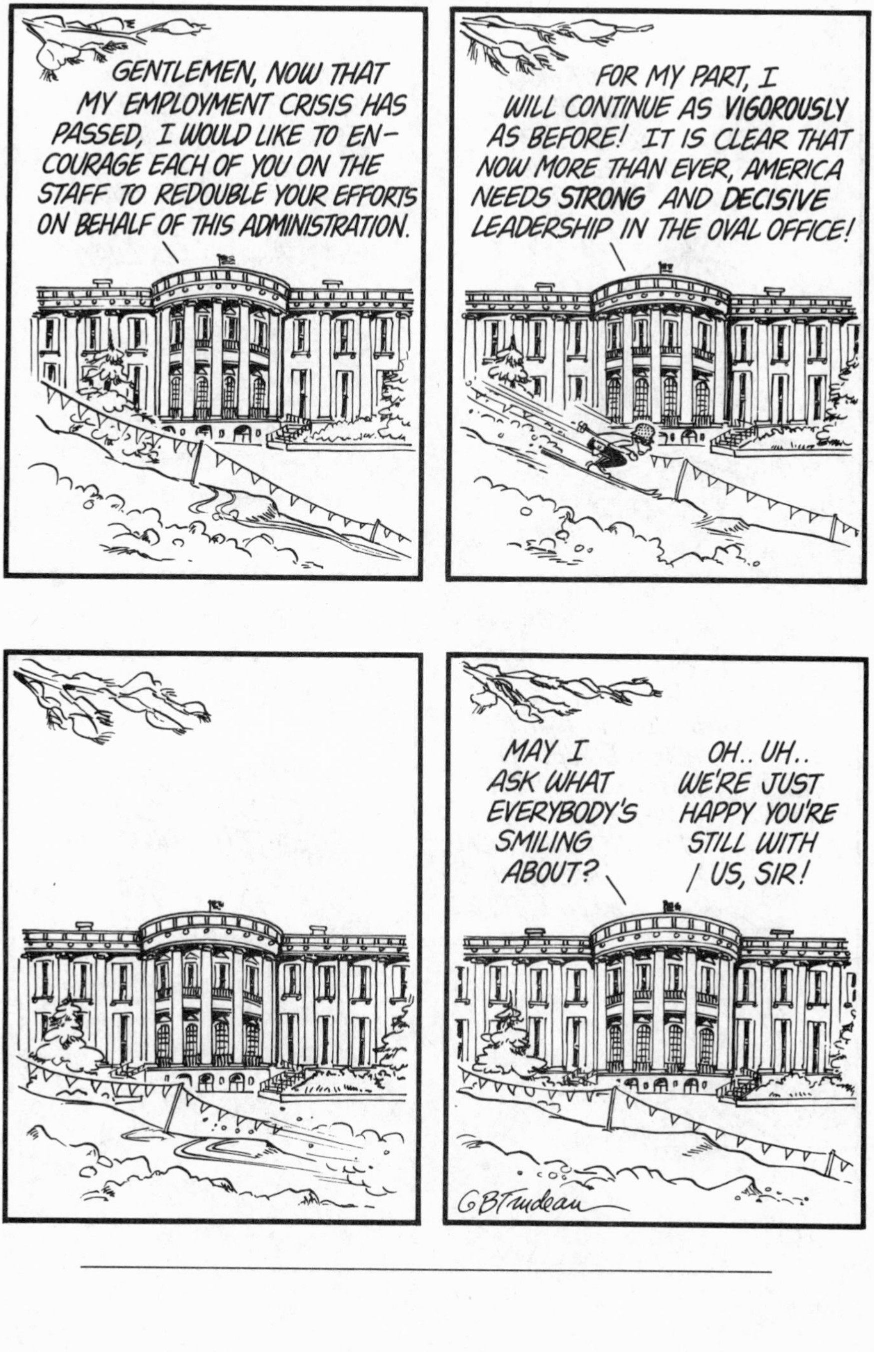
GENTLEMEN, NOW THAT MY EMPLOYMENT CRISIS HAS PASSED, I WOULD LIKE TO ENCOURAGE EACH OF YOU ON THE STAFF TO REDOUBLE YOUR EFFORTS ON BEHALF OF THIS ADMINISTRATION.
FOR MY PART, I WILL CONTINUE AS VIGOROUSLY AS BEFORE! IT IS CLEAR THAT NOW MORE THAN EVER, AMERICA NEEDS STRONG AND DECISIVE LEADERSHIP IN THE OVAL OFFICE!
MAY I ASK WHAT EVERYBODY'S SMILING ABOUT?
OH.. UH.. WE'RE JUST HAPPY YOU'RE STILL WITH US, SIR!
GBTrudeau

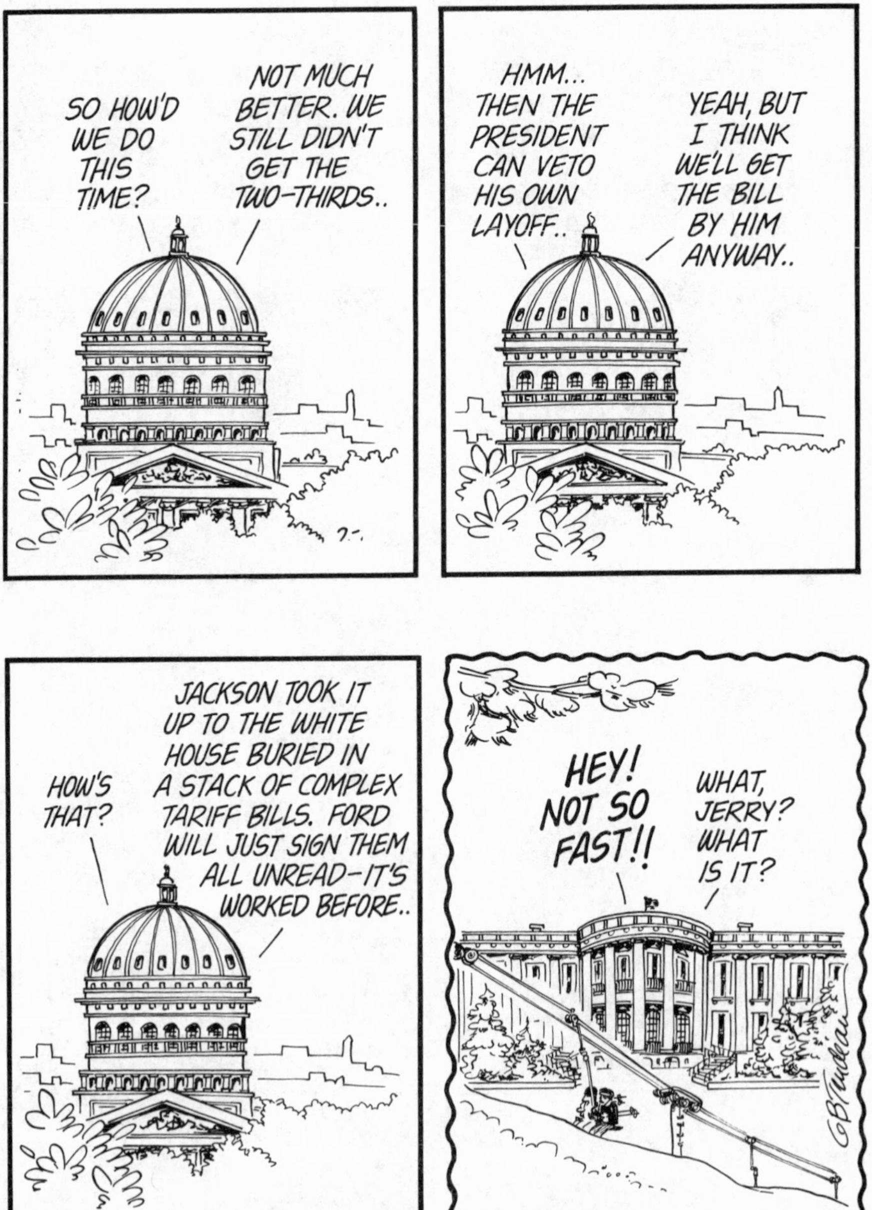
SO HOW'D WE DO THIS TIME?
NOT MUCH BETTER. WE STILL DIDN'T GET THE TWO-THIRDS..
HMM... THEN THE PRESIDENT CAN VETO HIS OWN LAYOFF..
YEAH, BUT I THINK WE'LL GET THE BILL BY HIM ANYWAY..
HOW'S THAT?
JACKSON TOOK IT UP TO THE WHITE HOUSE BURIED IN A STACK OF COMPLEX TARIFF BILLS. FORD WILL JUST SIGN THEM ALL UNREAD-IT'S WORKED BEFORE..
HEY! NOT SO FAST!!
WHAT, JERRY? WHAT IS IT?

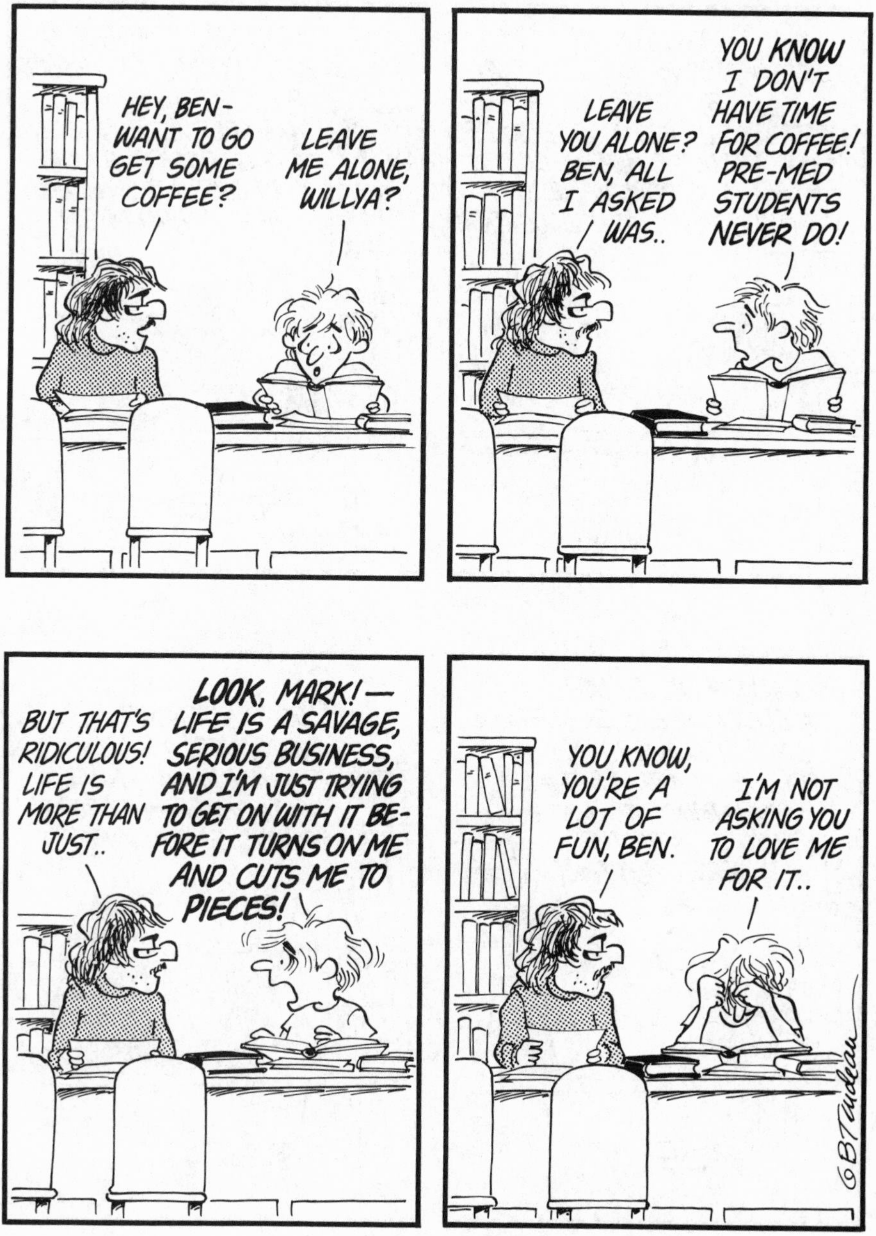
HEY, BEN- WANT TO GO GET SOME COFFEE?
LEAVE ME ALONE, WILLYA?
LEAVE YOU ALONE? BEN, ALL I ASKED WAS..
YOU KNOW I DON'T HAVE TIME FOR COFFEE! PRE-MED STUDENTS NEVER DO!
BUT THAT'S RIDICULOUS! LIFE IS MORE THAN JUST..
LOOK, MARK!— LIFE IS A SAVAGE, SERIOUS BUSINESS, AND I'M JUST TRYING TO GET ON WITH IT BEFORE IT TURNS ON ME AND CUTS ME TO PIECES!
YOU KNOW, YOU'RE A LOT OF FUN, BEN.
I'M NOT ASKING YOU TO LOVE ME FOR IT..
© B Trudeau

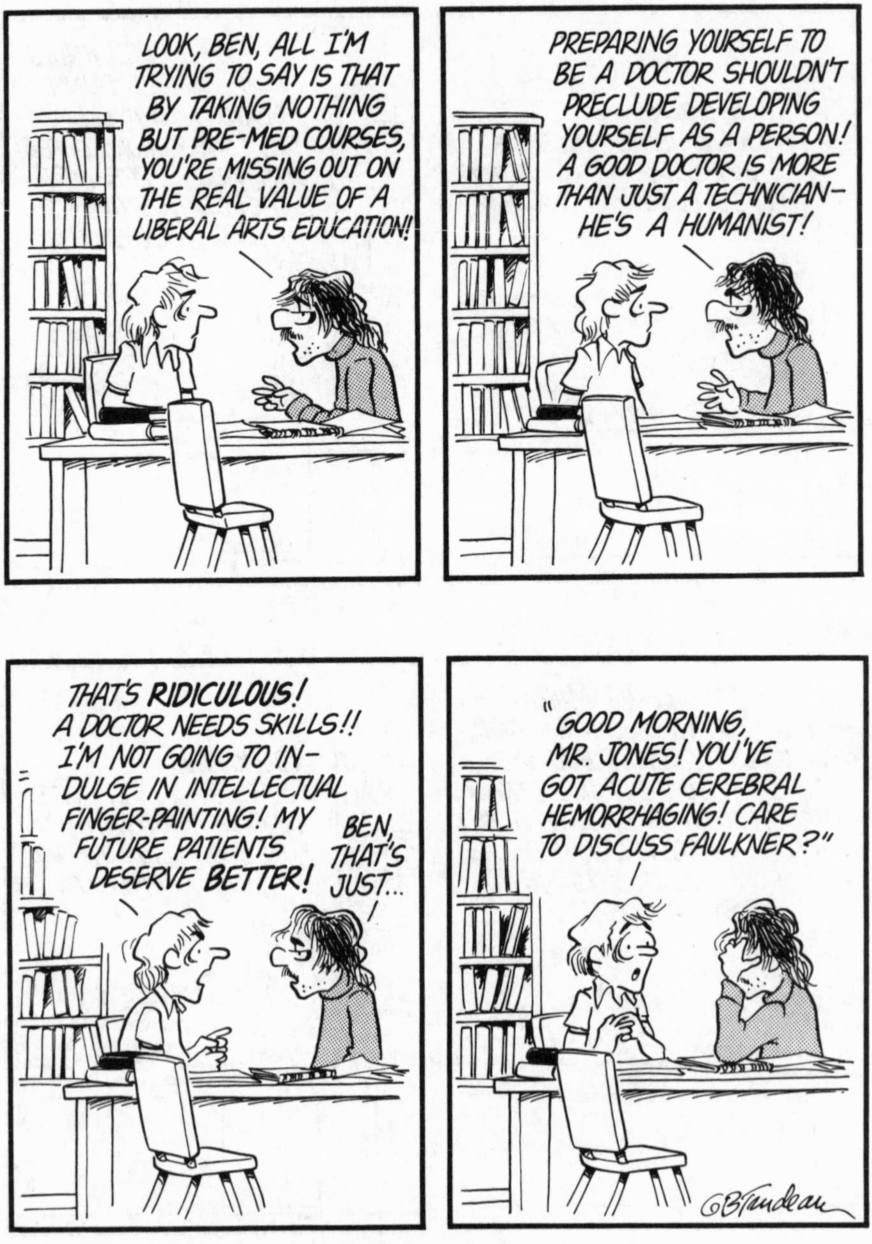
LOOK, BEN, ALL I'M TRYING TO SAY IS THAT BY TAKING NOTHING BUT PRE-MED COURSES, YOU'RE MISSING OUT ON THE REAL VALUE OF A LIBERAL ARTS EDUCATION!
PREPARING YOURSELF TO BE A DOCTOR SHOULDN'T PRECLUDE DEVELOPING YOURSELF AS A PERSON! A GOOD DOCTOR IS MORE THAN JUST A TECHNICIAN-HE'S A HUMANIST!
THAT'S RIDICULOUS! A DOCTOR NEEDS SKILLS!! I'M NOT GOING TO IN-DULGE IN INTELLECTUAL FINGER-PAINTING! MY FUTURE PATIENTS DESERVE BETTER!
BEN, THAT'S JUST...
"GOOD MORNING, MR. JONES! YOU'VE GOT ACUTE CEREBRAL HEMORRHAGING! CARE TO DISCUSS FAULKNER?"
©BTrudeau

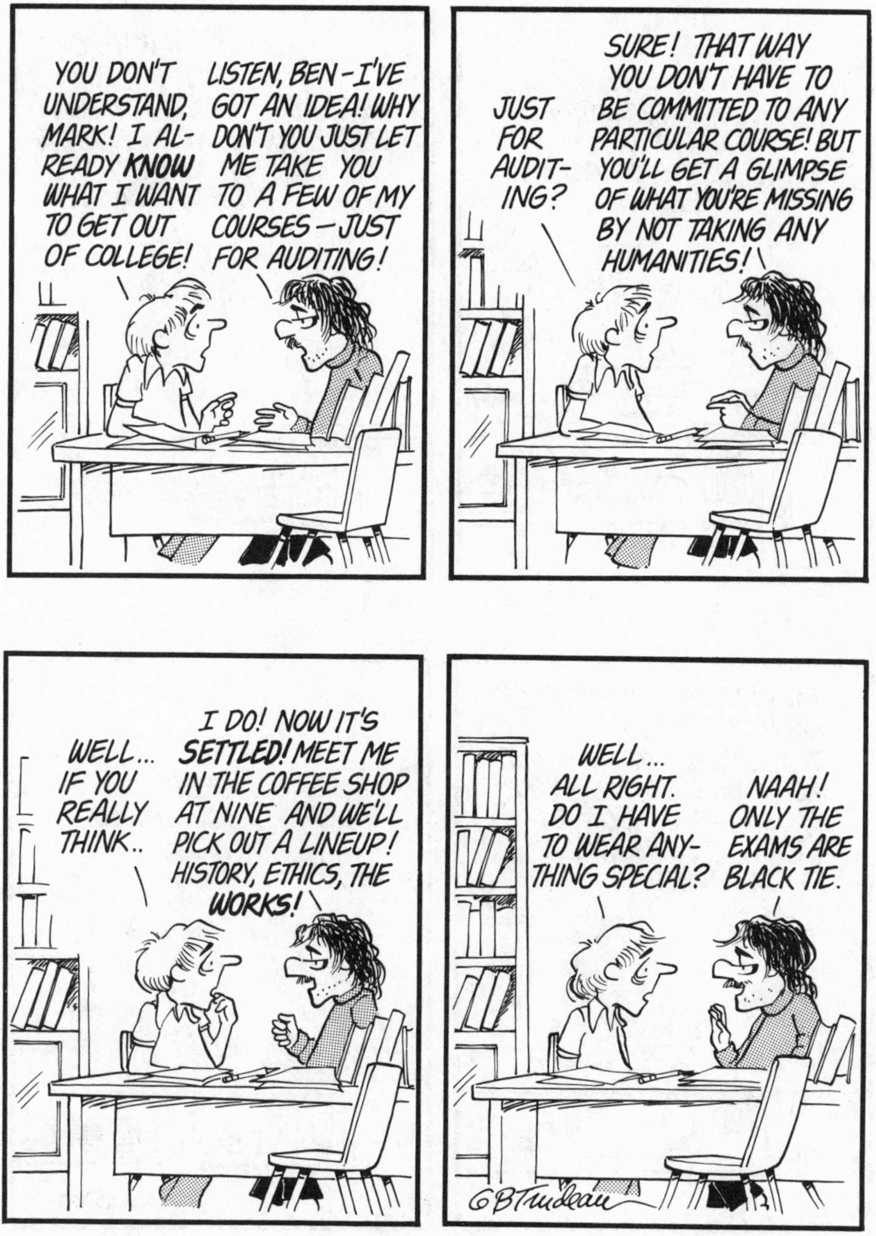

YOU DON'T UNDERSTAND, MARK! I ALREADY **KNOW** WHAT I WANT TO GET OUT OF COLLEGE!
LISTEN, BEN - I'VE GOT AN IDEA! WHY DON'T YOU JUST LET ME TAKE YOU TO A FEW OF MY COURSES - JUST FOR AUDITING!
JUST FOR AUDITING?
SURE! THAT WAY YOU DON'T HAVE TO BE COMMITTED TO ANY PARTICULAR COURSE! BUT YOU'LL GET A GLIMPSE OF WHAT YOU'RE MISSING BY NOT TAKING ANY HUMANITIES!
WELL... IF YOU REALLY THINK..
I DO! NOW IT'S **SETTLED!** MEET ME IN THE COFFEE SHOP AT NINE AND WE'LL PICK OUT A LINEUP! HISTORY, ETHICS, THE **WORKS!**
WELL... ALL RIGHT. DO I HAVE TO WEAR ANYTHING SPECIAL?
NAAH! ONLY THE EXAMS ARE BLACK TIE.
GBTrudeau

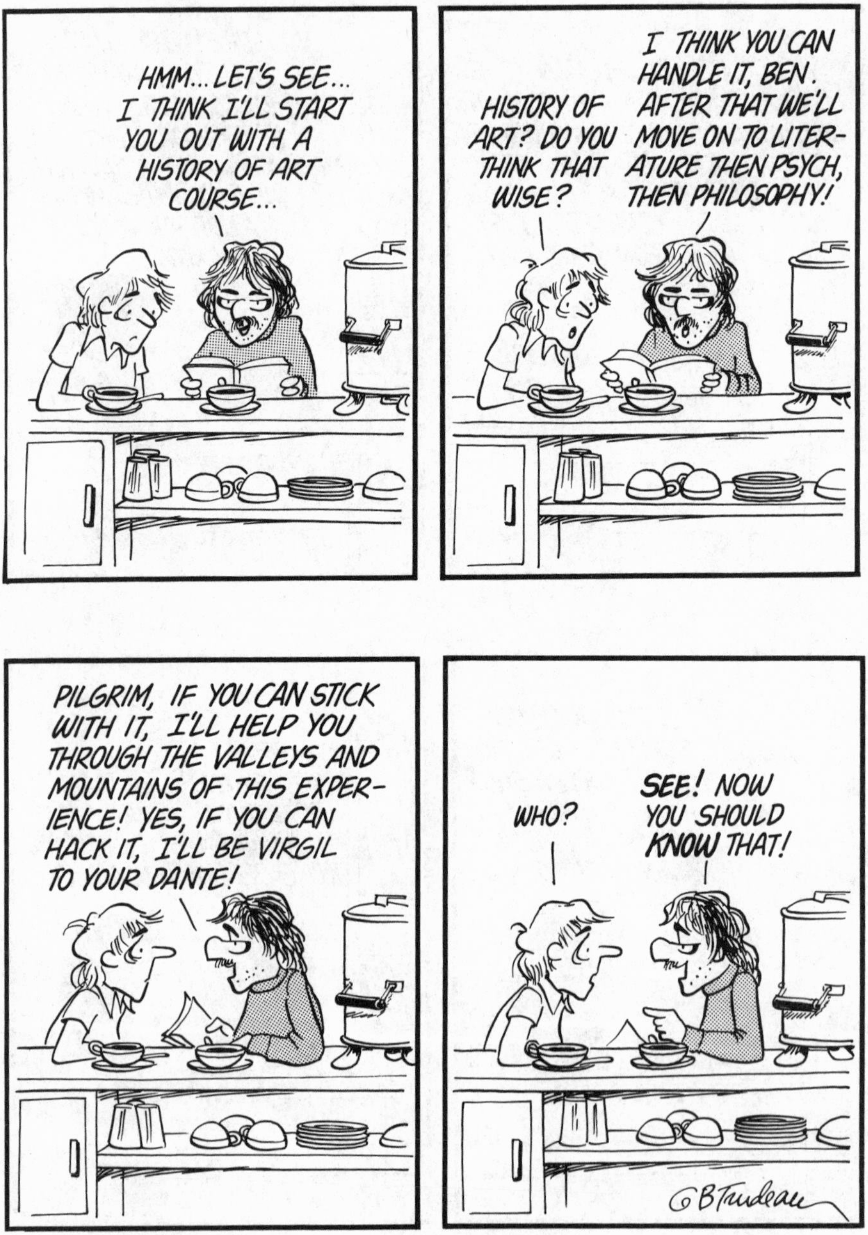
HMM... LET'S SEE... I THINK I'LL START YOU OUT WITH A HISTORY OF ART COURSE...
HISTORY OF ART? DO YOU THINK THAT WISE?
I THINK YOU CAN HANDLE IT, BEN. AFTER THAT WE'LL MOVE ON TO LITER-ATURE THEN PSYCH, THEN PHILOSOPHY!
PILGRIM, IF YOU CAN STICK WITH IT, I'LL HELP YOU THROUGH THE VALLEYS AND MOUNTAINS OF THIS EXPER-IENCE! YES, IF YOU CAN HACK IT, I'LL BE VIRGIL TO YOUR DANTE!
WHO?
SEE! NOW YOU SHOULD KNOW THAT!
GBTrudeau

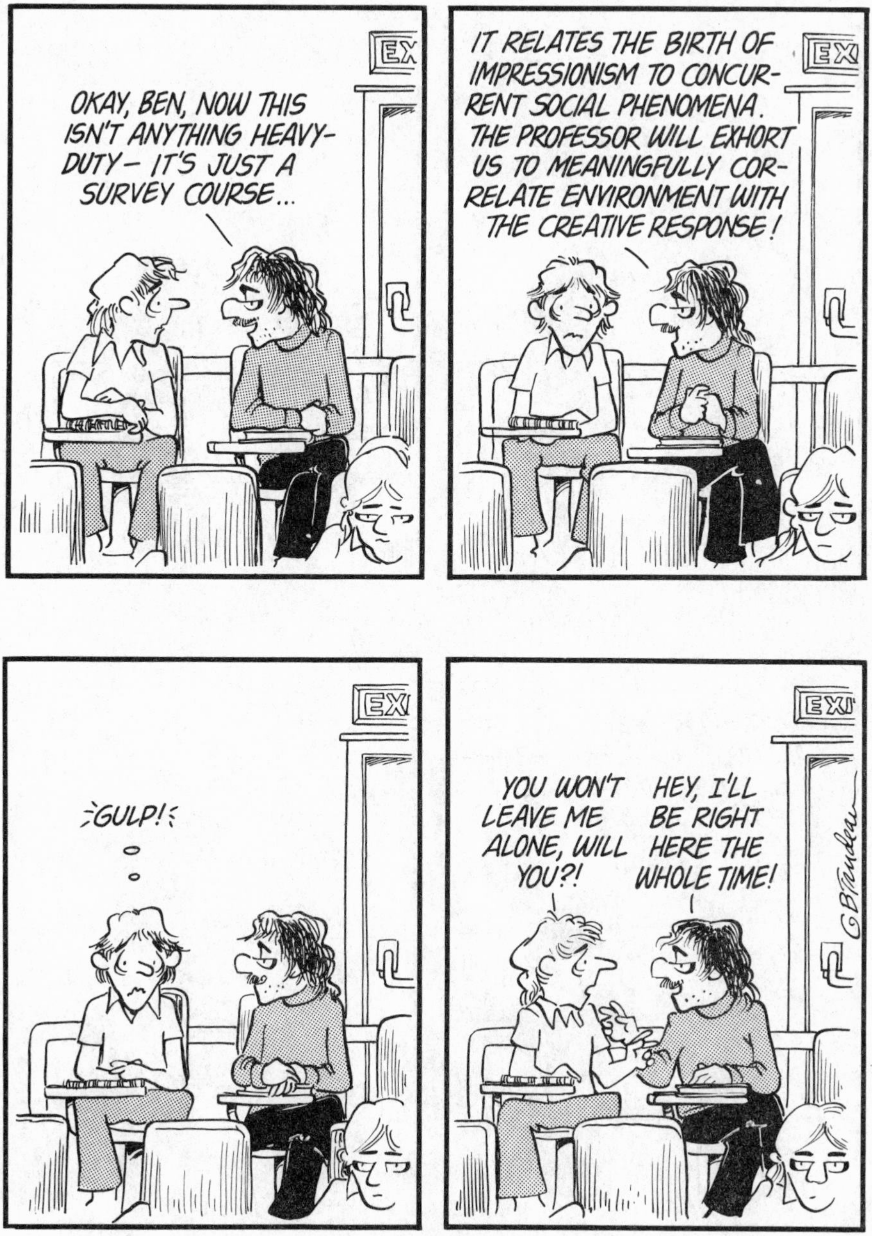
OKAY, BEN, NOW THIS ISN'T ANYTHING HEAVY-DUTY— IT'S JUST A SURVEY COURSE...
IT RELATES THE BIRTH OF IMPRESSIONISM TO CONCURRENT SOCIAL PHENOMENA. THE PROFESSOR WILL EXHORT US TO MEANINGFULLY CORRELATE ENVIRONMENT WITH THE CREATIVE RESPONSE!
GULP!
YOU WON'T LEAVE ME ALONE, WILL YOU?!
HEY, I'LL BE RIGHT HERE THE WHOLE TIME!
© G B Trudeau

WELL? WHATJA THINK?
WOW... OH, WOW...
THAT STUFF HE SAID ABOUT MANET... IT WAS INSPIRING!... I MEAN.. I MEAN.. I.. I LIKED IT! I REALLY LIKED IT!
AND ON MY FIRST TRY!
GREAT FEELING, ISN'T IT?
© GBTrudeau

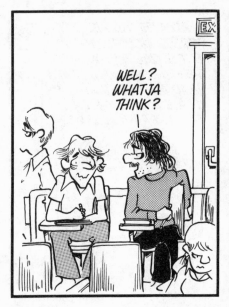

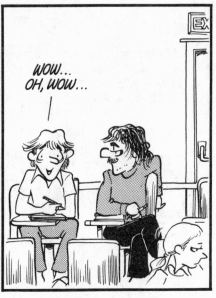

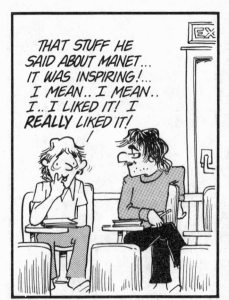

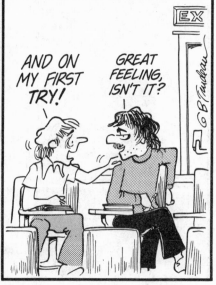

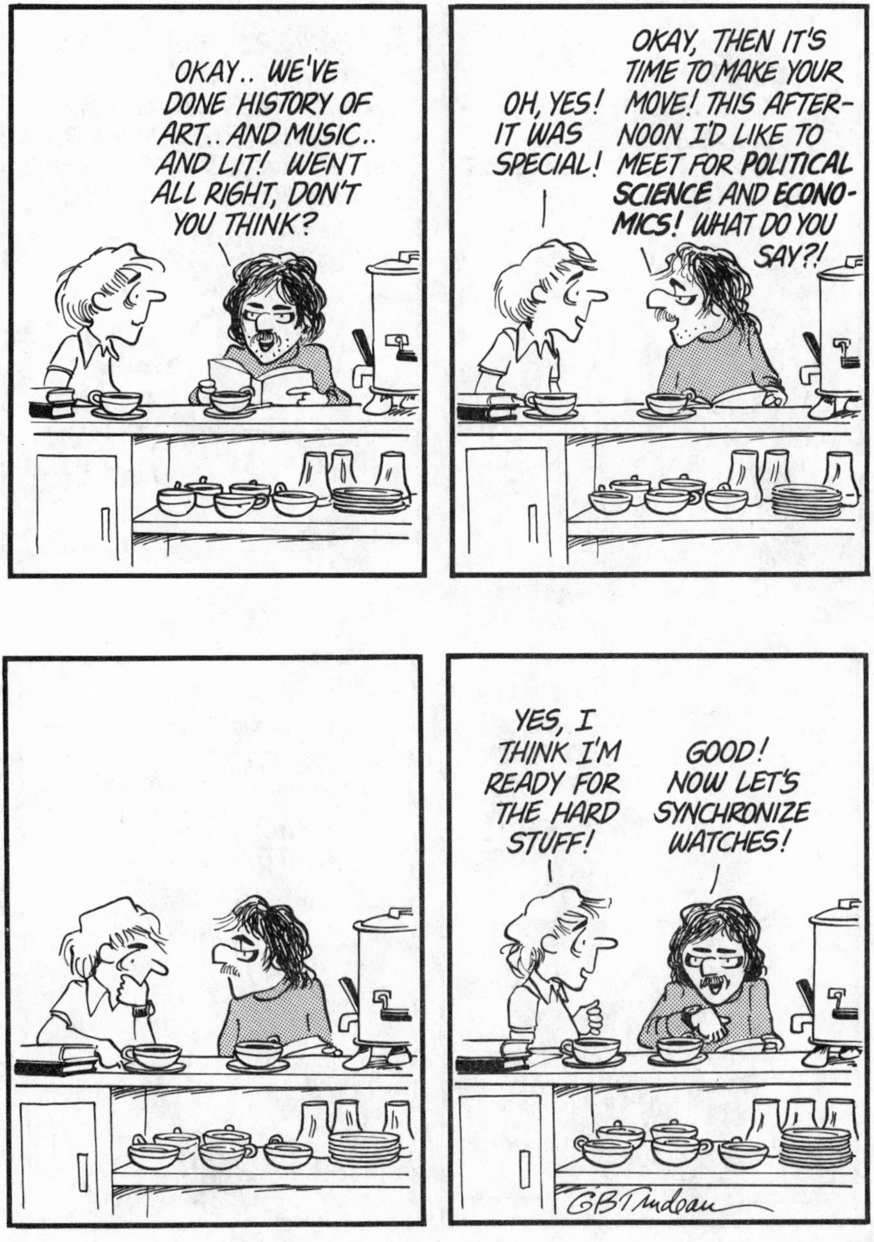
OKAY.. WE'VE DONE HISTORY OF ART.. AND MUSIC.. AND LIT! WENT ALL RIGHT, DON'T YOU THINK?
OH, YES! IT WAS SPECIAL!
OKAY, THEN IT'S TIME TO MAKE YOUR MOVE! THIS AFTERNOON I'D LIKE TO MEET FOR POLITICAL SCIENCE AND ECONOMICS! WHAT DO YOU SAY?!
YES, I THINK I'M READY FOR THE HARD STUFF!
GOOD! NOW LET'S SYNCHRONIZE WATCHES!
GBTrudeau

WHERE'D MARK GO? I THOUGHT HE WAS GOING TO HELP CLEAN UP...
HE HAD A CLASS.
ANOTHER CLASS?! SAY, WHAT'S WITH HIM? HE HASN'T STOPPED GOING TO CLASSES ALL WEEK!
BELIEVE IT OR NOT, HE'S BEEN SHOWING BEN THE LIBERAL ARTS!
BEN? REALLY?
YUP! AND AS I UNDERSTAND IT, BEN HAS QUITE TAKEN TO IT!
CAN WE SIT IN THE FRONT ROW TODAY?! CAN WE?! CAN WE?!
IF WE HURRY!
GBTrudeau

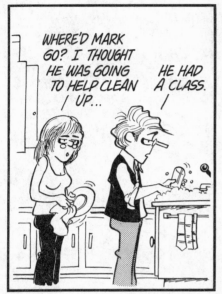

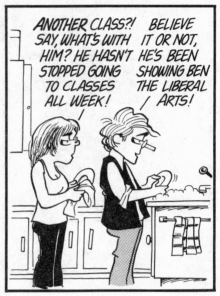

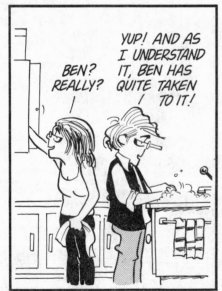

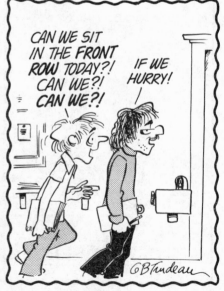

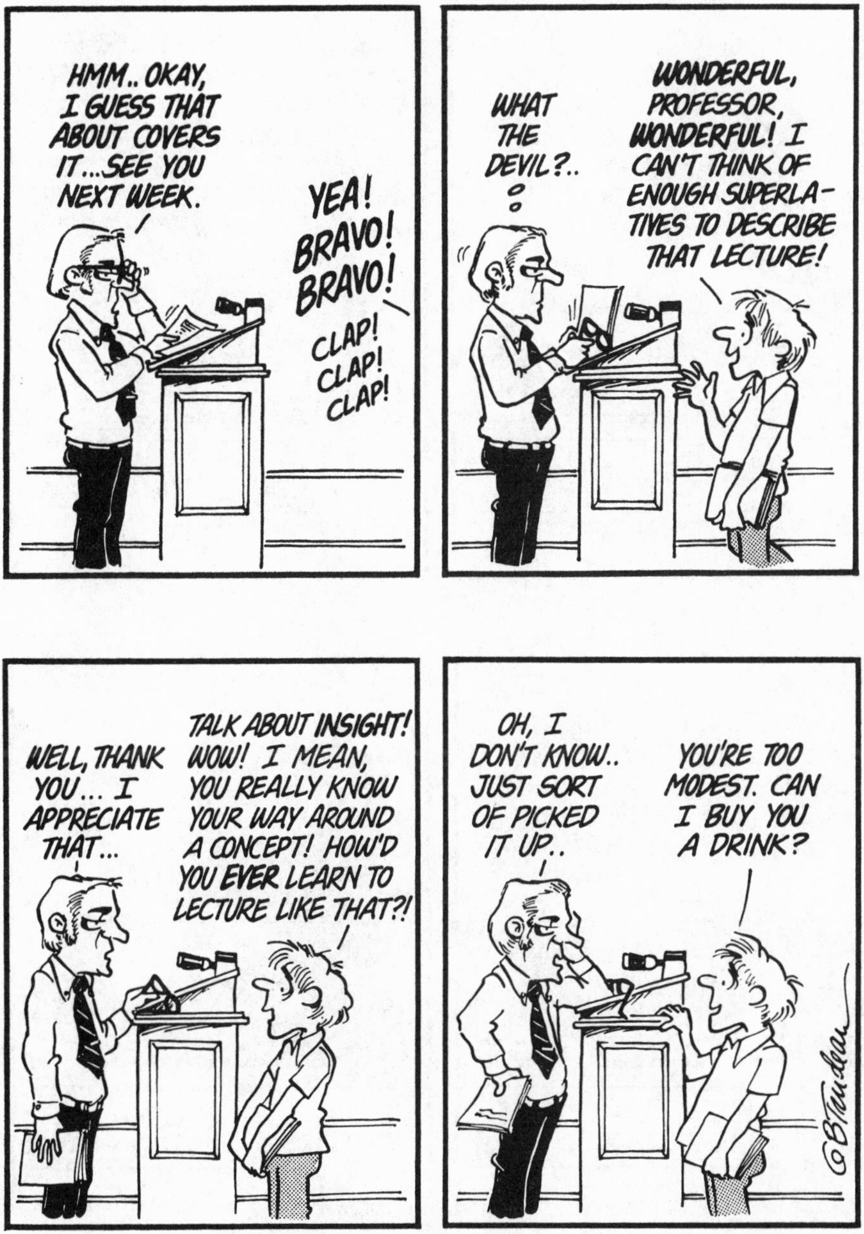

HMM.. OKAY, I GUESS THAT ABOUT COVERS IT...SEE YOU NEXT WEEK.
YEA! BRAVO! BRAVO!
CLAP! CLAP! CLAP!
WHAT THE DEVIL?..
WONDERFUL, PROFESSOR, WONDERFUL! I CAN'T THINK OF ENOUGH SUPERLA-TIVES TO DESCRIBE THAT LECTURE!
WELL, THANK YOU... I APPRECIATE THAT...
TALK ABOUT INSIGHT! WOW! I MEAN, YOU REALLY KNOW YOUR WAY AROUND A CONCEPT! HOW'D YOU EVER LEARN TO LECTURE LIKE THAT?!
OH, I DON'T KNOW.. JUST SORT OF PICKED IT UP..
YOU'RE TOO MODEST. CAN I BUY YOU A DRINK?
©BTrudeau

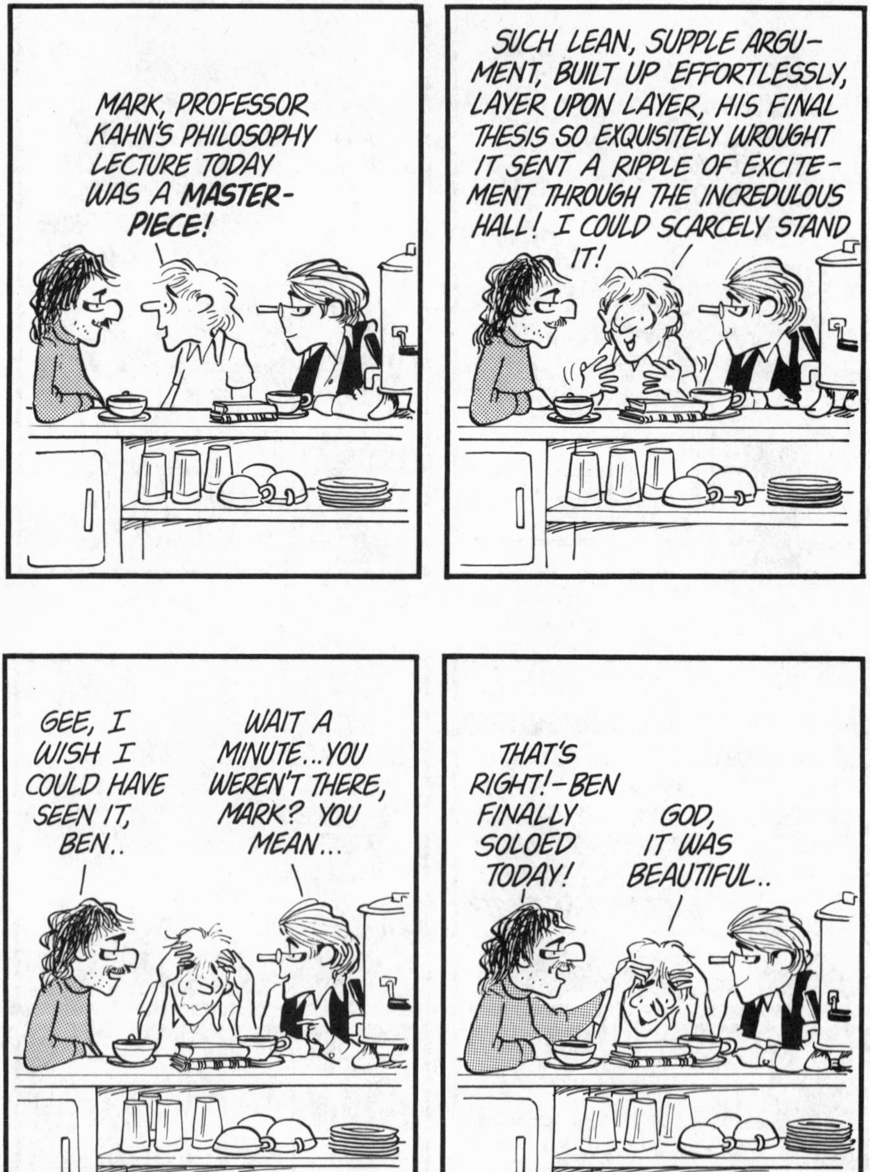
MARK, PROFESSOR KAHN'S PHILOSOPHY LECTURE TODAY WAS A **MASTER-PIECE!**
SUCH LEAN, SUPPLE ARGU-MENT, BUILT UP EFFORTLESSLY, LAYER UPON LAYER, HIS FINAL THESIS SO EXQUISITELY WROUGHT IT SENT A RIPPLE OF EXCITE-MENT THROUGH THE INCREDULOUS HALL! I COULD SCARCELY STAND IT!
GEE, I WISH I COULD HAVE SEEN IT, BEN..
WAIT A MINUTE...YOU WEREN'T THERE, MARK? YOU MEAN...
THAT'S RIGHT!–BEN FINALLY SOLOED TODAY!
GOD, IT WAS BEAUTIFUL..
GBTrudeau

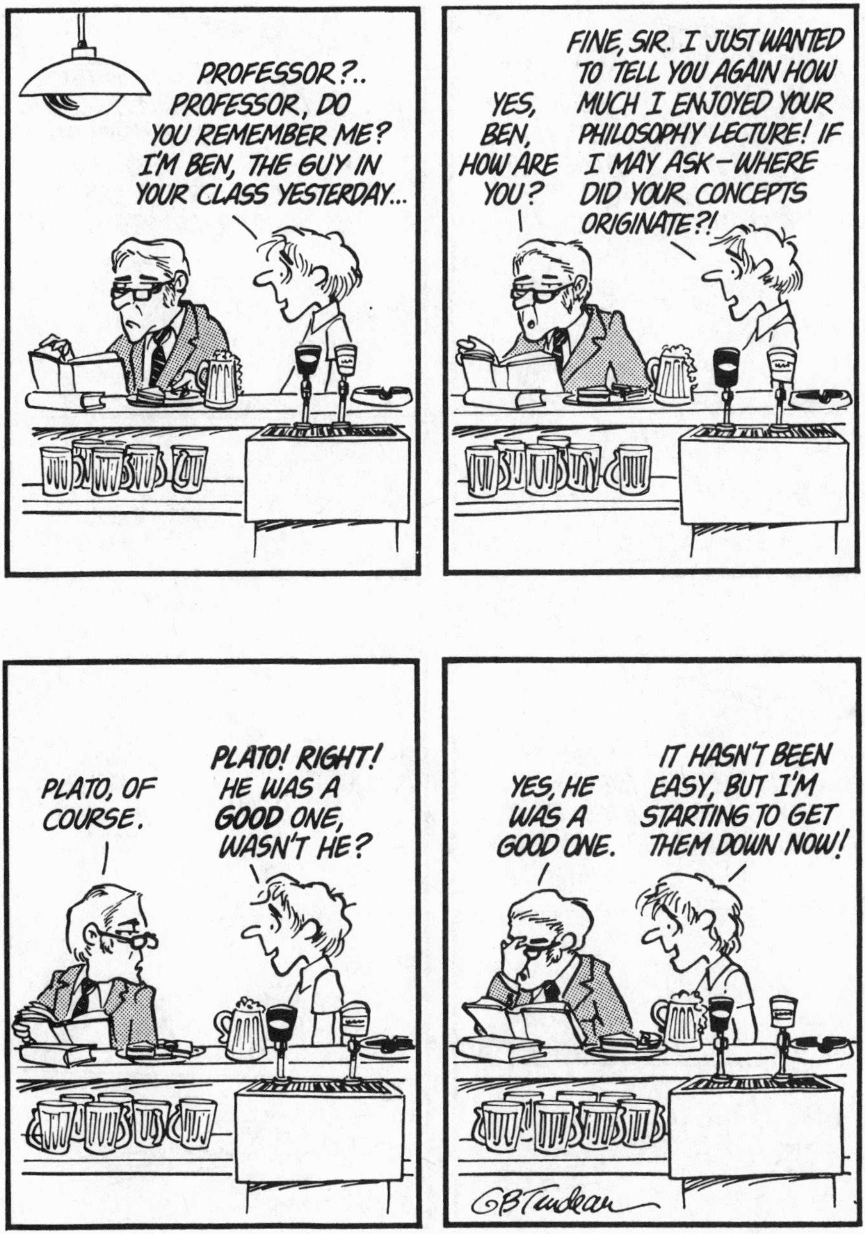
PROFESSOR?.. PROFESSOR, DO YOU REMEMBER ME? I'M BEN, THE GUY IN YOUR CLASS YESTERDAY...
YES, BEN, HOW ARE YOU?
FINE, SIR. I JUST WANTED TO TELL YOU AGAIN HOW MUCH I ENJOYED YOUR PHILOSOPHY LECTURE! IF I MAY ASK–WHERE DID YOUR CONCEPTS ORIGINATE?!
PLATO, OF COURSE.
PLATO! RIGHT! HE WAS A GOOD ONE, WASN'T HE?
YES, HE WAS A GOOD ONE.
IT HASN'T BEEN EASY, BUT I'M STARTING TO GET THEM DOWN NOW!
GBTrudeau

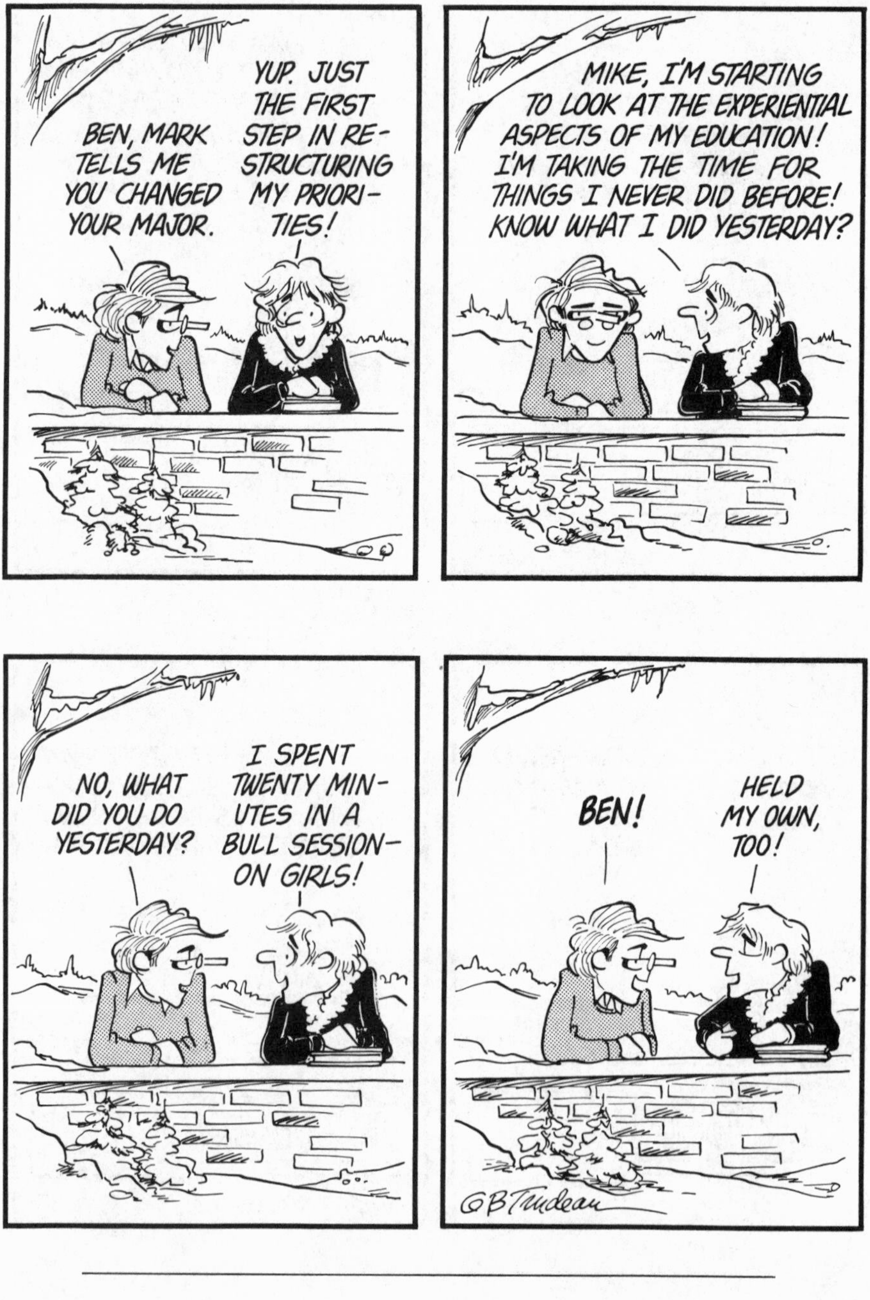
BEN, MARK TELLS ME YOU CHANGED YOUR MAJOR.
YUP. JUST THE FIRST STEP IN RE-STRUCTURING MY PRIORI-TIES!
MIKE, I'M STARTING TO LOOK AT THE EXPERIENTIAL ASPECTS OF MY EDUCATION! I'M TAKING THE TIME FOR THINGS I NEVER DID BEFORE! KNOW WHAT I DID YESTERDAY?
NO, WHAT DID YOU DO YESTERDAY?
I SPENT TWENTY MIN-UTES IN A BULL SESSION-ON GIRLS!
BEN!
HELD MY OWN, TOO!
GBTrudeau

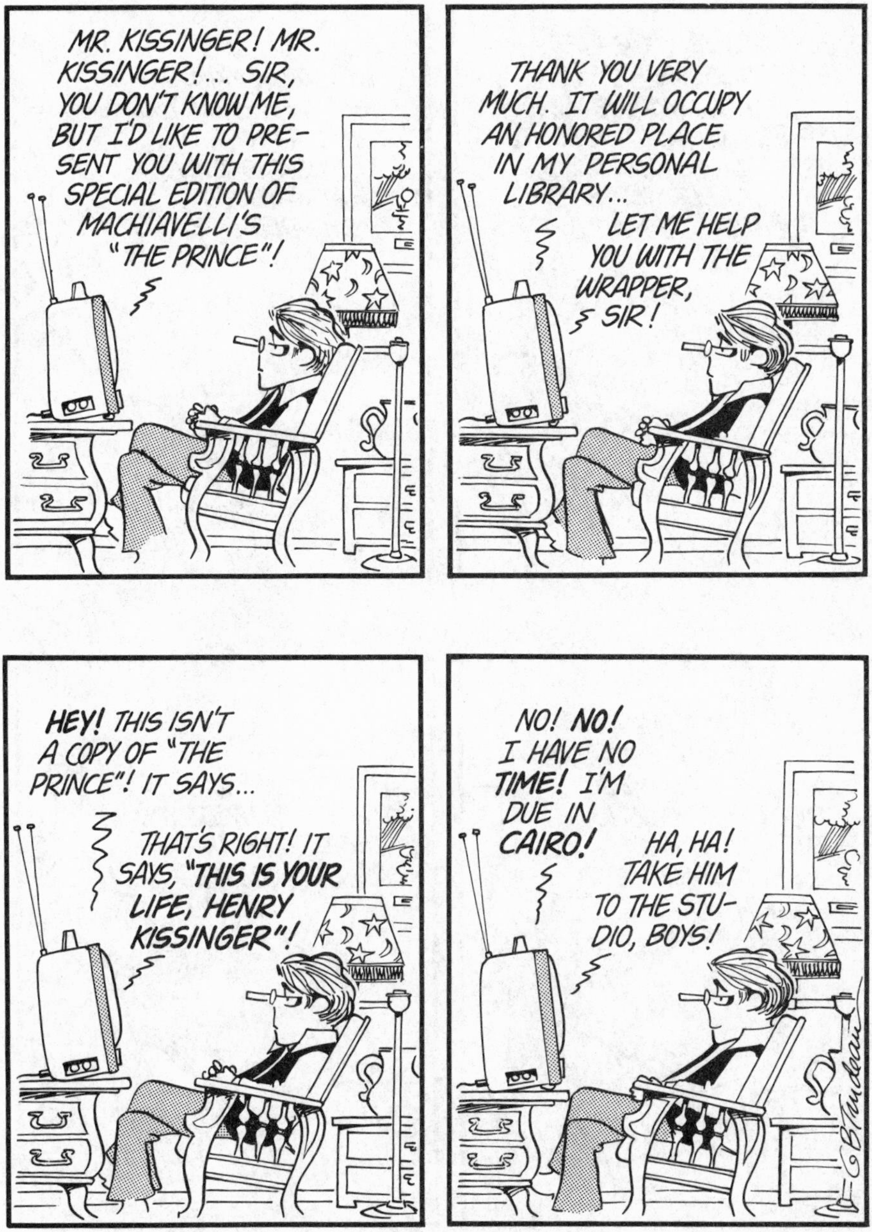
MR. KISSINGER! MR. KISSINGER!... SIR, YOU DON'T KNOW ME, BUT I'D LIKE TO PRE-SENT YOU WITH THIS SPECIAL EDITION OF MACHIAVELLI'S "THE PRINCE"!
THANK YOU VERY MUCH. IT WILL OCCUPY AN HONORED PLACE IN MY PERSONAL LIBRARY...
LET ME HELP YOU WITH THE WRAPPER, SIR!
HEY! THIS ISN'T A COPY OF "THE PRINCE"! IT SAYS...
THAT'S RIGHT! IT SAYS, "THIS IS YOUR LIFE, HENRY KISSINGER"!
NO! NO! I HAVE NO TIME! I'M DUE IN CAIRO!
HA, HA! TAKE HIM TO THE STU-DIO, BOYS!
©B Trudeau

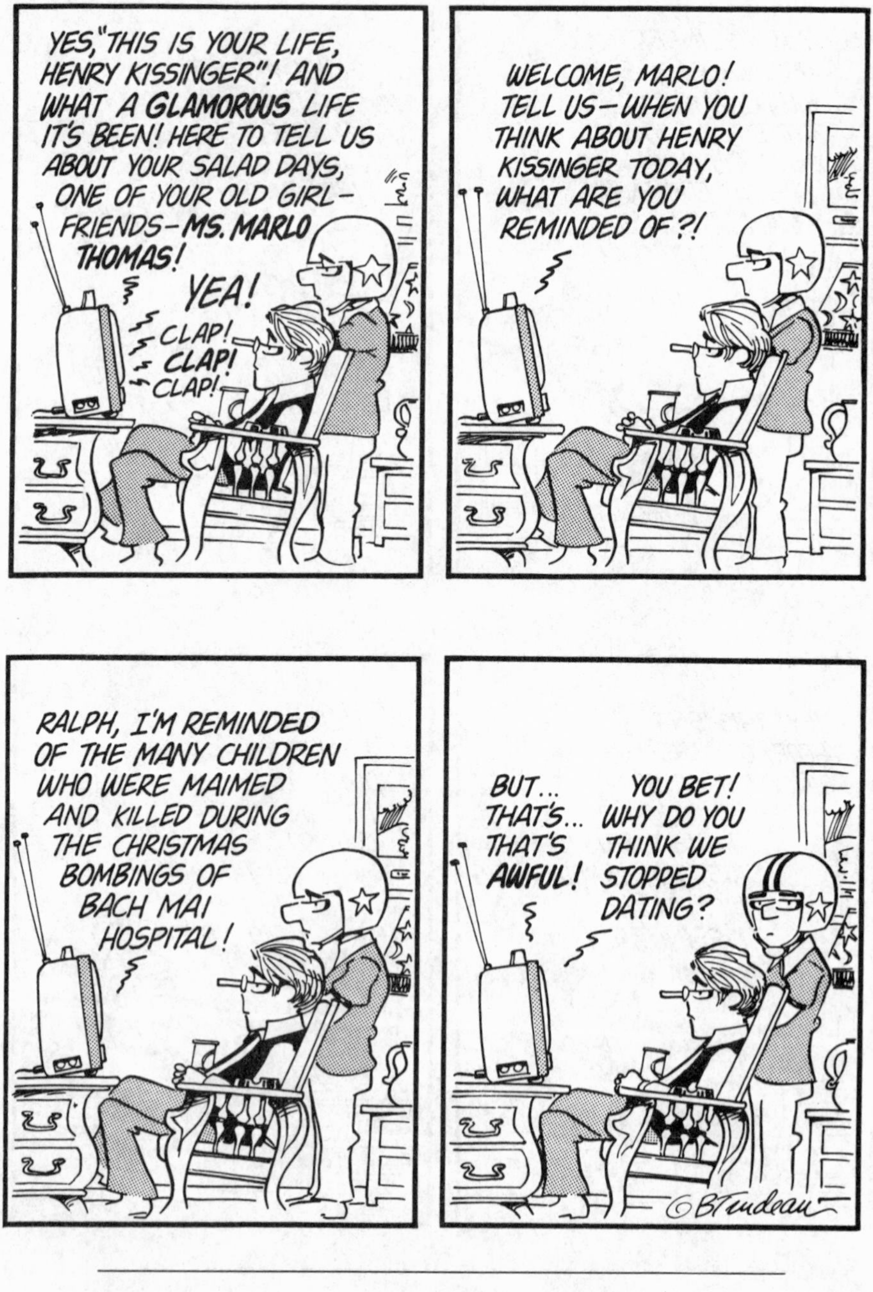
YES, "THIS IS YOUR LIFE, HENRY KISSINGER"! AND WHAT A GLAMOROUS LIFE IT'S BEEN! HERE TO TELL US ABOUT YOUR SALAD DAYS, ONE OF YOUR OLD GIRL-FRIENDS—MS. MARLO THOMAS!
YEA!
CLAP! CLAP! CLAP!
WELCOME, MARLO! TELL US—WHEN YOU THINK ABOUT HENRY KISSINGER TODAY, WHAT ARE YOU REMINDED OF?!
RALPH, I'M REMINDED OF THE MANY CHILDREN WHO WERE MAIMED AND KILLED DURING THE CHRISTMAS BOMBINGS OF BACH MAI HOSPITAL!
BUT... THAT'S... THAT'S AWFUL!
YOU BET! WHY DO YOU THINK WE STOPPED DATING?
© BTrudeau

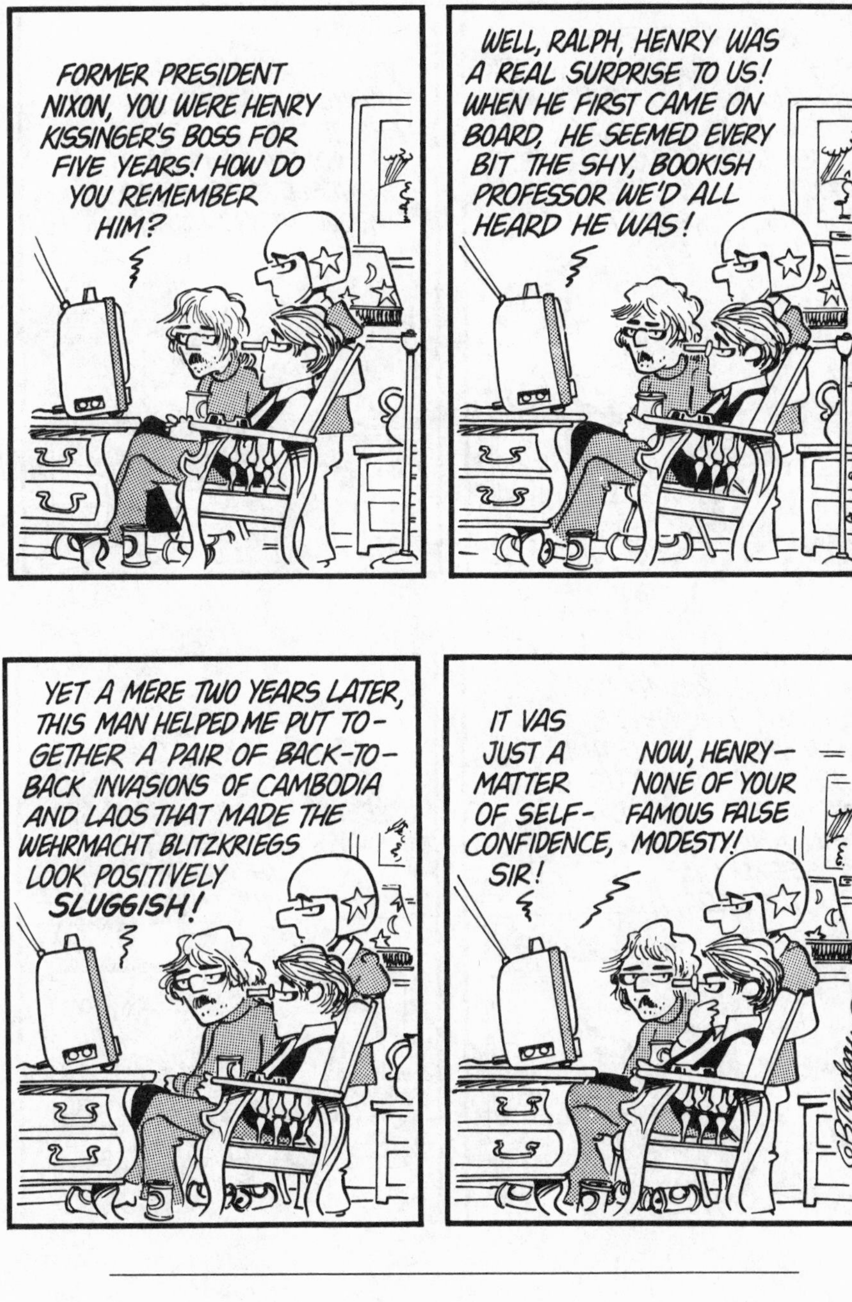
FORMER PRESIDENT NIXON, YOU WERE HENRY KISSINGER'S BOSS FOR FIVE YEARS! HOW DO YOU REMEMBER HIM?
WELL, RALPH, HENRY WAS A REAL SURPRISE TO US! WHEN HE FIRST CAME ON BOARD, HE SEEMED EVERY BIT THE SHY, BOOKISH PROFESSOR WE'D ALL HEARD HE WAS!
YET A MERE TWO YEARS LATER, THIS MAN HELPED ME PUT TOGETHER A PAIR OF BACK-TO-BACK INVASIONS OF CAMBODIA AND LAOS THAT MADE THE WEHRMACHT BLITZKRIEGS LOOK POSITIVELY **SLUGGISH**!
NOW, HENRY— NONE OF YOUR FAMOUS FALSE MODESTY!
IT VAS JUST A MATTER OF SELF-CONFIDENCE, SIR!
©BTrudeau

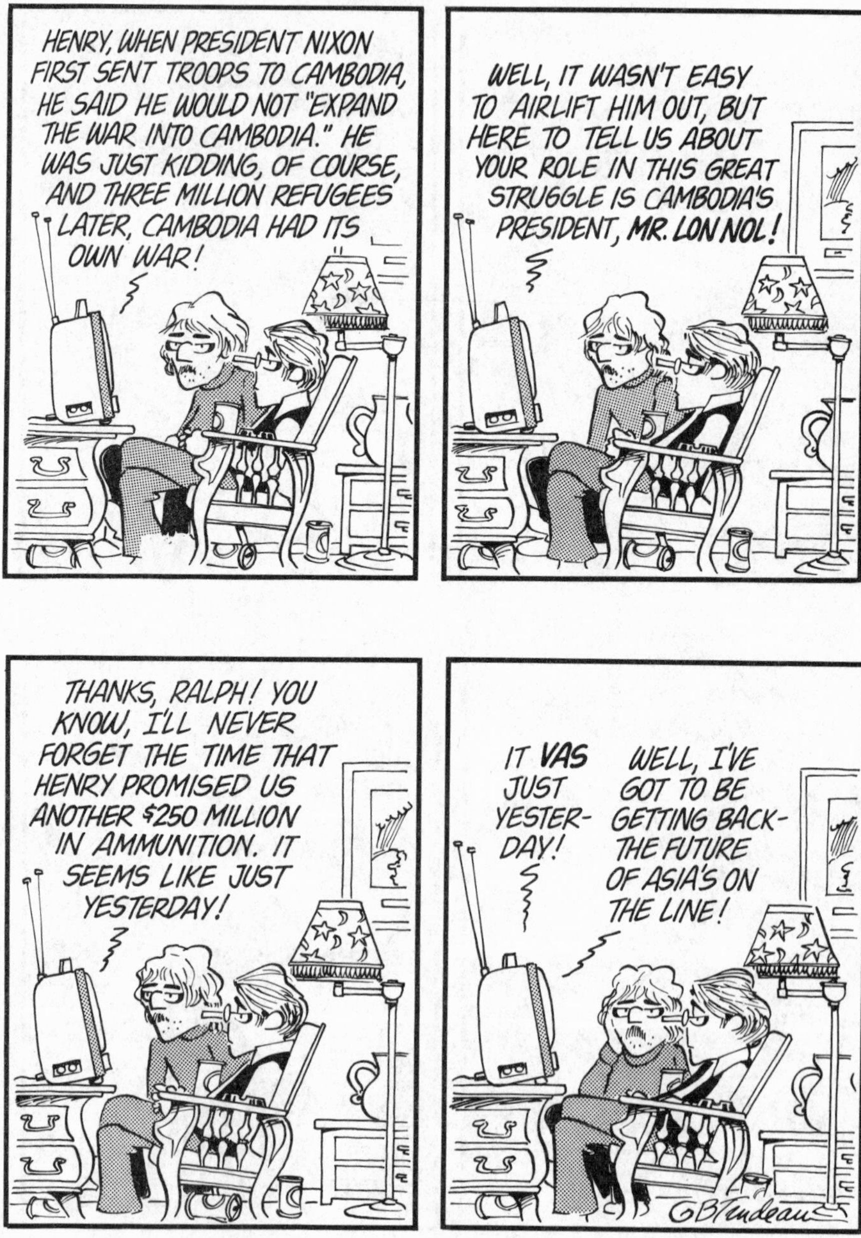
HENRY, WHEN PRESIDENT NIXON FIRST SENT TROOPS TO CAMBODIA, HE SAID HE WOULD NOT "EXPAND THE WAR INTO CAMBODIA." HE WAS JUST KIDDING, OF COURSE, AND THREE MILLION REFUGEES LATER, CAMBODIA HAD ITS OWN WAR!
WELL, IT WASN'T EASY TO AIRLIFT HIM OUT, BUT HERE TO TELL US ABOUT YOUR ROLE IN THIS GREAT STRUGGLE IS CAMBODIA'S PRESIDENT, **MR. LON NOL**!
THANKS, RALPH! YOU KNOW, I'LL NEVER FORGET THE TIME THAT HENRY PROMISED US ANOTHER $250 MILLION IN AMMUNITION. IT SEEMS LIKE JUST YESTERDAY!
IT **VAS** JUST YESTER-DAY!
WELL, I'VE GOT TO BE GETTING BACK- THE FUTURE OF ASIA'S ON THE LINE!
GBTrudeau

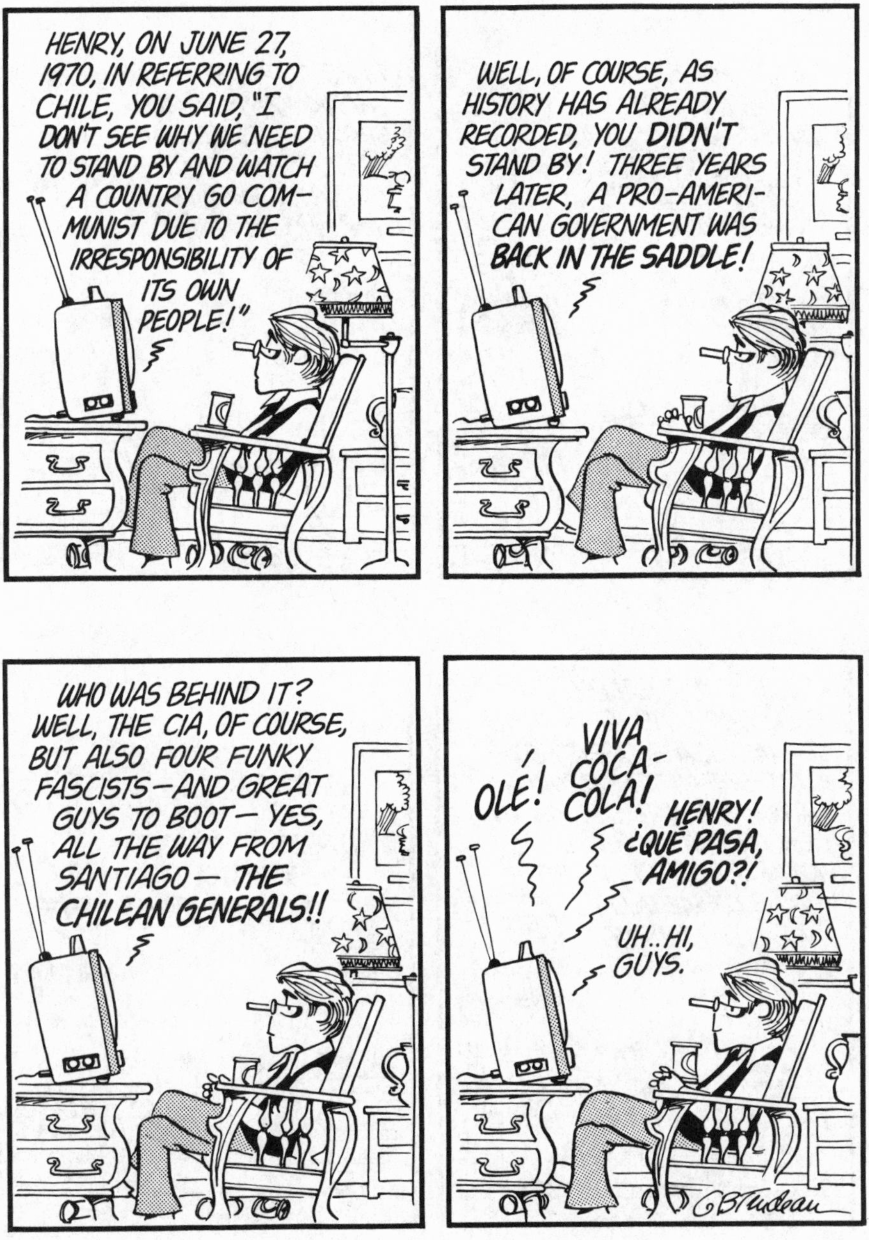

HENRY, ON JUNE 27, 1970, IN REFERRING TO CHILE, YOU SAID, "I DON'T SEE WHY WE NEED TO STAND BY AND WATCH A COUNTRY GO COMMUNIST DUE TO THE IRRESPONSIBILITY OF ITS OWN PEOPLE!"
WELL, OF COURSE, AS HISTORY HAS ALREADY RECORDED, YOU **DIDN'T** STAND BY! THREE YEARS LATER, A PRO-AMERICAN GOVERNMENT WAS **BACK IN THE SADDLE!**
WHO WAS BEHIND IT? WELL, THE CIA, OF COURSE, BUT ALSO FOUR FUNKY FASCISTS—AND GREAT GUYS TO BOOT—YES, ALL THE WAY FROM SANTIAGO—**THE CHILEAN GENERALS!!**
OLÉ!
VIVA COCA-COLA!
HENRY! ¿QUÉ PASA, AMIGO?!
UH..HI, GUYS.
GBTrudeau

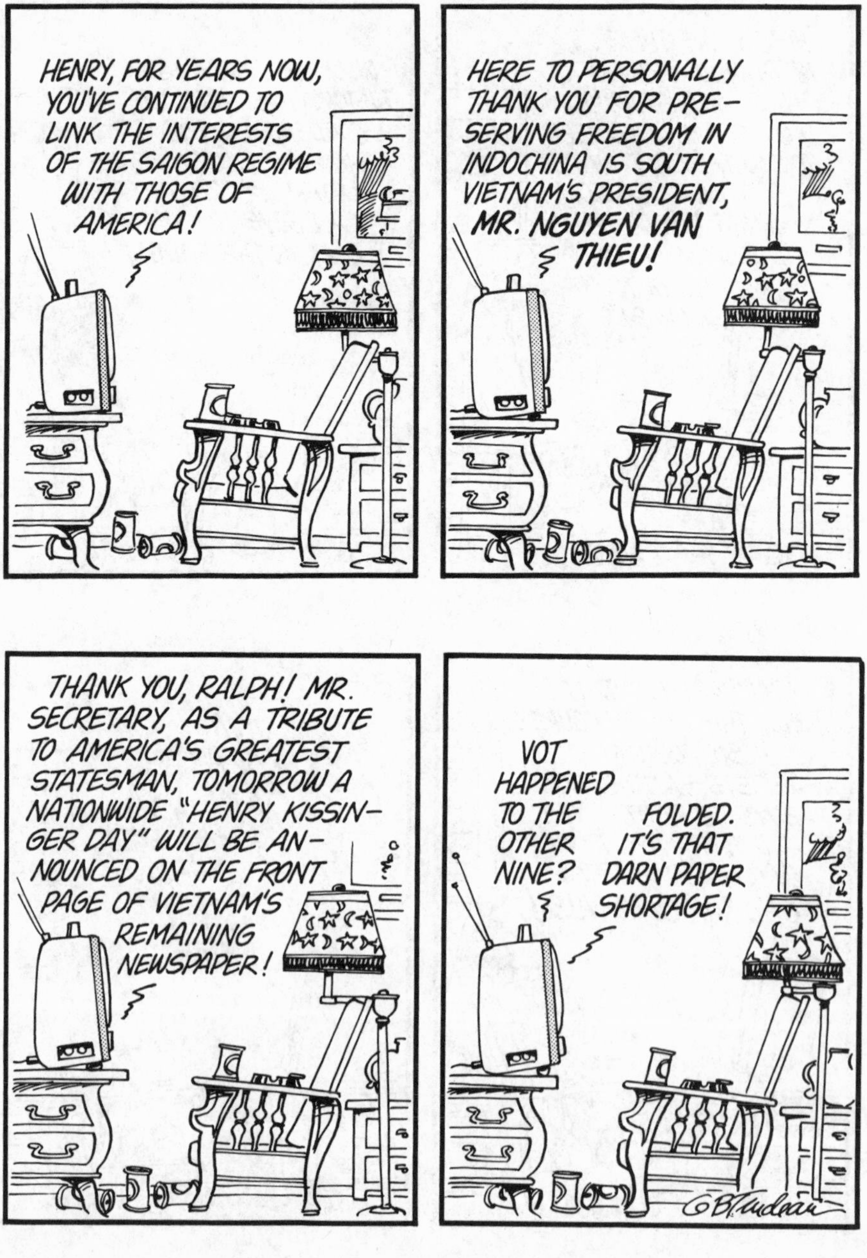
HENRY, FOR YEARS NOW, YOU'VE CONTINUED TO LINK THE INTERESTS OF THE SAIGON REGIME WITH THOSE OF AMERICA!
HERE TO PERSONALLY THANK YOU FOR PRE-SERVING FREEDOM IN INDOCHINA IS SOUTH VIETNAM'S PRESIDENT, MR. NGUYEN VAN THIEU!
THANK YOU, RALPH! MR. SECRETARY, AS A TRIBUTE TO AMERICA'S GREATEST STATESMAN, TOMORROW A NATIONWIDE "HENRY KISSIN-GER DAY" WILL BE AN-NOUNCED ON THE FRONT PAGE OF VIETNAM'S REMAINING NEWSPAPER!
VOT HAPPENED TO THE OTHER NINE?
FOLDED. IT'S THAT DARN PAPER SHORTAGE!
© B. Trudeau

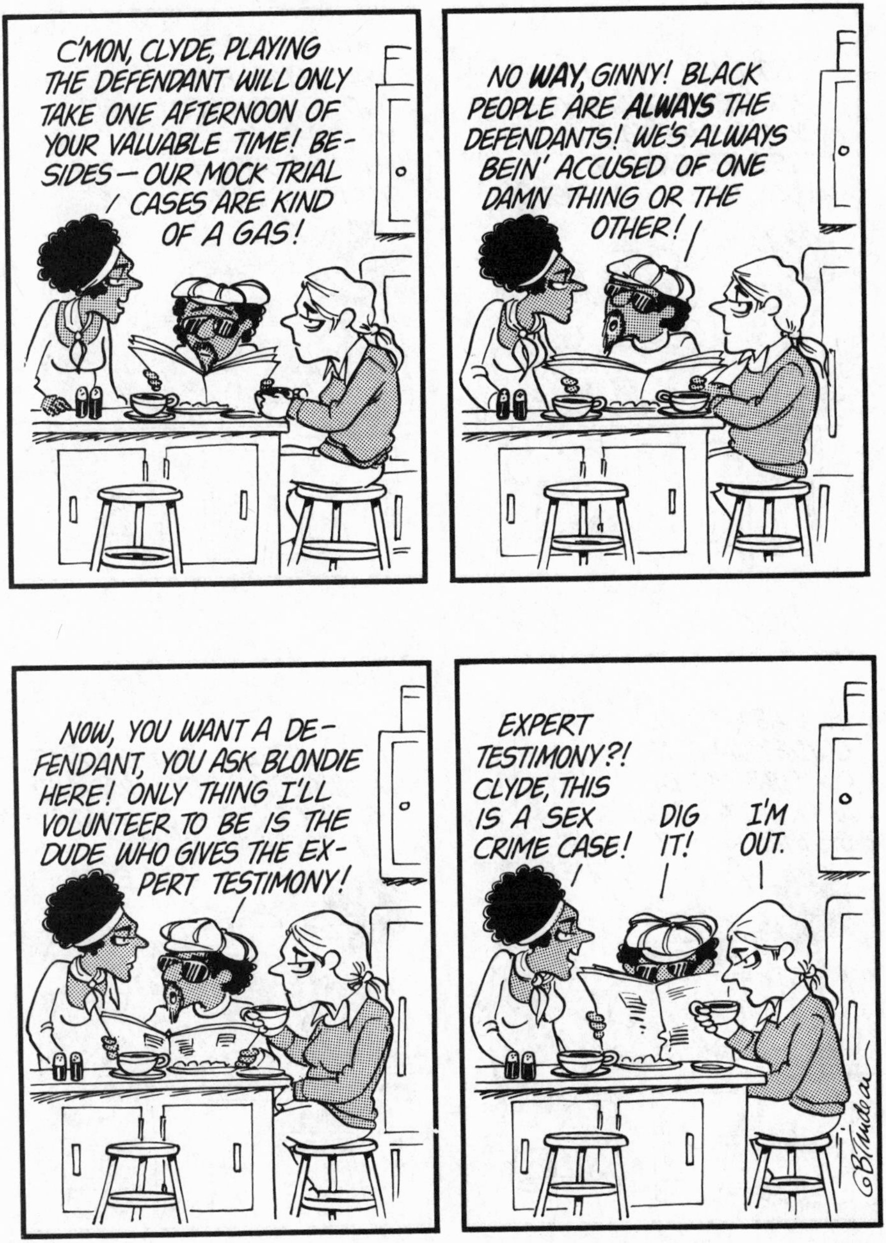

C'MON, CLYDE, PLAYING THE DEFENDANT WILL ONLY TAKE ONE AFTERNOON OF YOUR VALUABLE TIME! BESIDES—OUR MOCK TRIAL CASES ARE KIND OF A GAS!
NO **WAY**, GINNY! BLACK PEOPLE ARE **ALWAYS** THE DEFENDANTS! WE'S ALWAYS BEIN' ACCUSED OF ONE DAMN THING OR THE OTHER!
NOW, YOU WANT A DEFENDANT, YOU ASK BLONDIE HERE! ONLY THING I'LL VOLUNTEER TO BE IS THE DUDE WHO GIVES THE EXPERT TESTIMONY!
EXPERT TESTIMONY?! CLYDE, THIS IS A SEX CRIME CASE!
DIG IT!
I'M OUT.
©BTrudeau

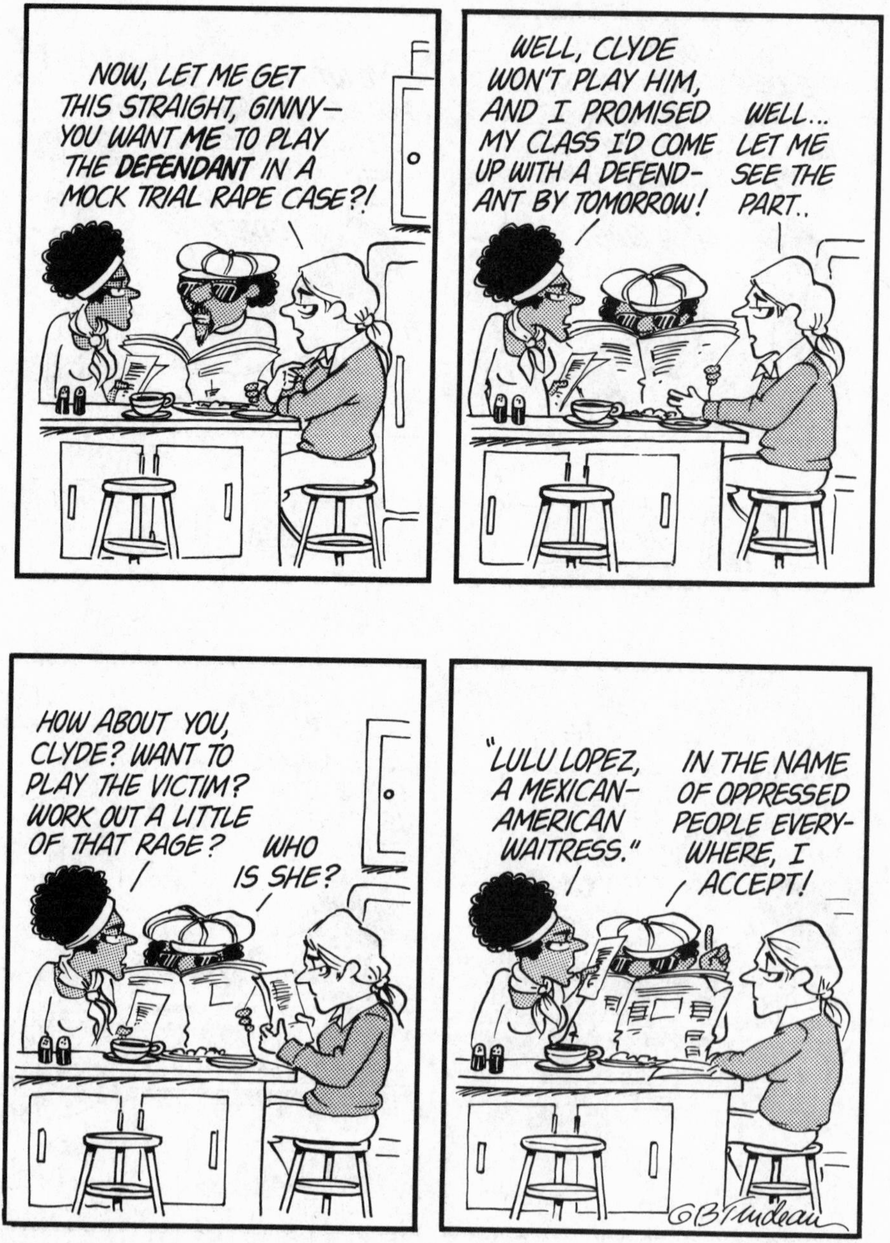
NOW, LET ME GET THIS STRAIGHT, GINNY– YOU WANT ME TO PLAY THE DEFENDANT IN A MOCK TRIAL RAPE CASE?!
WELL, CLYDE WON'T PLAY HIM, AND I PROMISED MY CLASS I'D COME UP WITH A DEFEND-ANT BY TOMORROW!
WELL... LET ME SEE THE PART..
HOW ABOUT YOU, CLYDE? WANT TO PLAY THE VICTIM? WORK OUT A LITTLE OF THAT RAGE?
WHO IS SHE?
"LULU LOPEZ, A MEXICAN-AMERICAN WAITRESS."
IN THE NAME OF OPPRESSED PEOPLE EVERY-WHERE, I ACCEPT!
GBTrudeau

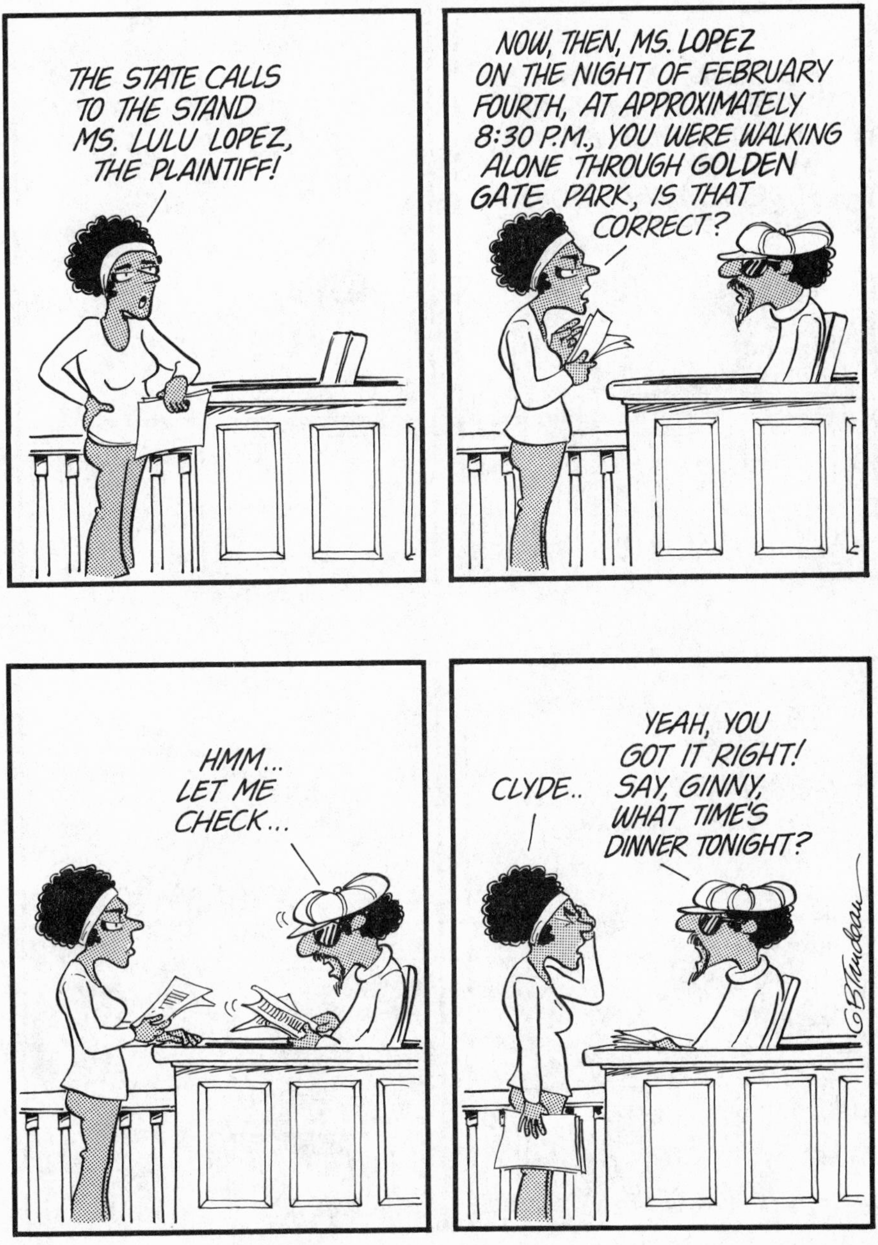
THE STATE CALLS TO THE STAND MS. LULU LOPEZ, THE PLAINTIFF!
NOW, THEN, MS. LOPEZ ON THE NIGHT OF FEBRUARY FOURTH, AT APPROXIMATELY 8:30 P.M., YOU WERE WALKING ALONE THROUGH GOLDEN GATE PARK, IS THAT CORRECT?
HMM... LET ME CHECK...
YEAH, YOU GOT IT RIGHT! SAY, GINNY, WHAT TIME'S DINNER TONIGHT?
CLYDE..
©GBTrudeau

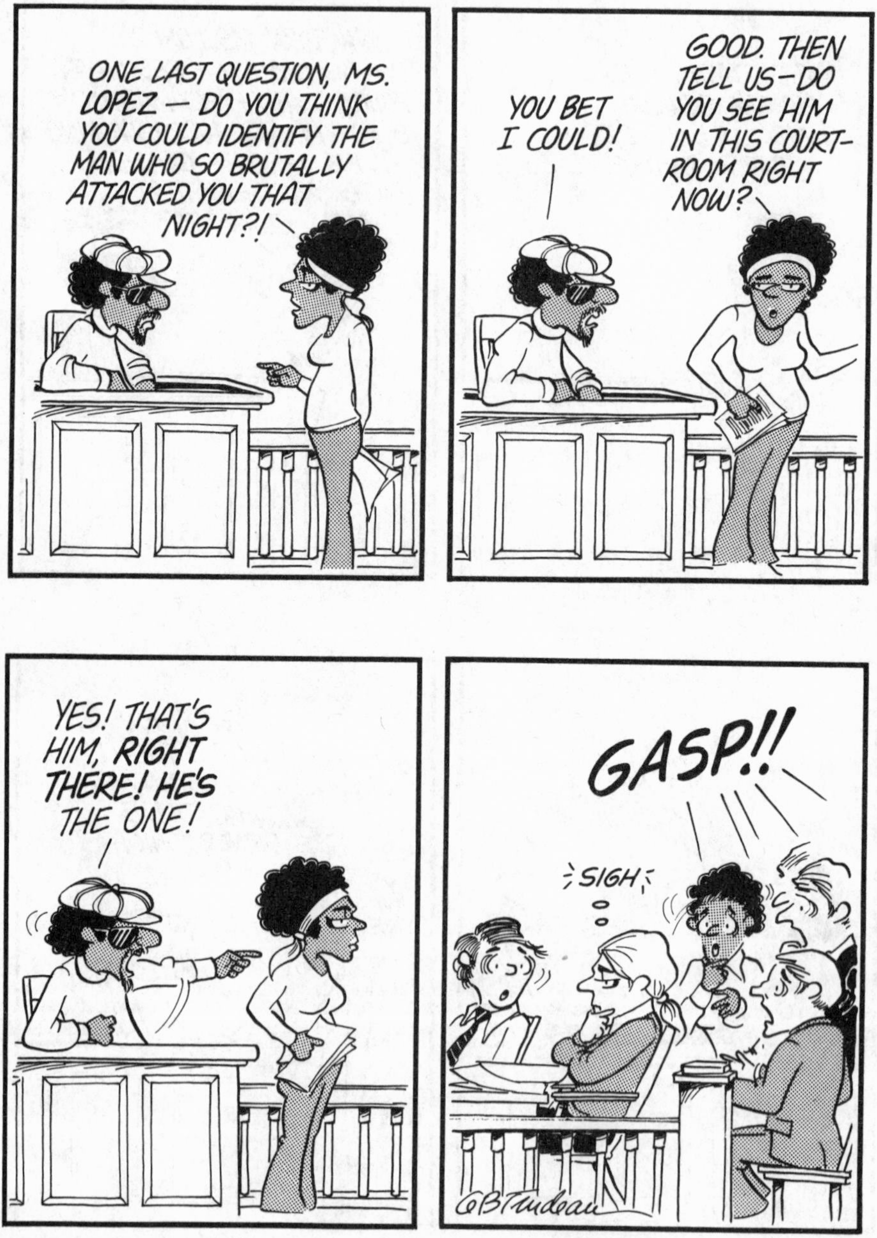
ONE LAST QUESTION, MS. LOPEZ — DO YOU THINK YOU COULD IDENTIFY THE MAN WHO SO BRUTALLY ATTACKED YOU THAT NIGHT?!
YOU BET I COULD!
GOOD. THEN TELL US—DO YOU SEE HIM IN THIS COURTROOM RIGHT NOW?
YES! THAT'S HIM, RIGHT THERE! HE'S THE ONE!
GASP!!
SIGH
©BTrudeau

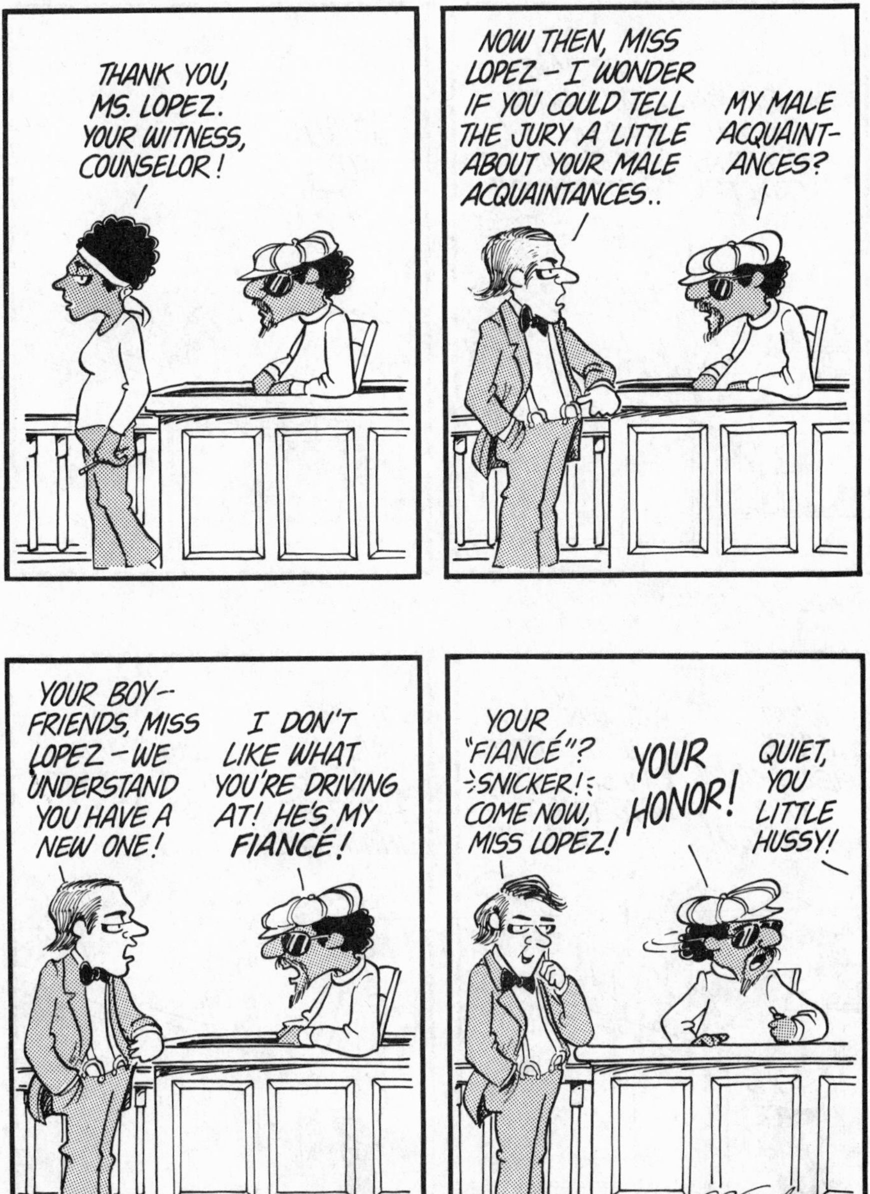
THANK YOU, MS. LOPEZ. YOUR WITNESS, COUNSELOR!
NOW THEN, MISS LOPEZ - I WONDER IF YOU COULD TELL THE JURY A LITTLE ABOUT YOUR MALE ACQUAINTANCES..
MY MALE ACQUAINT-ANCES?
YOUR BOY-FRIENDS, MISS LOPEZ - WE UNDERSTAND YOU HAVE A NEW ONE!
I DON'T LIKE WHAT YOU'RE DRIVING AT! HE'S MY FIANCÉ!
YOUR "FIANCÉ"? SNICKER! COME NOW, MISS LOPEZ!
YOUR HONOR!
QUIET, YOU LITTLE HUSSY!
GBTrudeau

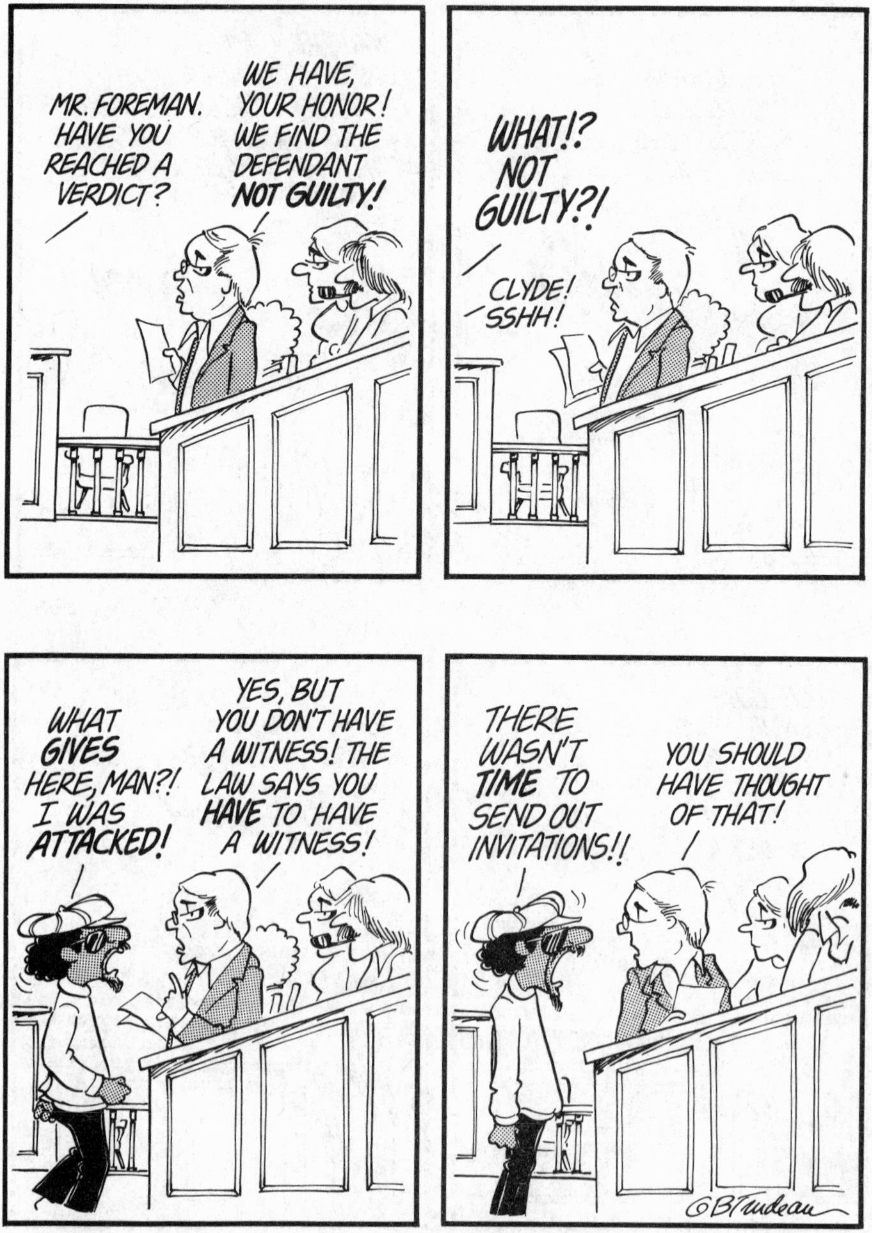
MR. FOREMAN. HAVE YOU REACHED A VERDICT?
WE HAVE, YOUR HONOR! WE FIND THE DEFENDANT NOT GUILTY!
WHAT!? NOT GUILTY?!
CLYDE! SSHH!
WHAT GIVES HERE, MAN?! I WAS ATTACKED!
YES, BUT YOU DON'T HAVE A WITNESS! THE LAW SAYS YOU HAVE TO HAVE A WITNESS!
THERE WASN'T TIME TO SEND OUT INVITATIONS!!
YOU SHOULD HAVE THOUGHT OF THAT!
©BTrudeau

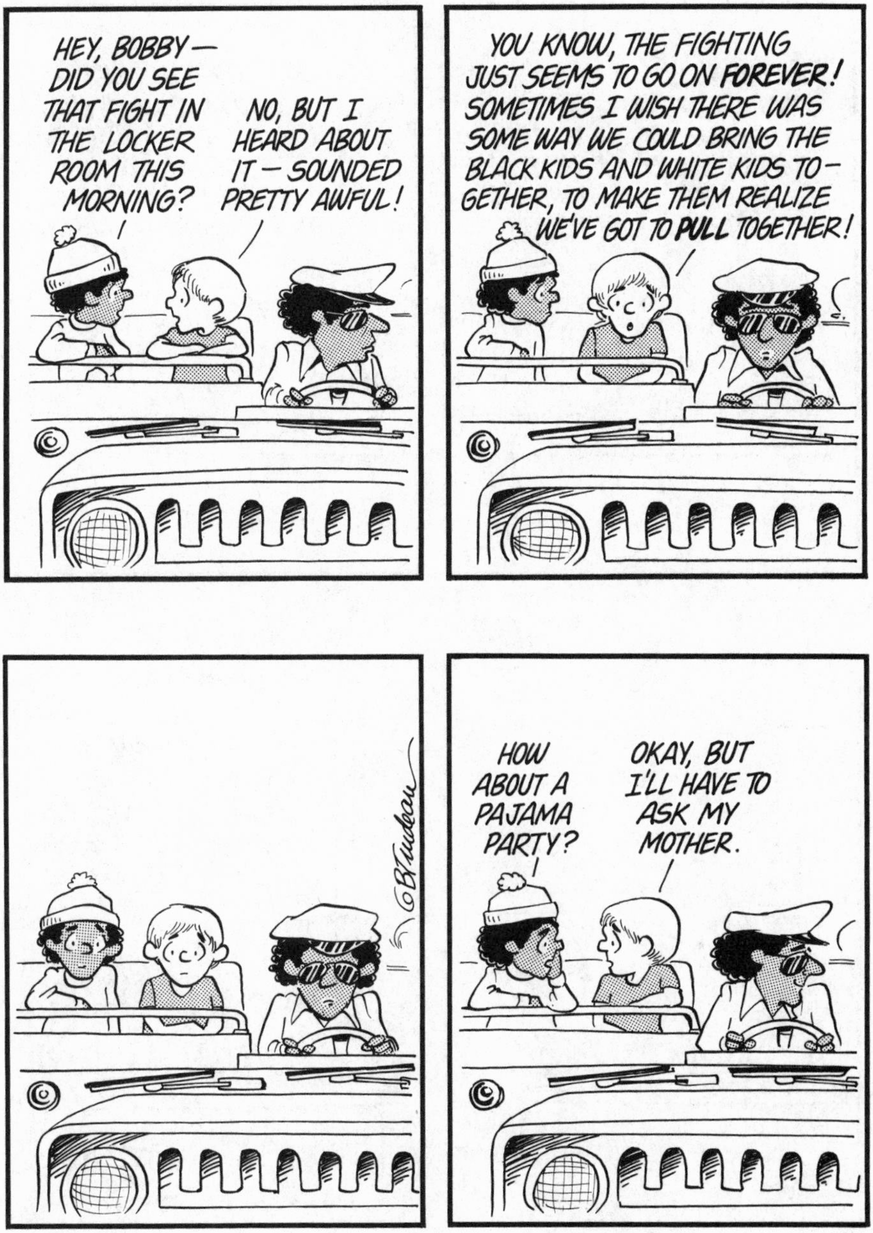
HEY, BOBBY— DID YOU SEE THAT FIGHT IN THE LOCKER ROOM THIS MORNING?
NO, BUT I HEARD ABOUT IT — SOUNDED PRETTY AWFUL!
YOU KNOW, THE FIGHTING JUST SEEMS TO GO ON FOREVER! SOMETIMES I WISH THERE WAS SOME WAY WE COULD BRING THE BLACK KIDS AND WHITE KIDS TOGETHER, TO MAKE THEM REALIZE WE'VE GOT TO PULL TOGETHER!
©BTrudeau
HOW ABOUT A PAJAMA PARTY?
OKAY, BUT I'LL HAVE TO ASK MY MOTHER.

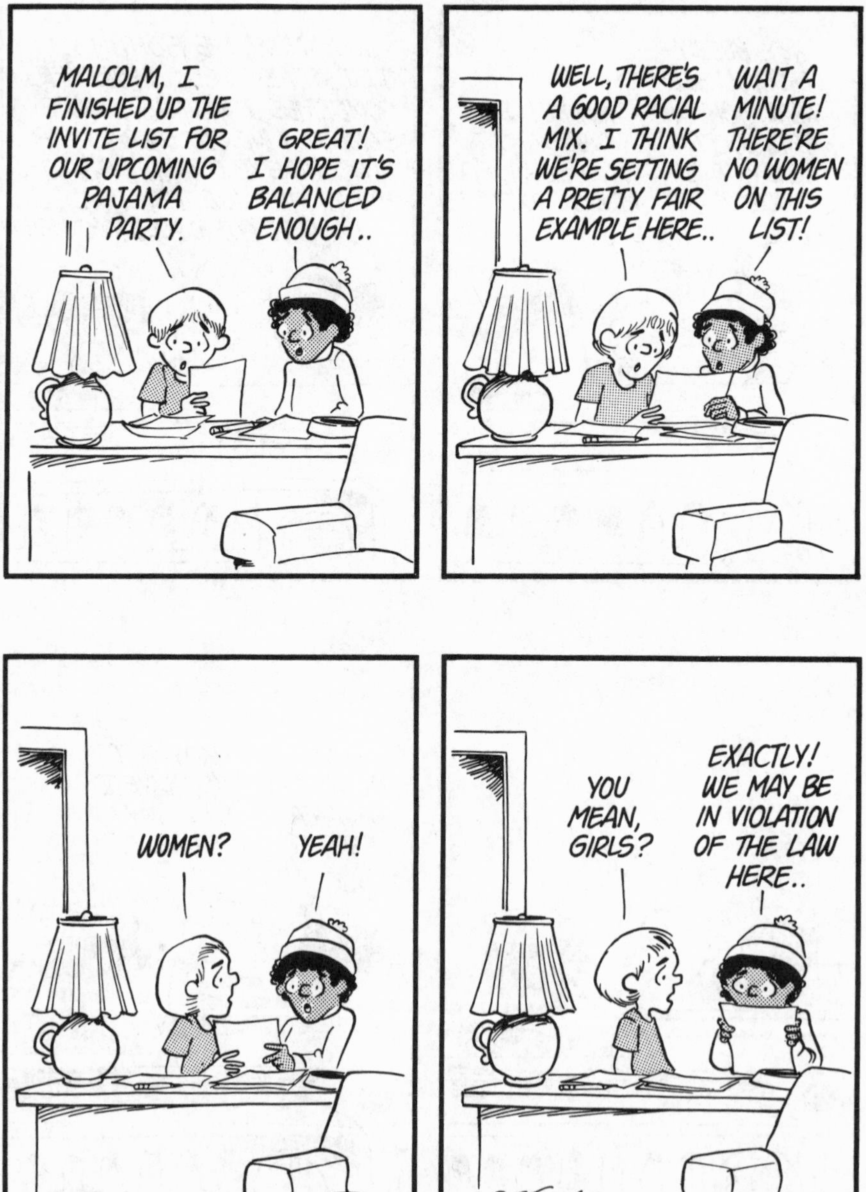

MALCOLM, I FINISHED UP THE INVITE LIST FOR OUR UPCOMING PAJAMA PARTY.
GREAT! I HOPE IT'S BALANCED ENOUGH..
WELL, THERE'S A GOOD RACIAL MIX. I THINK WE'RE SETTING A PRETTY FAIR EXAMPLE HERE..
WAIT A MINUTE! THERE'RE NO WOMEN ON THIS LIST!
WOMEN?
YEAH!
YOU MEAN, GIRLS?
EXACTLY! WE MAY BE IN VIOLATION OF THE LAW HERE..
© BTrudeau

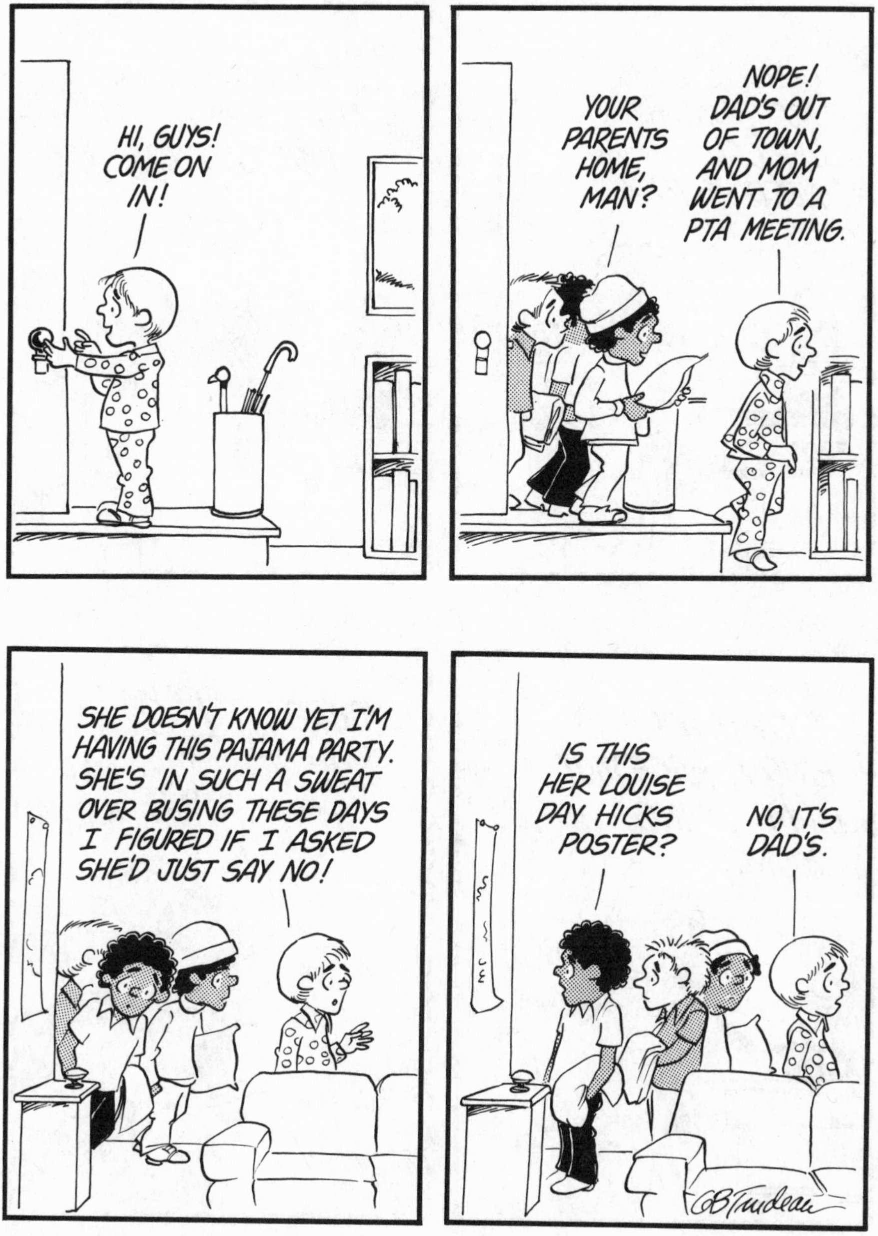
HI, GUYS! COME ON IN!
YOUR PARENTS HOME, MAN?
NOPE! DAD'S OUT OF TOWN, AND MOM WENT TO A PTA MEETING.
SHE DOESN'T KNOW YET I'M HAVING THIS PAJAMA PARTY. SHE'S IN SUCH A SWEAT OVER BUSING THESE DAYS I FIGURED IF I ASKED SHE'D JUST SAY NO!
IS THIS HER LOUISE DAY HICKS POSTER?
NO, IT'S DAD'S.
GBTrudeau

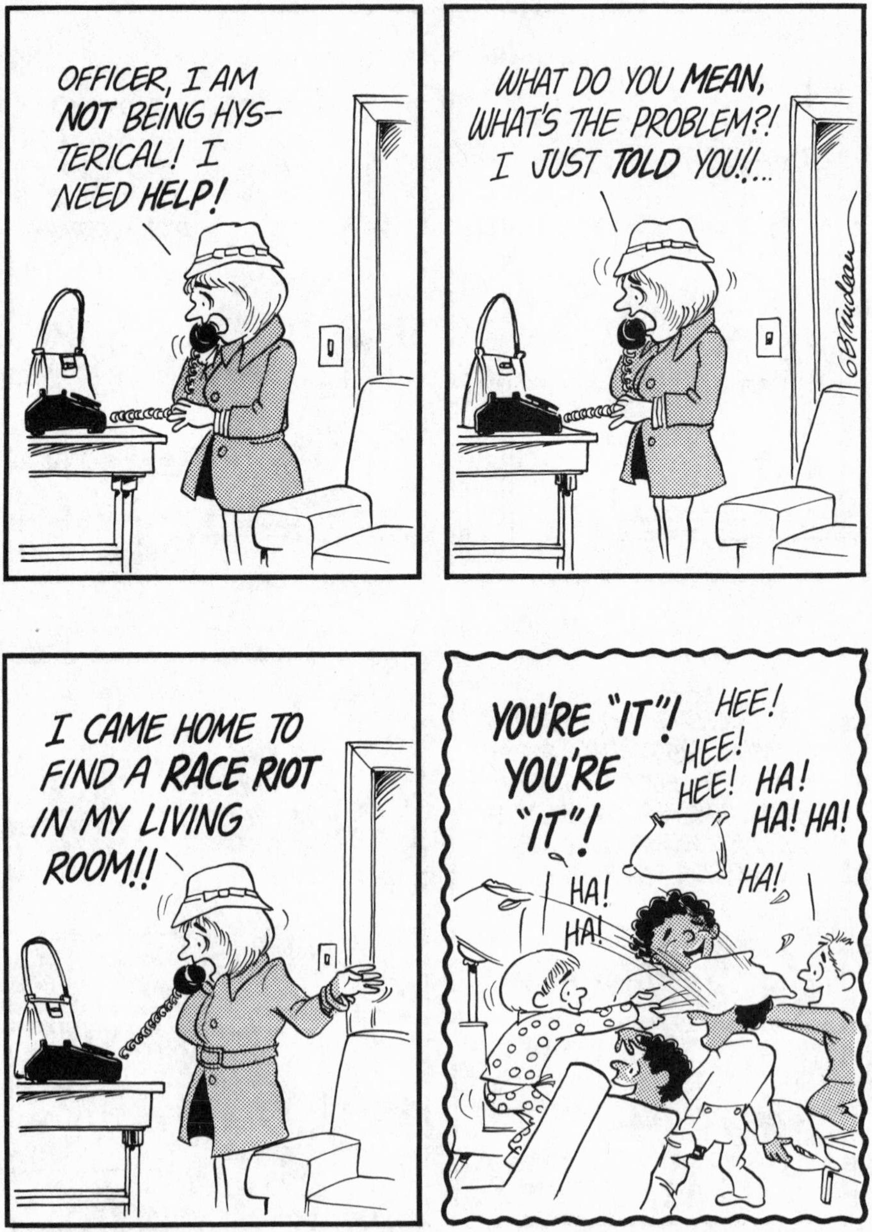
OFFICER, I AM NOT BEING HYS-TERICAL! I NEED HELP!
WHAT DO YOU MEAN, WHAT'S THE PROBLEM?! I JUST TOLD YOU!!...
GBTrudeau
I CAME HOME TO FIND A RACE RIOT IN MY LIVING ROOM!!
YOU'RE "IT"! YOU'RE "IT"!
HEE! HEE! HEE!
HA! HA! HA!
HA!
HA! HA!

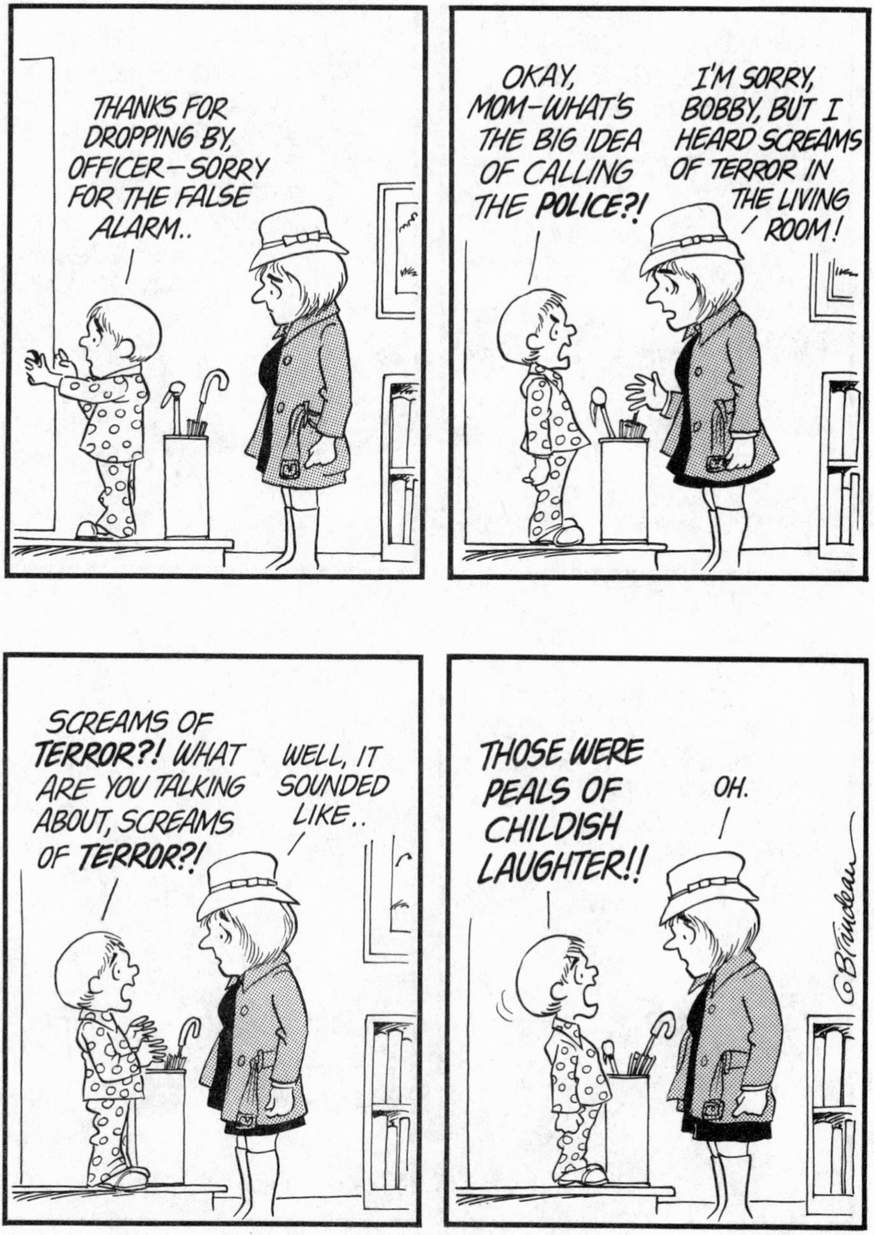
THANKS FOR DROPPING BY, OFFICER—SORRY FOR THE FALSE ALARM..
OKAY, MOM—WHAT'S THE BIG IDEA OF CALLING THE POLICE?!
I'M SORRY, BOBBY, BUT I HEARD SCREAMS OF TERROR IN THE LIVING ROOM!
SCREAMS OF TERROR?! WHAT ARE YOU TALKING ABOUT, SCREAMS OF TERROR?!
WELL, IT SOUNDED LIKE..
THOSE WERE PEALS OF CHILDISH LAUGHTER!!
OH.
© B Trudeau

CAREFUL! CAREFUL! MAN, YOU'VE GOT THE SENSITIVITY OF A MACK TRUCK!
HEY, BERT– WHY DON'T YOU GO FLY A KITE?
GBTrudeau
YOU KNOW, WHAT THIS COUNTRY NEEDS IS A COMPREHENSIVE PLANT CARE PLAN– TO KEEP PLANT CARE OUT OF THE HANDS OF HACKS LIKE YOU!
HEY, MIKE! MIST MY BLOSSOMS, WILLYA?
DID YOU KNOW THAT 45% OF ALL PRIVATELY OWNED PLANTS GO TO BED INADEQUATELY FERTILIZED?!
APPALLING.
DO YOU CARE?!
FRANKLY..
HEY! NOT DOWN MY PISTILS, DAMMIT!

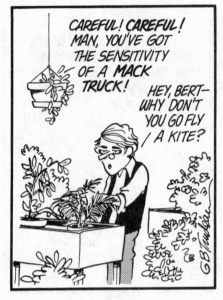

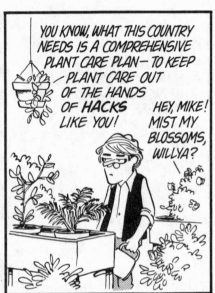

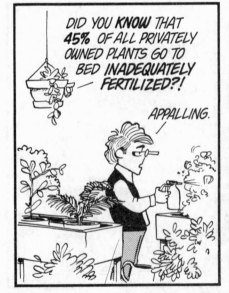

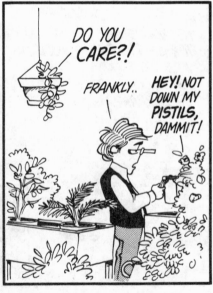

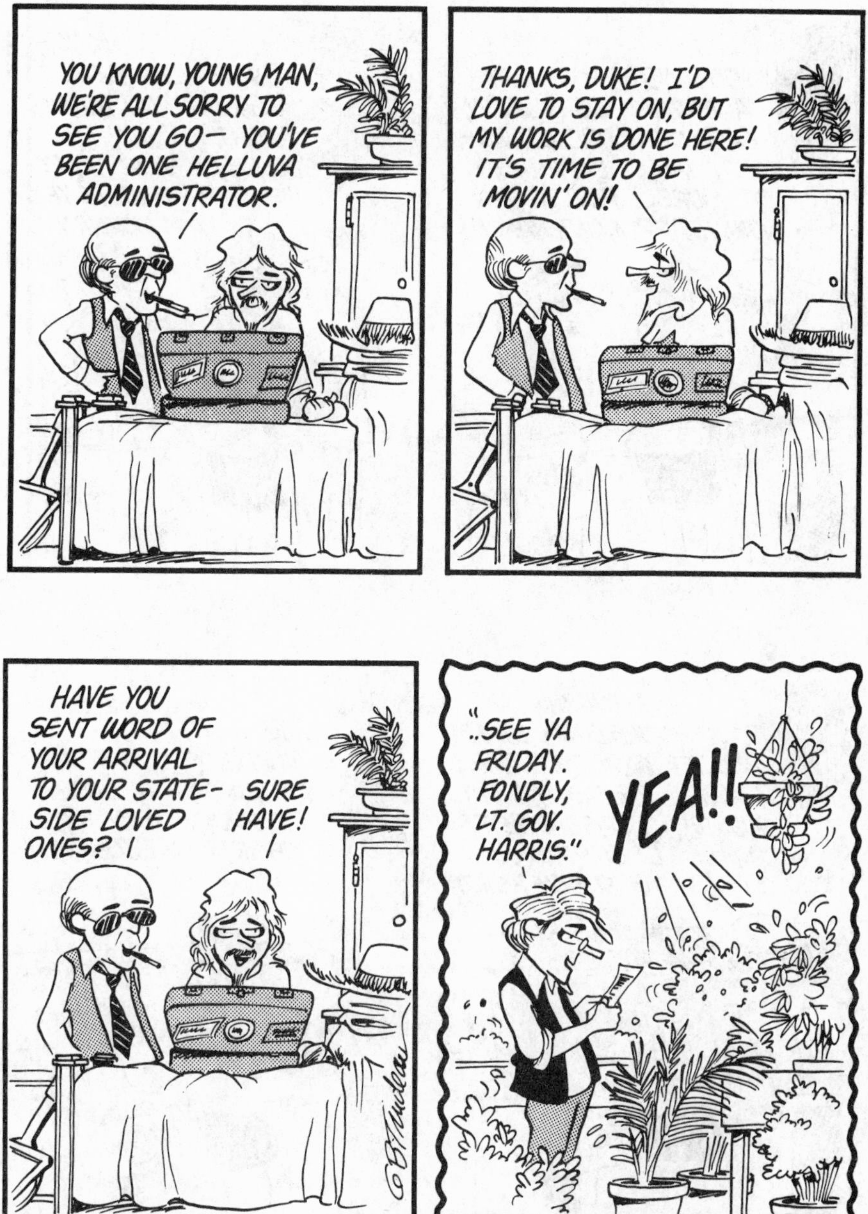
YOU KNOW, YOUNG MAN, WE'RE ALL SORRY TO SEE YOU GO— YOU'VE BEEN ONE HELLUVA ADMINISTRATOR.
THANKS, DUKE! I'D LOVE TO STAY ON, BUT MY WORK IS DONE HERE! IT'S TIME TO BE MOVIN' ON!
HAVE YOU SENT WORD OF YOUR ARRIVAL TO YOUR STATE-SIDE LOVED ONES?
SURE HAVE!
"..SEE YA FRIDAY. FONDLY, LT. GOV. HARRIS."
YEA!!

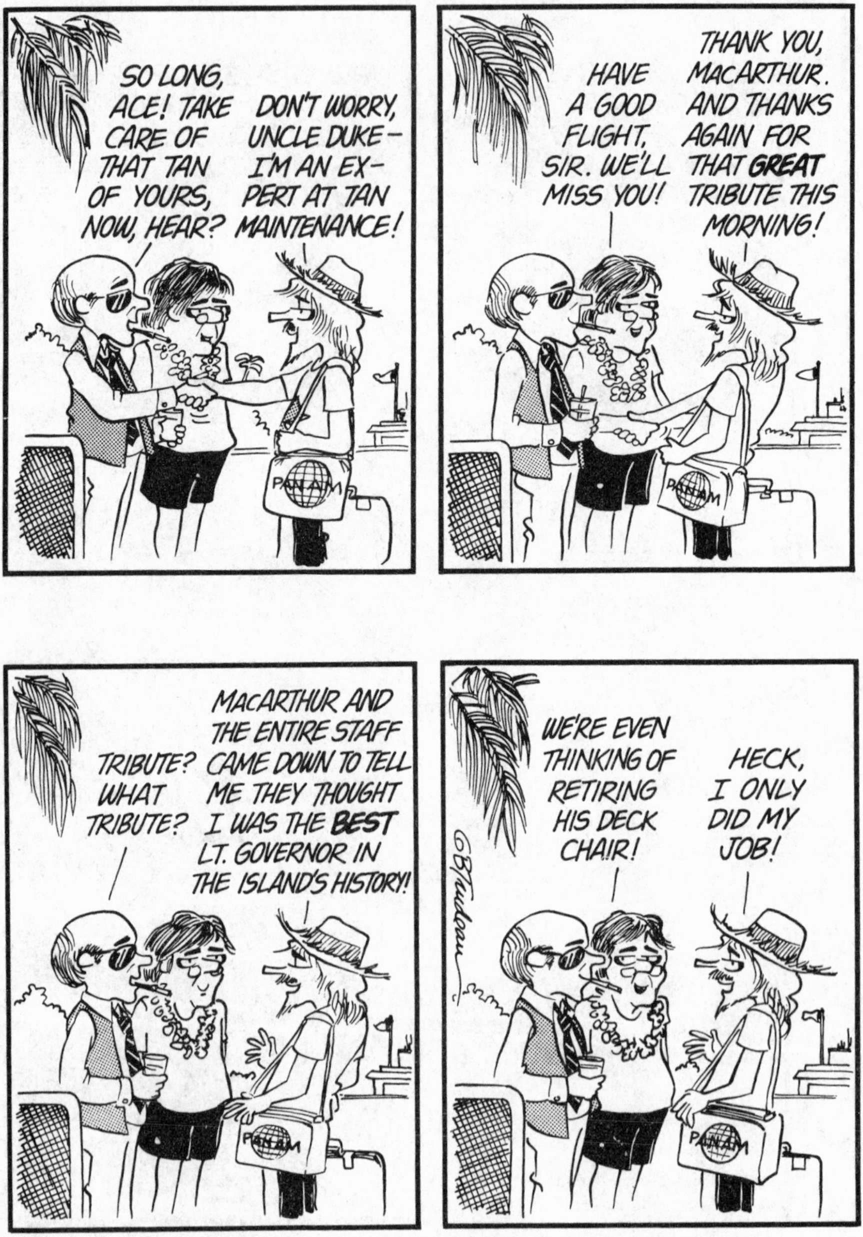
SO LONG, ACE! TAKE CARE OF THAT TAN OF YOURS, NOW, HEAR?
DON'T WORRY, UNCLE DUKE— I'M AN EXPERT AT TAN MAINTENANCE!
PAN AM
HAVE A GOOD FLIGHT, SIR. WE'LL MISS YOU!
THANK YOU, MacARTHUR. AND THANKS AGAIN FOR THAT **GREAT** TRIBUTE THIS MORNING!
PAN AM
TRIBUTE? WHAT TRIBUTE?
MacARTHUR AND THE ENTIRE STAFF CAME DOWN TO TELL ME THEY THOUGHT I WAS THE **BEST** LT. GOVERNOR IN THE ISLAND'S HISTORY!
PAN AM
©B Trudeau
WE'RE EVEN THINKING OF RETIRING HIS DECK CHAIR!
HECK, I ONLY DID MY JOB!
PAN AM

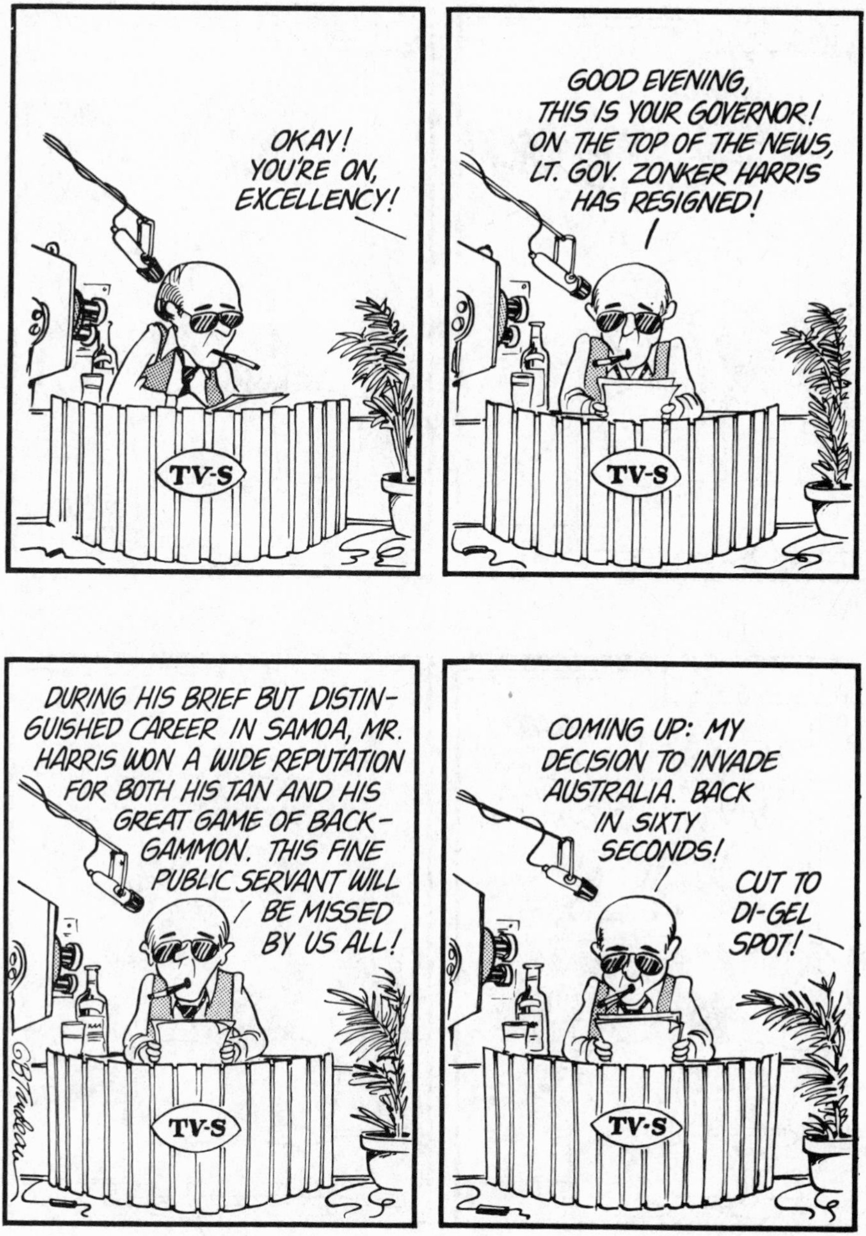
OKAY! YOU'RE ON, EXCELLENCY!
TV-S
GOOD EVENING, THIS IS YOUR GOVERNOR! ON THE TOP OF THE NEWS, LT. GOV. ZONKER HARRIS HAS RESIGNED!
TV-S
DURING HIS BRIEF BUT DISTINGUISHED CAREER IN SAMOA, MR. HARRIS WON A WIDE REPUTATION FOR BOTH HIS TAN AND HIS GREAT GAME OF BACKGAMMON. THIS FINE PUBLIC SERVANT WILL BE MISSED BY US ALL!
TV-S
COMING UP: MY DECISION TO INVADE AUSTRALIA. BACK IN SIXTY SECONDS!
CUT TO DI-GEL SPOT!
TV-S

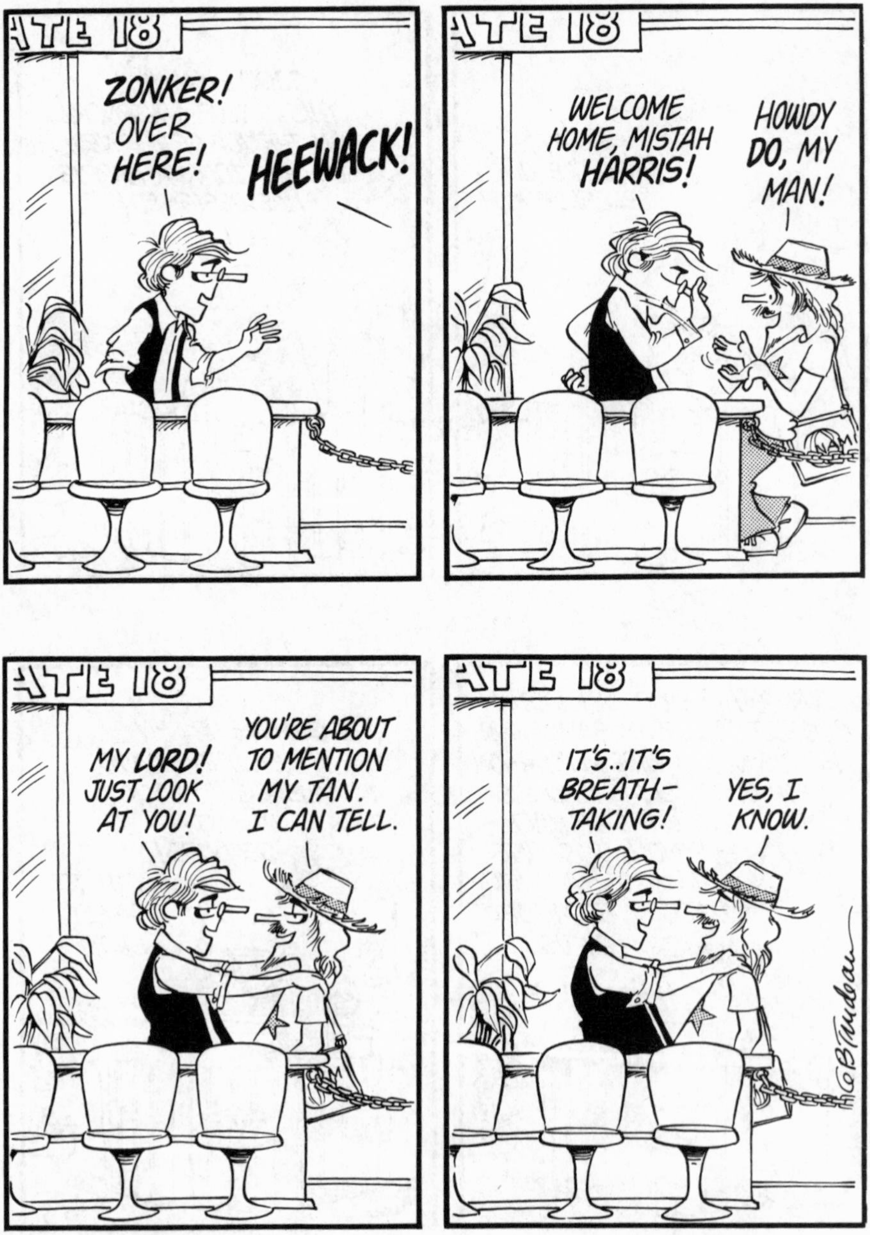
ATE 18
ZONKER! OVER HERE!
HEEWACK!
ATE 18
WELCOME HOME, MISTAH HARRIS!
HOWDY DO, MY MAN!
ATE 18
MY LORD! JUST LOOK AT YOU!
YOU'RE ABOUT TO MENTION MY TAN. I CAN TELL.
ATE 18
IT'S..IT'S BREATH-TAKING!
YES, I KNOW.
©BTrudeau

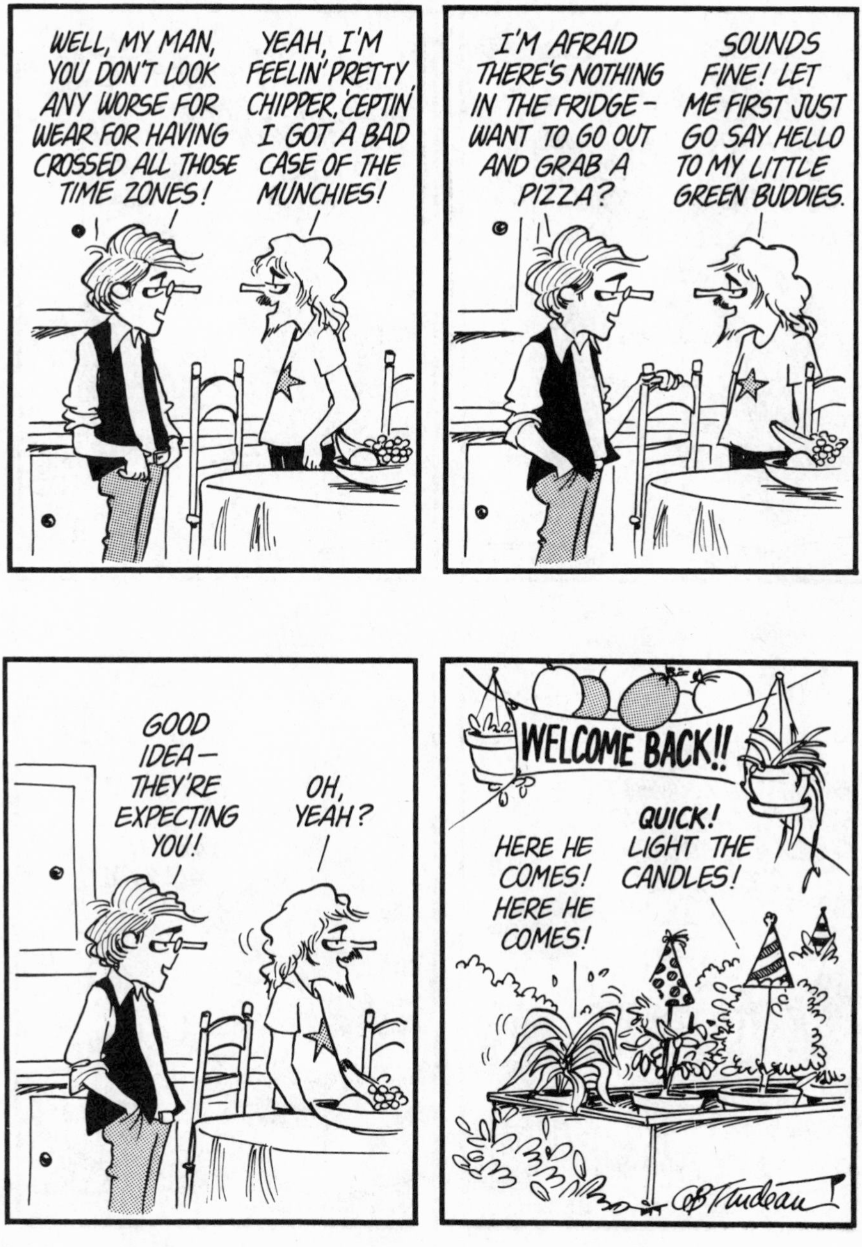
WELL, MY MAN, YOU DON'T LOOK ANY WORSE FOR WEAR FOR HAVING CROSSED ALL THOSE TIME ZONES!
YEAH, I'M FEELIN' PRETTY CHIPPER, 'CEPTIN' I GOT A BAD CASE OF THE MUNCHIES!
I'M AFRAID THERE'S NOTHING IN THE FRIDGE — WANT TO GO OUT AND GRAB A PIZZA?
SOUNDS FINE! LET ME FIRST JUST GO SAY HELLO TO MY LITTLE GREEN BUDDIES.
GOOD IDEA — THEY'RE EXPECTING YOU!
OH, YEAH?
WELCOME BACK!!
HERE HE COMES! HERE HE COMES!
QUICK! LIGHT THE CANDLES!
GBTrudeau

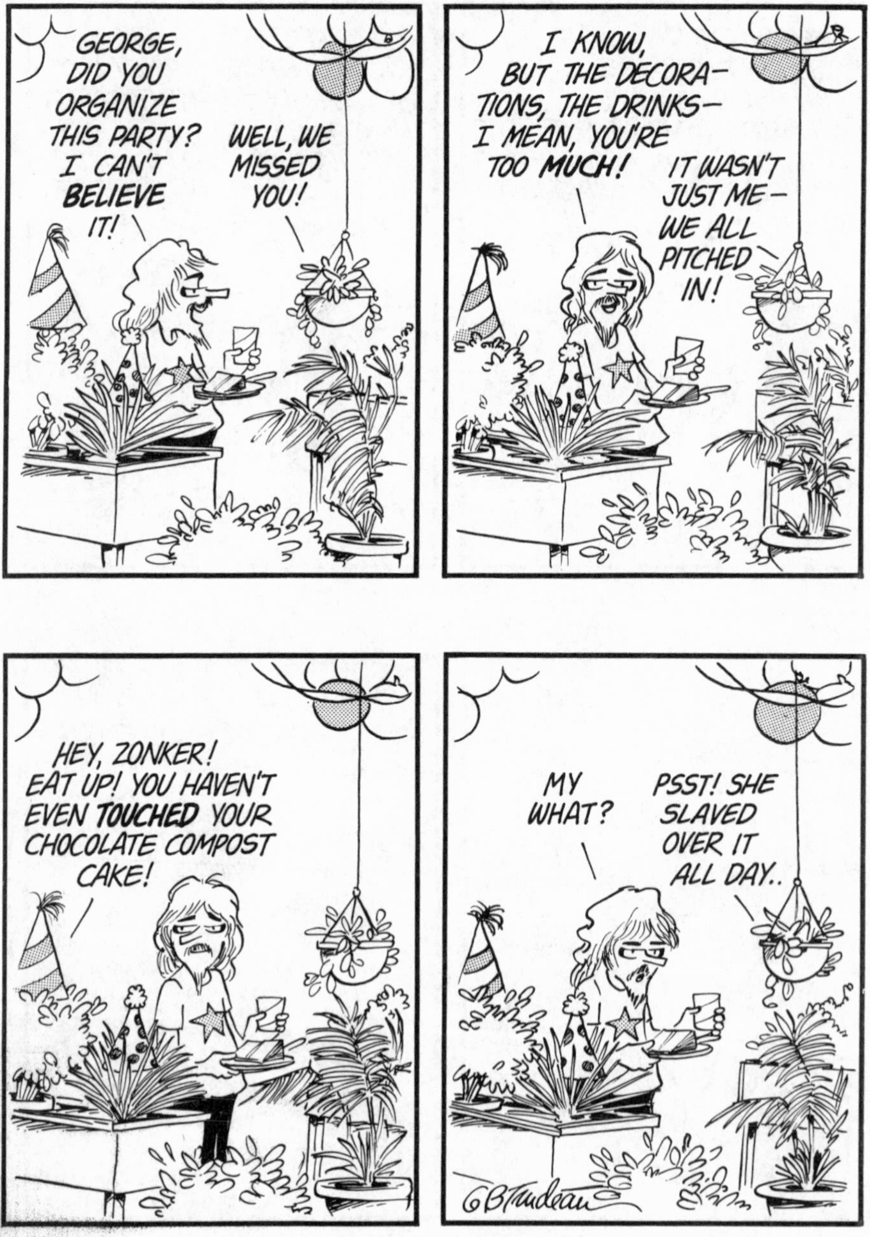
GEORGE, DID YOU ORGANIZE THIS PARTY? I CAN'T BELIEVE IT!
WELL, WE MISSED YOU!
I KNOW, BUT THE DECORATIONS, THE DRINKS— I MEAN, YOU'RE TOO MUCH!
IT WASN'T JUST ME— WE ALL PITCHED IN!
HEY, ZONKER! EAT UP! YOU HAVEN'T EVEN TOUCHED YOUR CHOCOLATE COMPOST CAKE!
MY WHAT?
PSST! SHE SLAVED OVER IT ALL DAY..
GBTrudeau

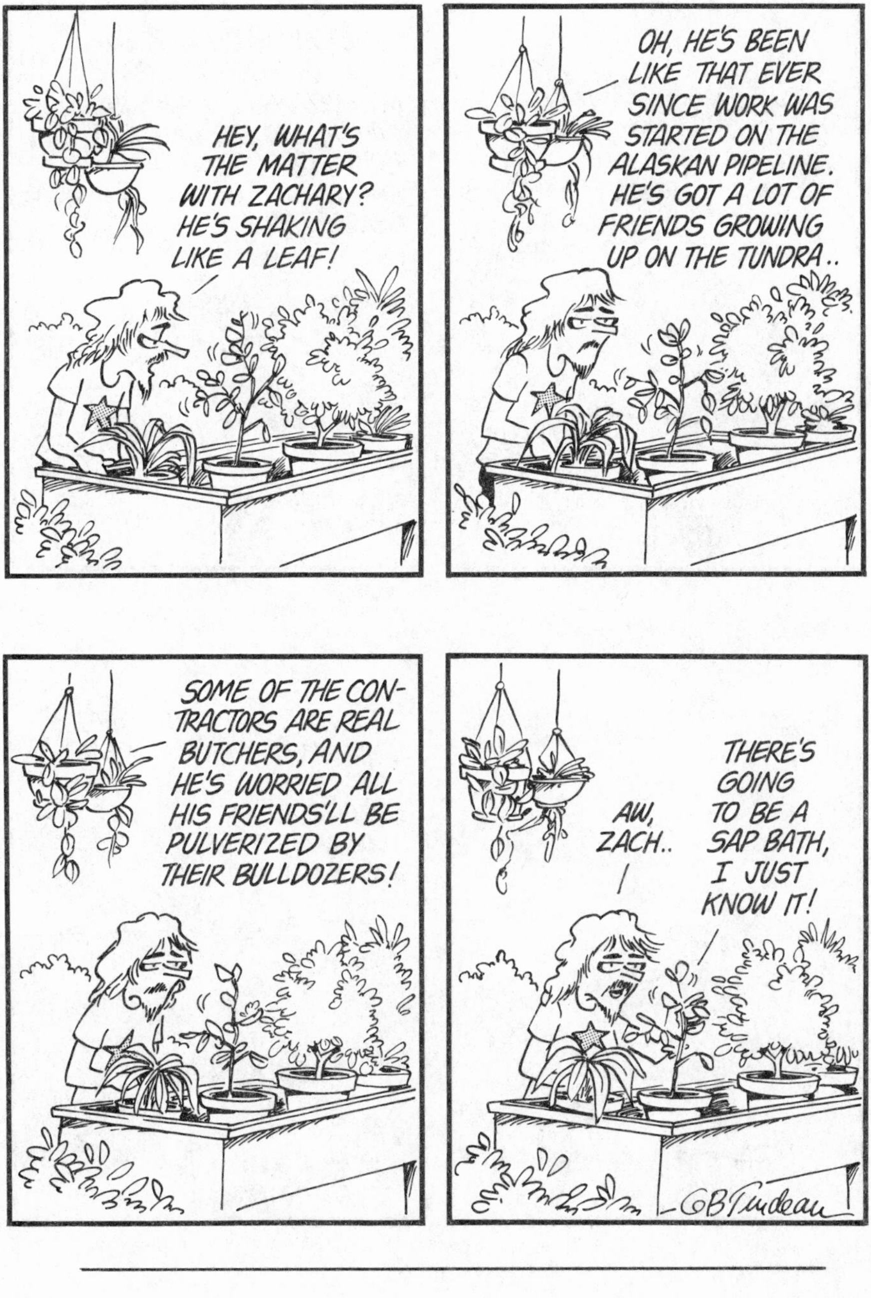
HEY, WHAT'S THE MATTER WITH ZACHARY? HE'S SHAKING LIKE A LEAF!
OH, HE'S BEEN LIKE THAT EVER SINCE WORK WAS STARTED ON THE ALASKAN PIPELINE. HE'S GOT A LOT OF FRIENDS GROWING UP ON THE TUNDRA..
SOME OF THE CONTRACTORS ARE REAL BUTCHERS, AND HE'S WORRIED ALL HIS FRIENDS'LL BE PULVERIZED BY THEIR BULLDOZERS!
AW, ZACH..
THERE'S GOING TO BE A SAP BATH, I JUST KNOW IT!
GBTrudeau

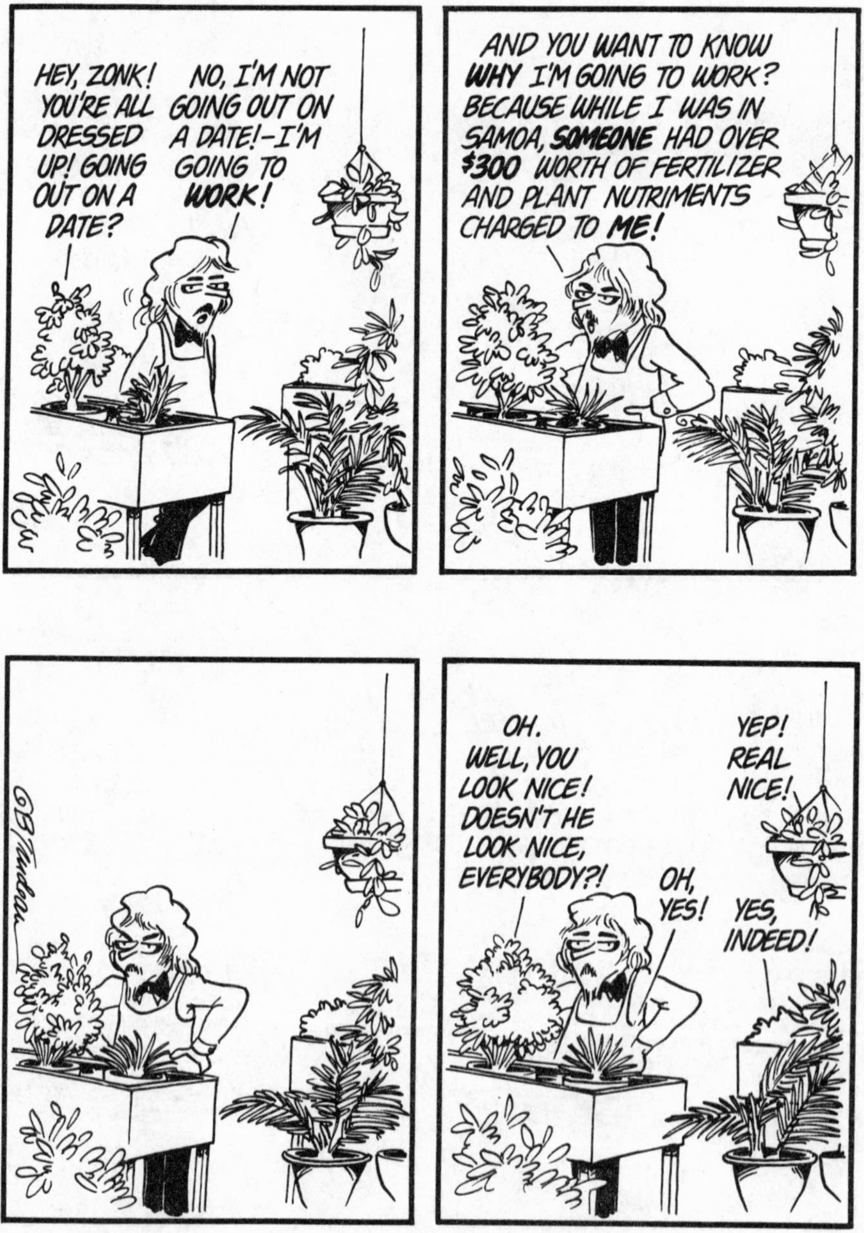
HEY, ZONK! YOU'RE ALL DRESSED UP! GOING OUT ON A DATE?
NO, I'M NOT GOING OUT ON A DATE!—I'M GOING TO WORK!
AND YOU WANT TO KNOW WHY I'M GOING TO WORK? BECAUSE WHILE I WAS IN SAMOA, SOMEONE HAD OVER $300 WORTH OF FERTILIZER AND PLANT NUTRIMENTS CHARGED TO ME!
OH. WELL, YOU LOOK NICE! DOESN'T HE LOOK NICE, EVERYBODY?!
OH, YES!
YEP! REAL NICE!
YES, INDEED!

AND THE WEATHER WAS GOOD?
IT SURE WAS, ALICE!.. EXCEPT FOR A FEW TYPHOONS!
TYPHOONS! REALLY?
UH-HUH. BUT WE GOT THROUGH THEM OKAY..
AND THE GOVERNOR? HOW'S HE DOIN'?
HE'S FINE! AT LEAST I HOPE HE IS—WHEN I LEFT, HE WAS WORKING ON SOME DUMB SCHEME TO INVADE AUSTRALIA!
IF WE COULD JUST SEIZE THE KEY TENNIS CAMPS NEAR SYDNEY!
GIVE IT UP, SIR—PLEASE!
©BTrudeau

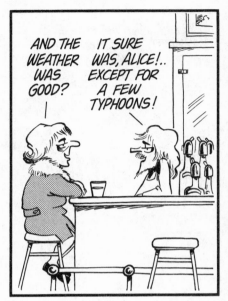

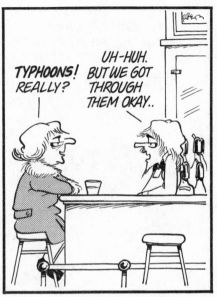

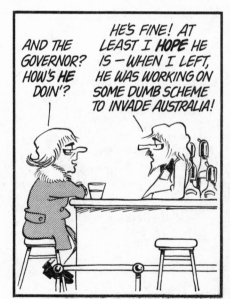

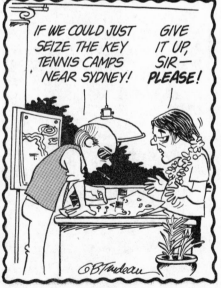

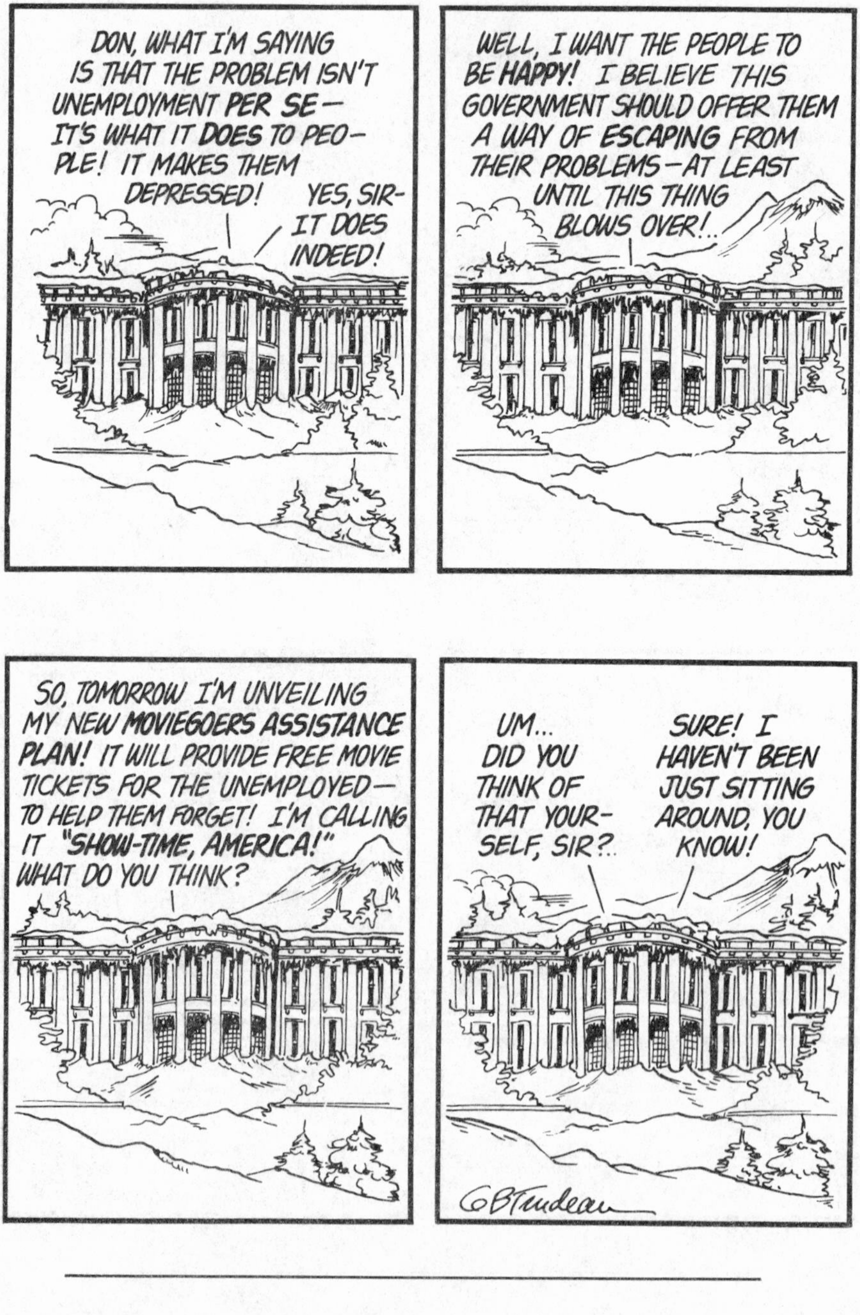
DON, WHAT I'M SAYING IS THAT THE PROBLEM ISN'T UNEMPLOYMENT PER SE— IT'S WHAT IT DOES TO PEOPLE! IT MAKES THEM DEPRESSED!
YES, SIR— IT DOES INDEED!
WELL, I WANT THE PEOPLE TO BE HAPPY! I BELIEVE THIS GOVERNMENT SHOULD OFFER THEM A WAY OF ESCAPING FROM THEIR PROBLEMS—AT LEAST UNTIL THIS THING BLOWS OVER!..
SO, TOMORROW I'M UNVEILING MY NEW MOVIEGOERS ASSISTANCE PLAN! IT WILL PROVIDE FREE MOVIE TICKETS FOR THE UNEMPLOYED— TO HELP THEM FORGET! I'M CALLING IT "SHOW-TIME, AMERICA!" WHAT DO YOU THINK?
UM... DID YOU THINK OF THAT YOURSELF, SIR?..
SURE! I HAVEN'T BEEN JUST SITTING AROUND, YOU KNOW!
GBTrudeau

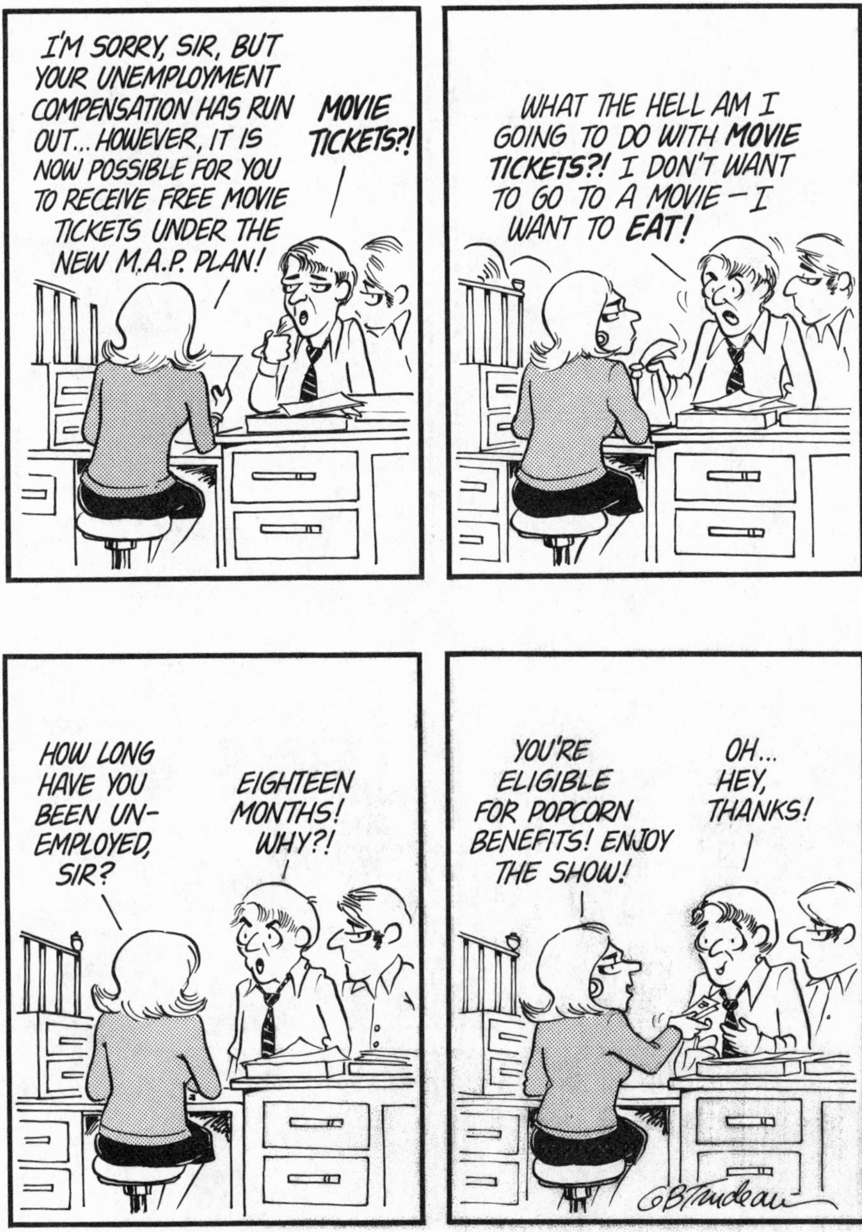
I'M SORRY, SIR, BUT YOUR UNEMPLOYMENT COMPENSATION HAS RUN OUT... HOWEVER, IT IS NOW POSSIBLE FOR YOU TO RECEIVE FREE MOVIE TICKETS UNDER THE NEW M.A.P. PLAN!
MOVIE TICKETS?!
WHAT THE HELL AM I GOING TO DO WITH MOVIE TICKETS?! I DON'T WANT TO GO TO A MOVIE — I WANT TO EAT!
HOW LONG HAVE YOU BEEN UN-EMPLOYED, SIR?
EIGHTEEN MONTHS! WHY?!
YOU'RE ELIGIBLE FOR POPCORN BENEFITS! ENJOY THE SHOW!
OH... HEY, THANKS!
GBTrudeau

ANYHOW, IT ALL WORKED OUT IN THE END, 'CAUSE I WON IT ALL BACK ON THE VIKINGS GAME!
HEE, HEE!
SAY, DARLIN'- WHAT TIME YOU GOT?
UM... QUARTER AFTER NINE, ALICE...
HOLY SMOKES! I'M LATE FOR THE FEDERAL FLICKS!
"FEDERAL FLICKS?"
TONIGHT! THE UNITED STATES GOVERNMENT PRESENTS- "SHAFT"!
CLAP! CLAP!
YEA! CLAP!
AW... SEEN IT! SEEN IT!
GBTrudeau

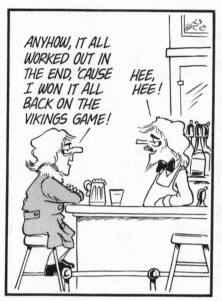

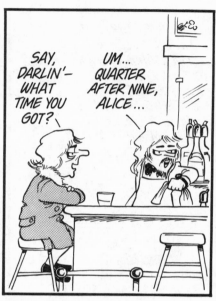

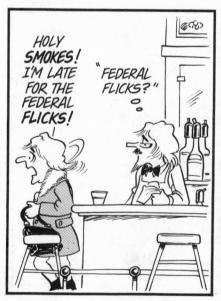

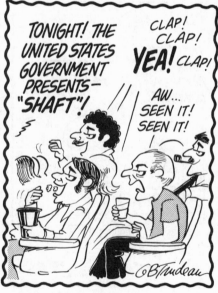

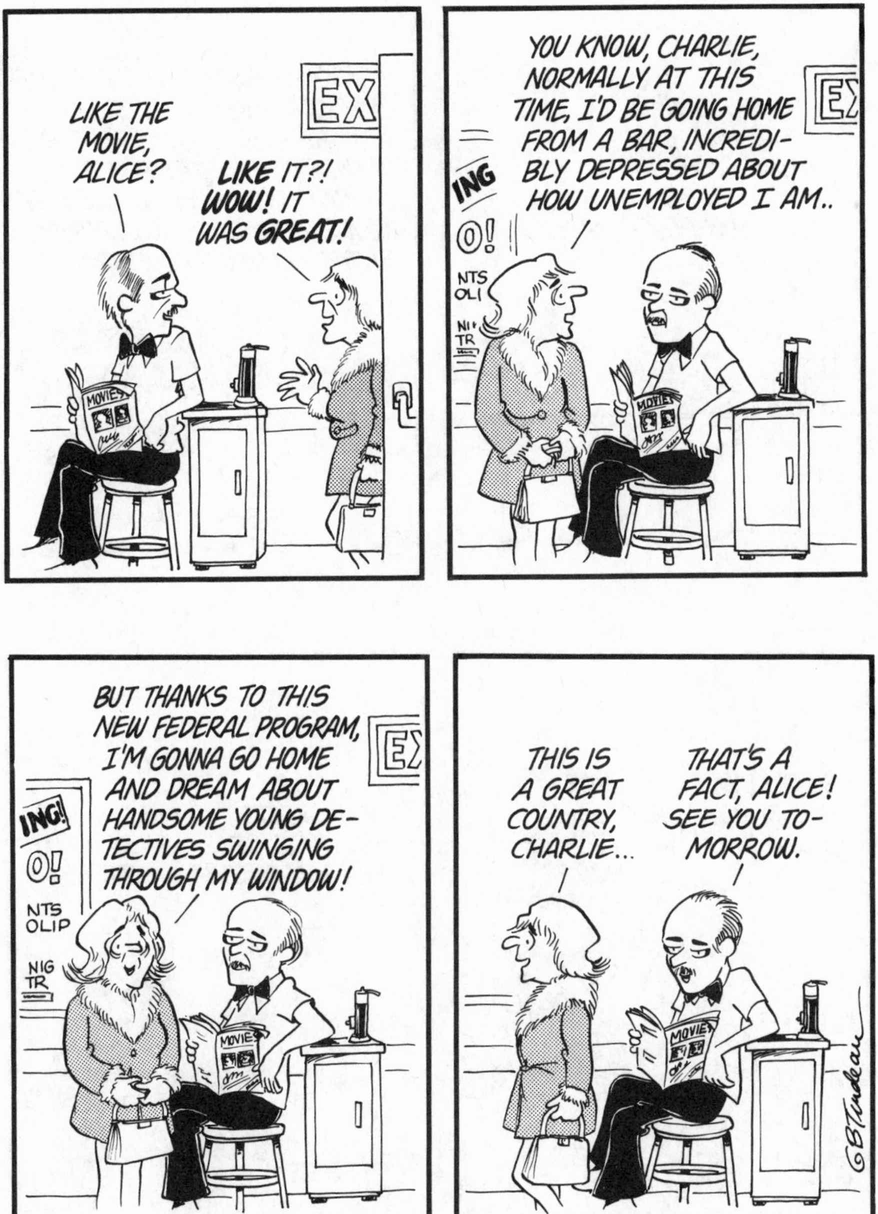

EX
LIKE THE MOVIE, ALICE?
LIKE IT?! WOW! IT WAS GREAT!
MOVIES
YOU KNOW, CHARLIE, NORMALLY AT THIS TIME, I'D BE GOING HOME FROM A BAR, INCREDIBLY DEPRESSED ABOUT HOW UNEMPLOYED I AM..
BUT THANKS TO THIS NEW FEDERAL PROGRAM, I'M GONNA GO HOME AND DREAM ABOUT HANDSOME YOUNG DETECTIVES SWINGING THROUGH MY WINDOW!
THIS IS A GREAT COUNTRY, CHARLIE...
THAT'S A FACT, ALICE! SEE YOU TOMORROW.
©BTrudeau

HEY, ALICE! COULD YOU AND EDDIE FILL IN THESE QUESTION-NAIRES BEFORE YOU GO?
SURE, LUV!
EXI
"PRESIDENT FORD AND 'SHOW-TIME, AMERICA!' THANK YOU FOR ATTENDING THIS WEEK'S MOVIE FEATURE. TO HELP US BE MORE RESPONSIVE TO YOUR FILM PREFERENCES, WE WOULD APPRECIATE YOUR RESPONSE TO THE FOLLOWING QUESTIONS."
"① HOW DID YOU ENJOY THE MOVIE?"
IT WAS EXCELLENT. RARELY HAVE I ENJOYED MYSELF MORE.
EX
"② WOULD YOU LIKE TO SEE MORE OF ANN-MARGRET?"
YES, INDEED-SHE'S A FINE ACTRESS!
GBTrudeau

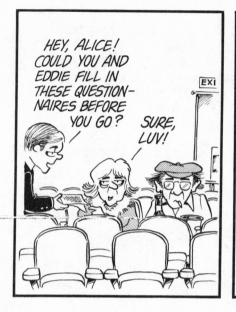

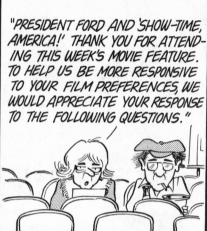

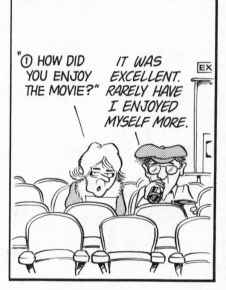

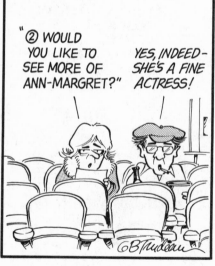

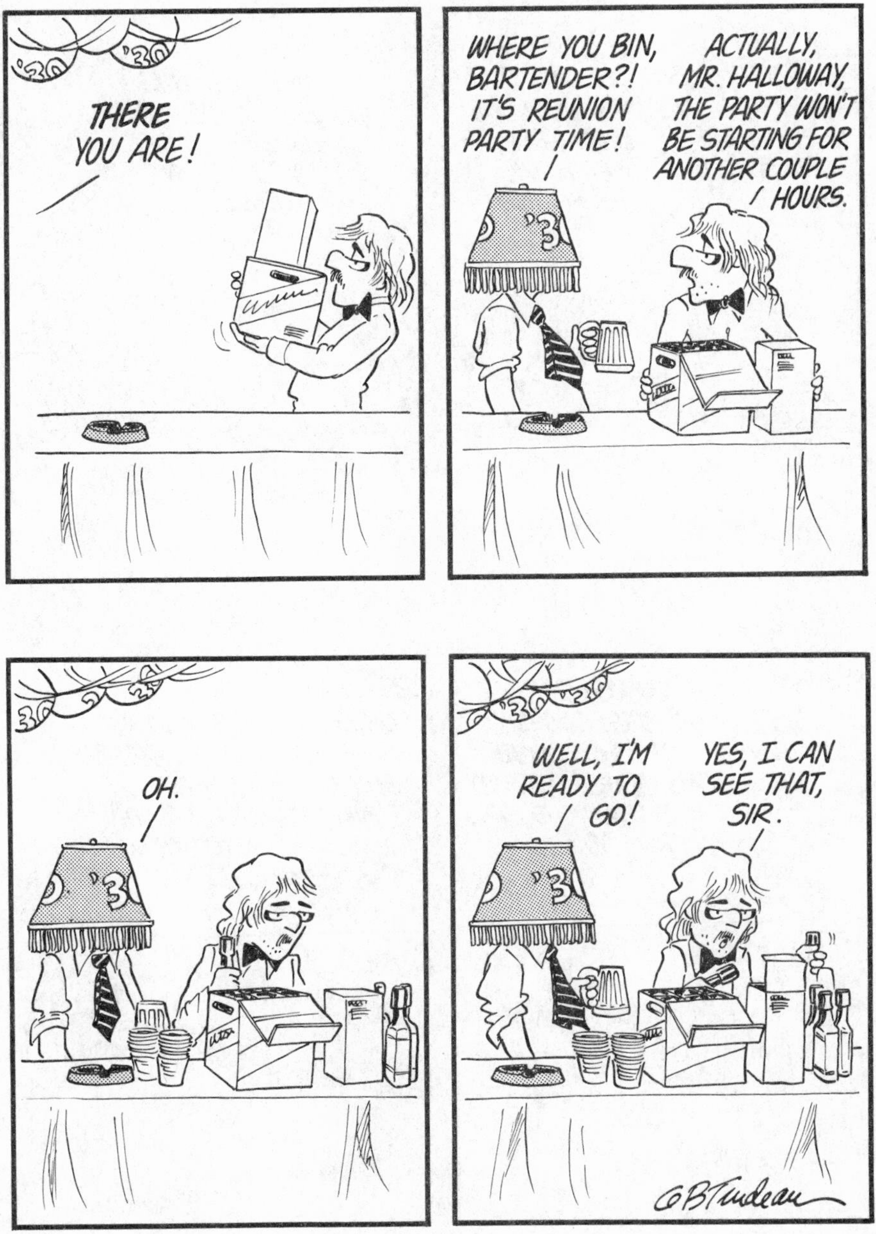
THERE YOU ARE!
WHERE YOU BIN, BARTENDER?! IT'S REUNION PARTY TIME!
ACTUALLY, MR. HALLOWAY, THE PARTY WON'T BE STARTING FOR ANOTHER COUPLE HOURS.
OH.
WELL, I'M READY TO GO!
YES, I CAN SEE THAT, SIR.
GBTrudeau

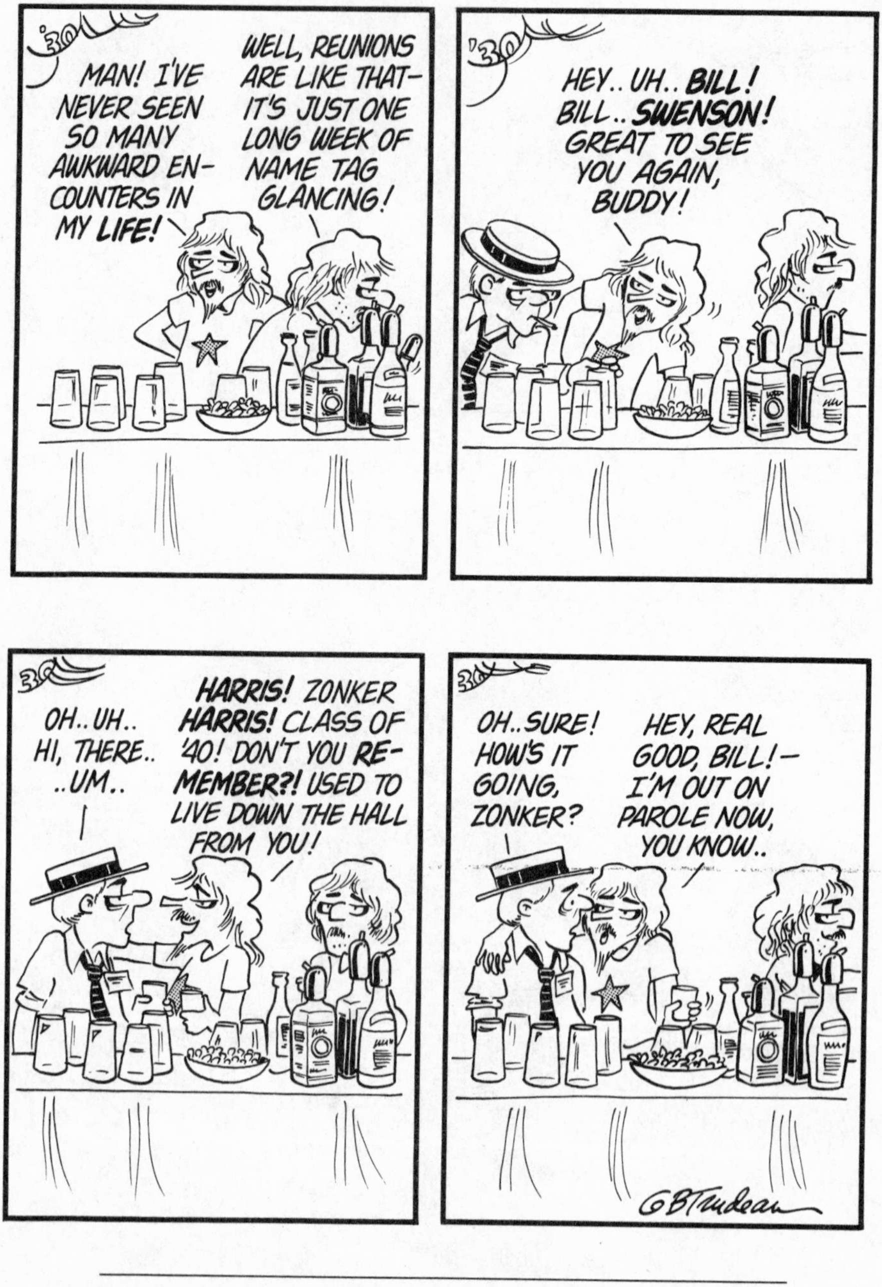
MAN! I'VE NEVER SEEN SO MANY AWKWARD EN-COUNTERS IN MY LIFE!
WELL, REUNIONS ARE LIKE THAT- IT'S JUST ONE LONG WEEK OF NAME TAG GLANCING!
HEY.. UH.. BILL! BILL.. SWENSON! GREAT TO SEE YOU AGAIN, BUDDY!
OH.. UH.. HI, THERE.. ..UM..
HARRIS! ZONKER HARRIS! CLASS OF '40! DON'T YOU RE-MEMBER?! USED TO LIVE DOWN THE HALL FROM YOU!
OH.. SURE! HOW'S IT GOING, ZONKER?
HEY, REAL GOOD, BILL!— I'M OUT ON PAROLE NOW, YOU KNOW..
GBTrudeau

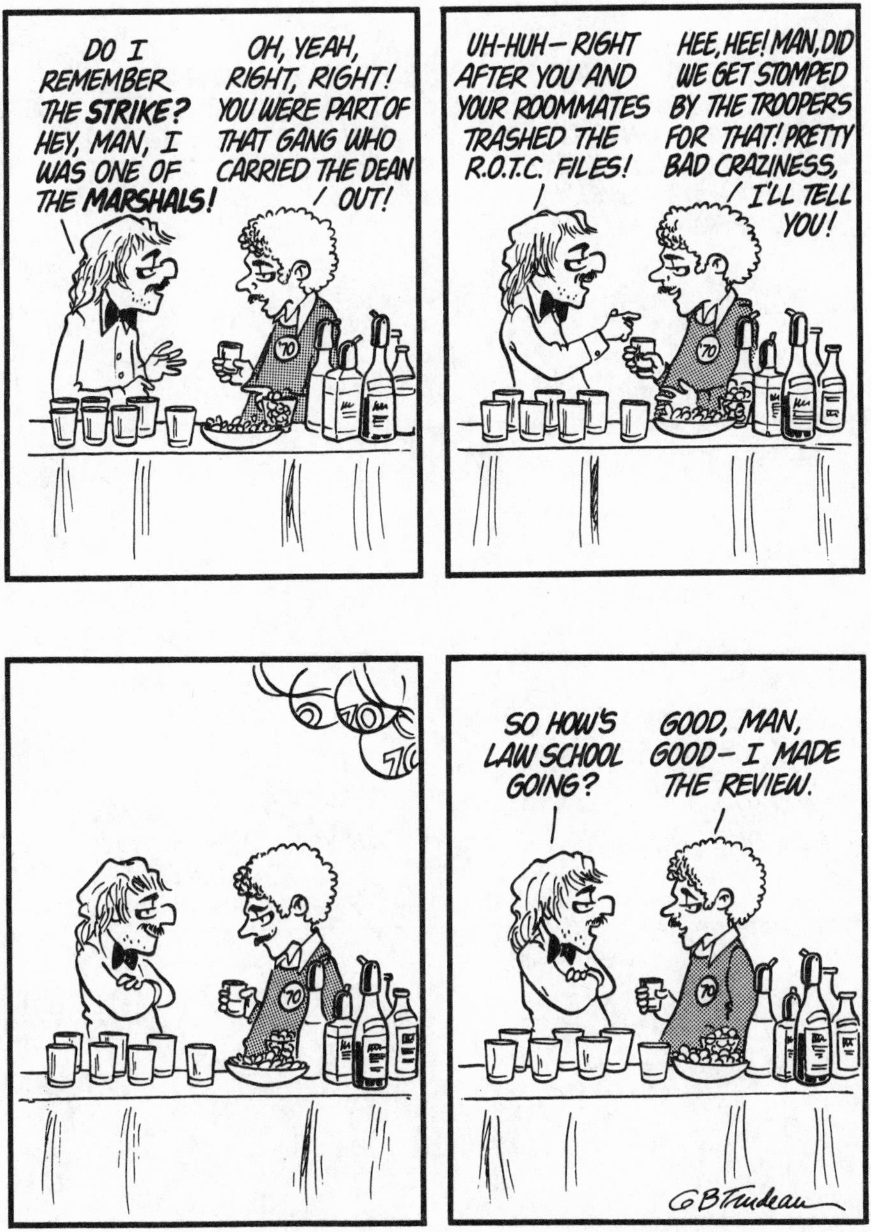
DO I REMEMBER THE **STRIKE?** HEY, MAN, I WAS ONE OF THE **MARSHALS!**
OH, YEAH, RIGHT, RIGHT! YOU WERE PART OF THAT GANG WHO CARRIED THE DEAN OUT!
UH-HUH—RIGHT AFTER YOU AND YOUR ROOMMATES TRASHED THE R.O.T.C. FILES!
HEE, HEE! MAN, DID WE GET STOMPED BY THE TROOPERS FOR THAT! PRETTY BAD CRAZINESS, I'LL TELL YOU!
SO HOW'S LAW SCHOOL GOING?
GOOD, MAN, GOOD—I MADE THE REVIEW.
GBTrudeau

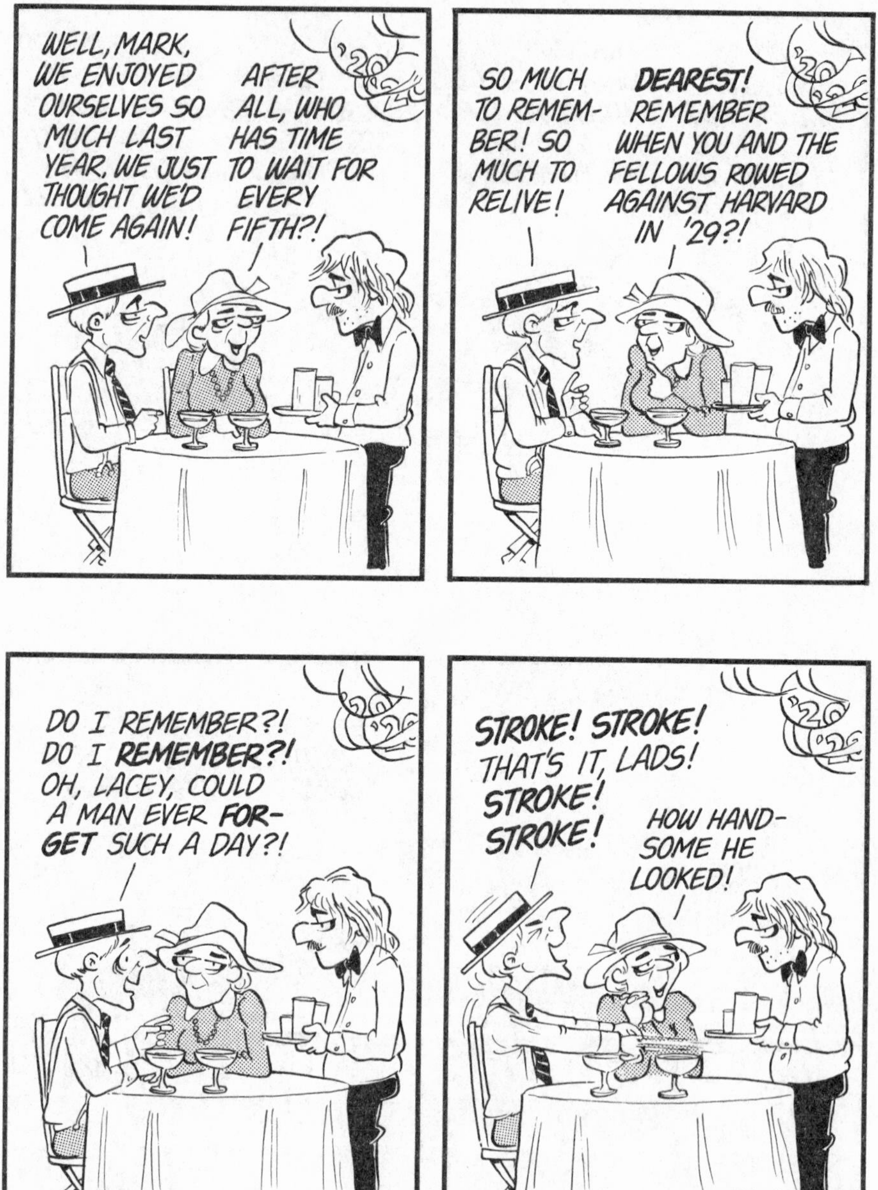
WELL, MARK, WE ENJOYED OURSELVES SO MUCH LAST YEAR, WE JUST THOUGHT WE'D COME AGAIN!
AFTER ALL, WHO HAS TIME TO WAIT FOR EVERY FIFTH?!
SO MUCH TO REMEMBER! SO MUCH TO RELIVE!
**DEAREST!** REMEMBER WHEN YOU AND THE FELLOWS ROWED AGAINST HARVARD IN '29?!
DO I REMEMBER?! DO I **REMEMBER?!** OH, LACEY, COULD A MAN EVER **FORGET** SUCH A DAY?!
**STROKE! STROKE!** THAT'S IT, LADS! **STROKE! STROKE!**
HOW HANDSOME HE LOOKED!
GBTrudeau

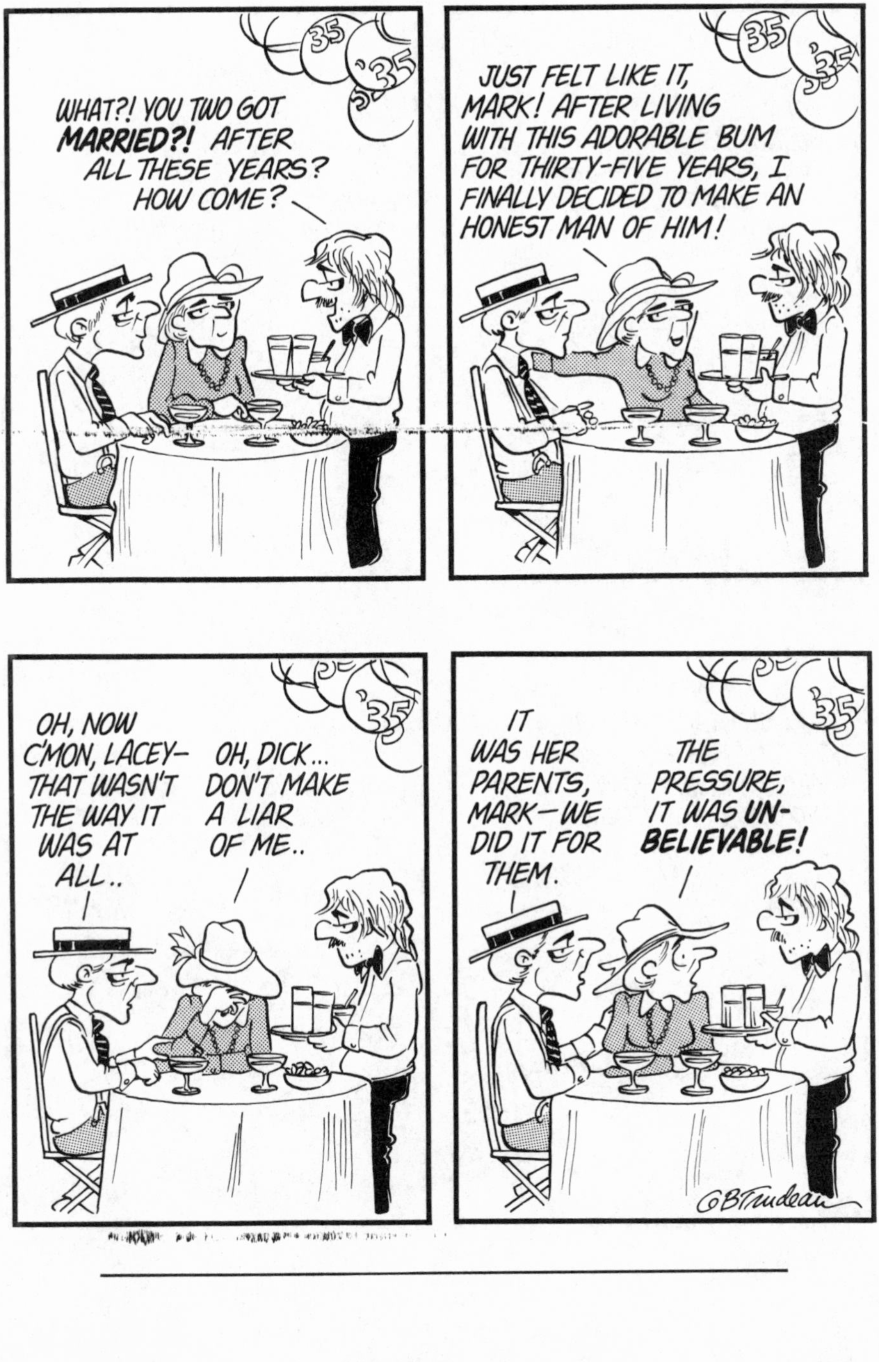
WHAT?! YOU TWO GOT **MARRIED?!** AFTER ALL THESE YEARS? HOW COME?
JUST FELT LIKE IT, MARK! AFTER LIVING WITH THIS ADORABLE BUM FOR THIRTY-FIVE YEARS, I FINALLY DECIDED TO MAKE AN HONEST MAN OF HIM!
OH, NOW C'MON, LACEY— THAT WASN'T THE WAY IT WAS AT ALL..
OH, DICK... DON'T MAKE A LIAR OF ME..
IT WAS HER PARENTS, MARK—WE DID IT FOR THEM.
THE PRESSURE, IT WAS **UN-BELIEVABLE!**
GBTrudeau

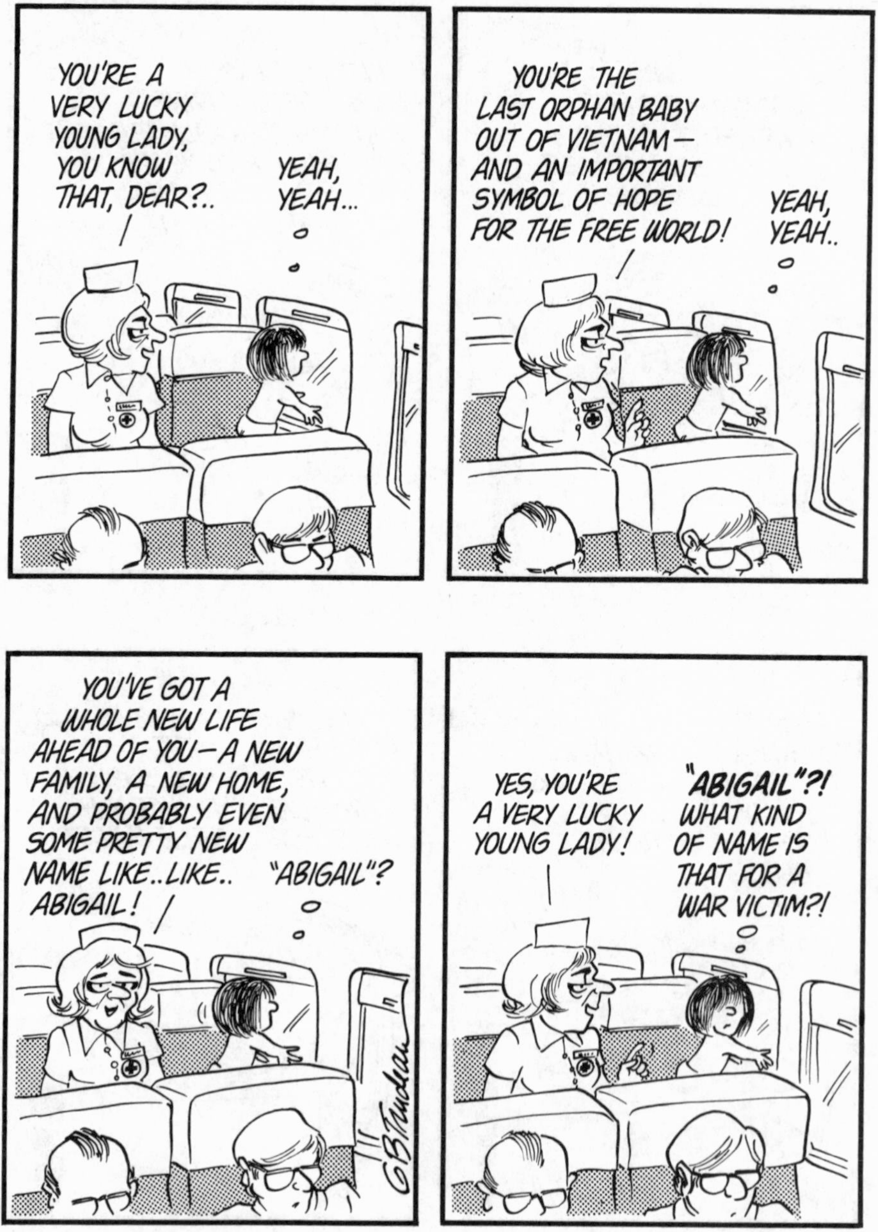
YOU'RE A VERY LUCKY YOUNG LADY, YOU KNOW THAT, DEAR?..
YEAH, YEAH...
YOU'RE THE LAST ORPHAN BABY OUT OF VIETNAM— AND AN IMPORTANT SYMBOL OF HOPE FOR THE FREE WORLD!
YEAH, YEAH..
YOU'VE GOT A WHOLE NEW LIFE AHEAD OF YOU—A NEW FAMILY, A NEW HOME, AND PROBABLY EVEN SOME PRETTY NEW NAME LIKE..LIKE.. ABIGAIL!
"ABIGAIL"?
YES, YOU'RE A VERY LUCKY YOUNG LADY!
"ABIGAIL"?! WHAT KIND OF NAME IS THAT FOR A WAR VICTIM?!
GBTrudeau

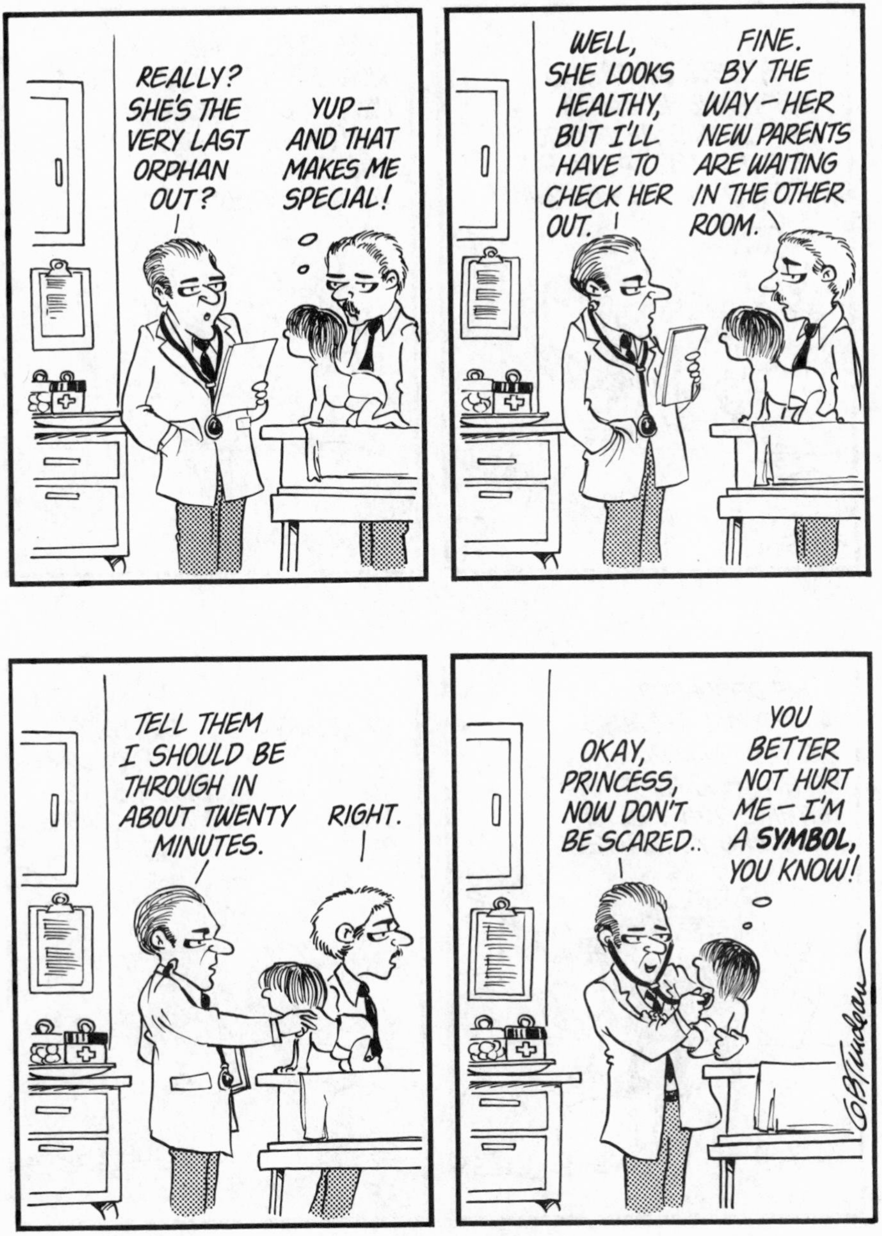
REALLY? SHE'S THE VERY LAST ORPHAN OUT?
YUP— AND THAT MAKES ME SPECIAL!
WELL, SHE LOOKS HEALTHY, BUT I'LL HAVE TO CHECK HER OUT.
FINE. BY THE WAY—HER NEW PARENTS ARE WAITING IN THE OTHER ROOM.
TELL THEM I SHOULD BE THROUGH IN ABOUT TWENTY MINUTES.
RIGHT.
OKAY, PRINCESS, NOW DON'T BE SCARED..
YOU BETTER NOT HURT ME—I'M A **SYMBOL,** YOU KNOW!
GBTrudeau

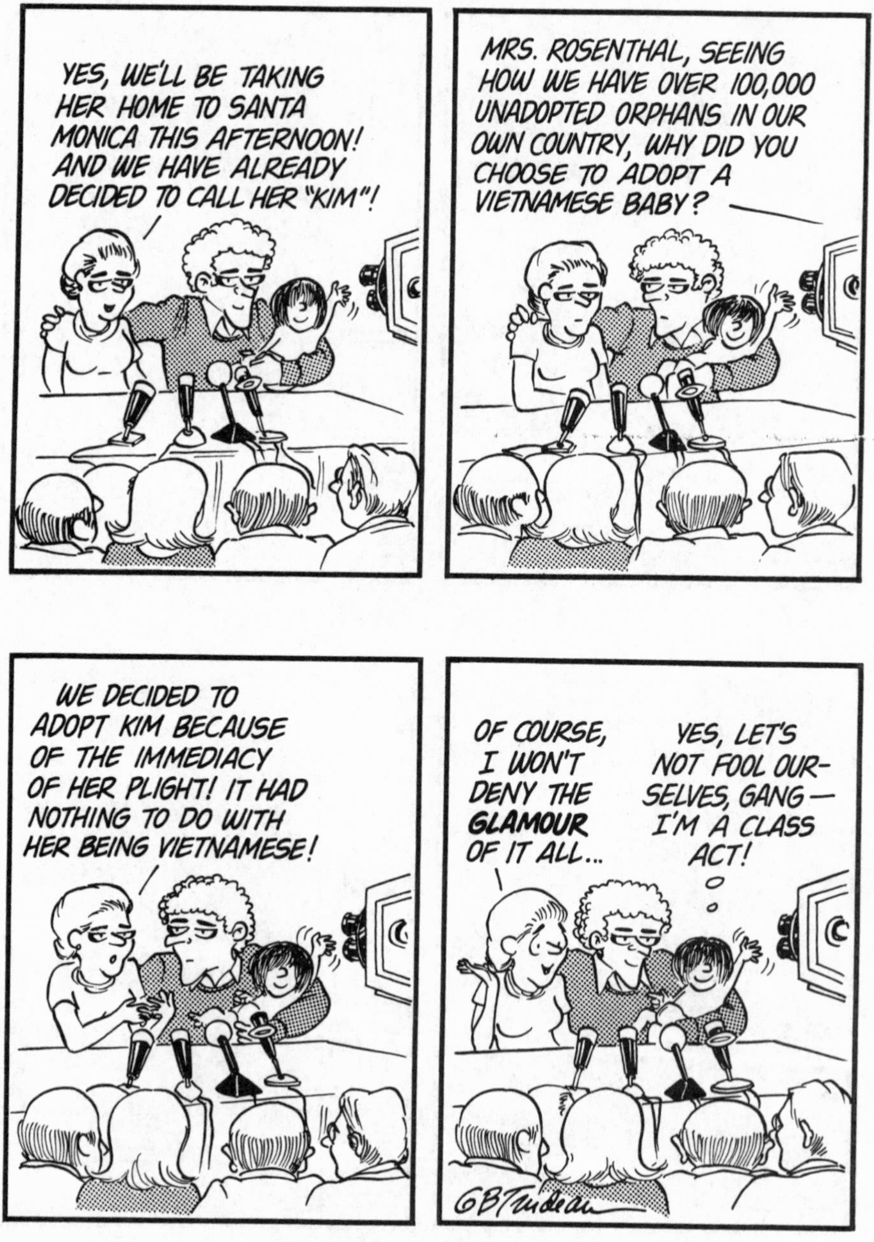

YES, WE'LL BE TAKING HER HOME TO SANTA MONICA THIS AFTERNOON! AND WE HAVE ALREADY DECIDED TO CALL HER "KIM"!
MRS. ROSENTHAL, SEEING HOW WE HAVE OVER 100,000 UNADOPTED ORPHANS IN OUR OWN COUNTRY, WHY DID YOU CHOOSE TO ADOPT A VIETNAMESE BABY?
WE DECIDED TO ADOPT KIM BECAUSE OF THE IMMEDIACY OF HER PLIGHT! IT HAD NOTHING TO DO WITH HER BEING VIETNAMESE!
OF COURSE, I WON'T DENY THE **GLAMOUR** OF IT ALL...
YES, LET'S NOT FOOL OURSELVES, GANG — I'M A CLASS ACT!
GBTrudeau

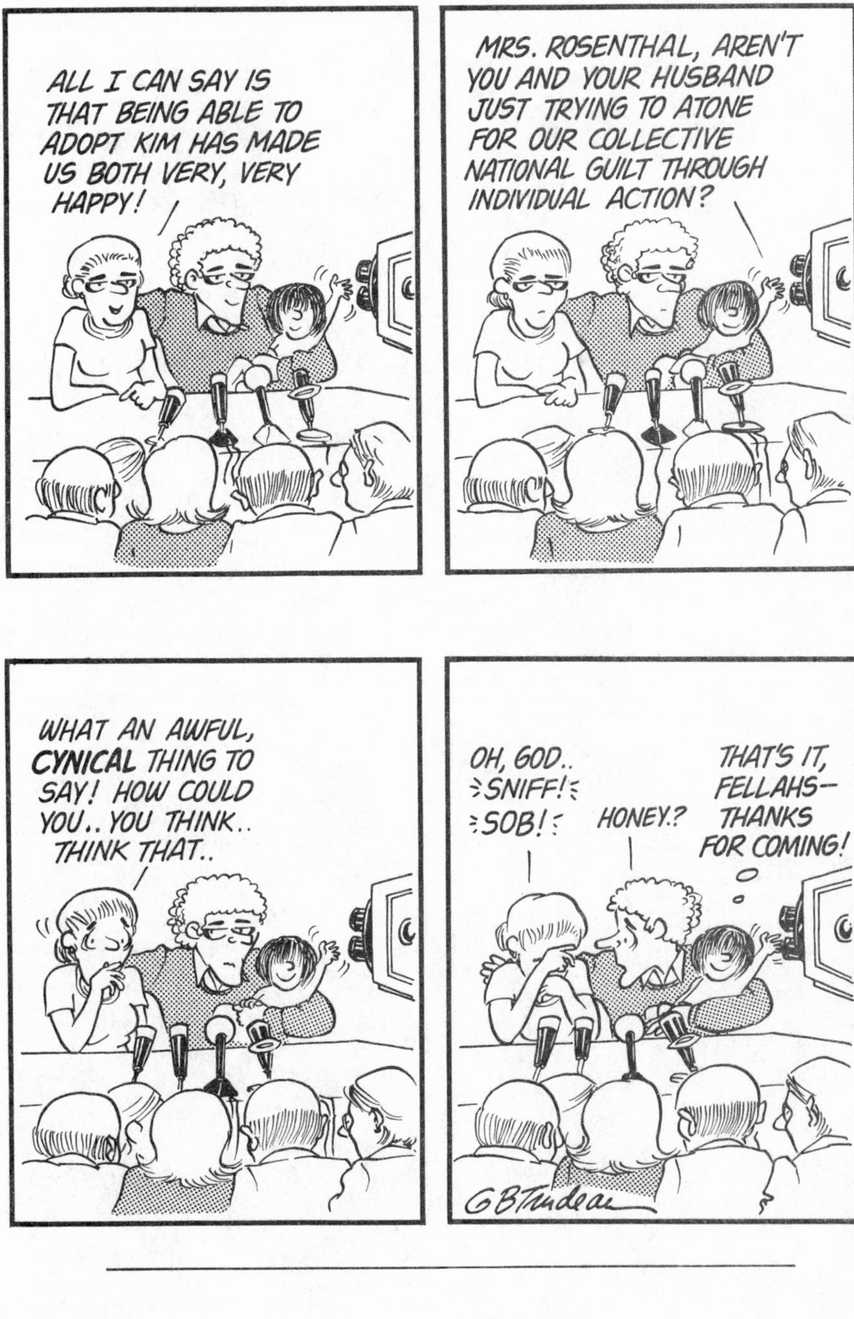
ALL I CAN SAY IS THAT BEING ABLE TO ADOPT KIM HAS MADE US BOTH VERY, VERY HAPPY!
MRS. ROSENTHAL, AREN'T YOU AND YOUR HUSBAND JUST TRYING TO ATONE FOR OUR COLLECTIVE NATIONAL GUILT THROUGH INDIVIDUAL ACTION?
WHAT AN AWFUL, **CYNICAL** THING TO SAY! HOW COULD YOU.. YOU THINK.. THINK THAT..
OH, GOD.. SNIFF! SOB!
HONEY.?
THAT'S IT, FELLAHS— THANKS FOR COMING!
GBTrudeau

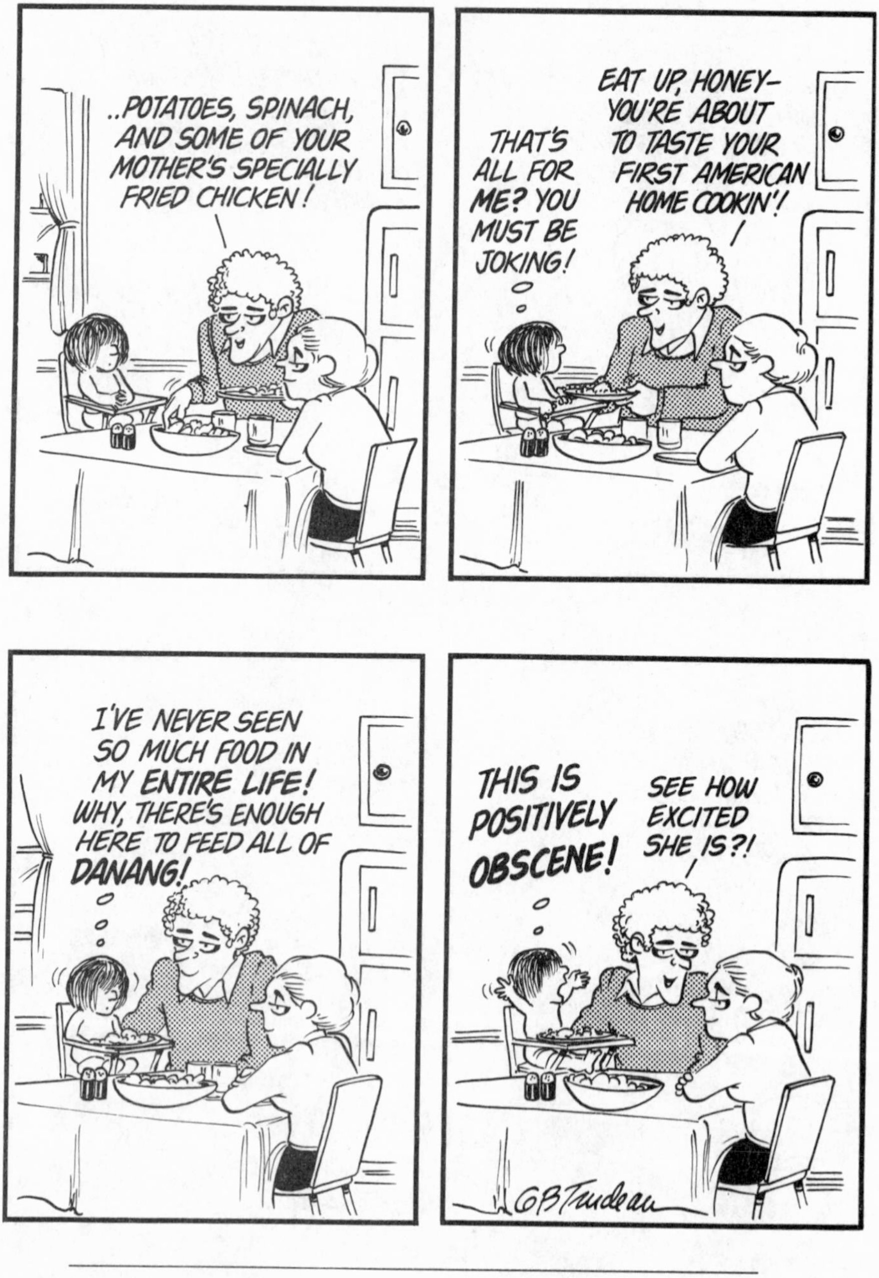
..POTATOES, SPINACH, AND SOME OF YOUR MOTHER'S SPECIALLY FRIED CHICKEN!
THAT'S ALL FOR ME? YOU MUST BE JOKING!
EAT UP, HONEY- YOU'RE ABOUT TO TASTE YOUR FIRST AMERICAN HOME COOKIN'!
I'VE NEVER SEEN SO MUCH FOOD IN MY ENTIRE LIFE! WHY, THERE'S ENOUGH HERE TO FEED ALL OF DANANG!
THIS IS POSITIVELY OBSCENE!
SEE HOW EXCITED SHE IS?!
GBTrudeau

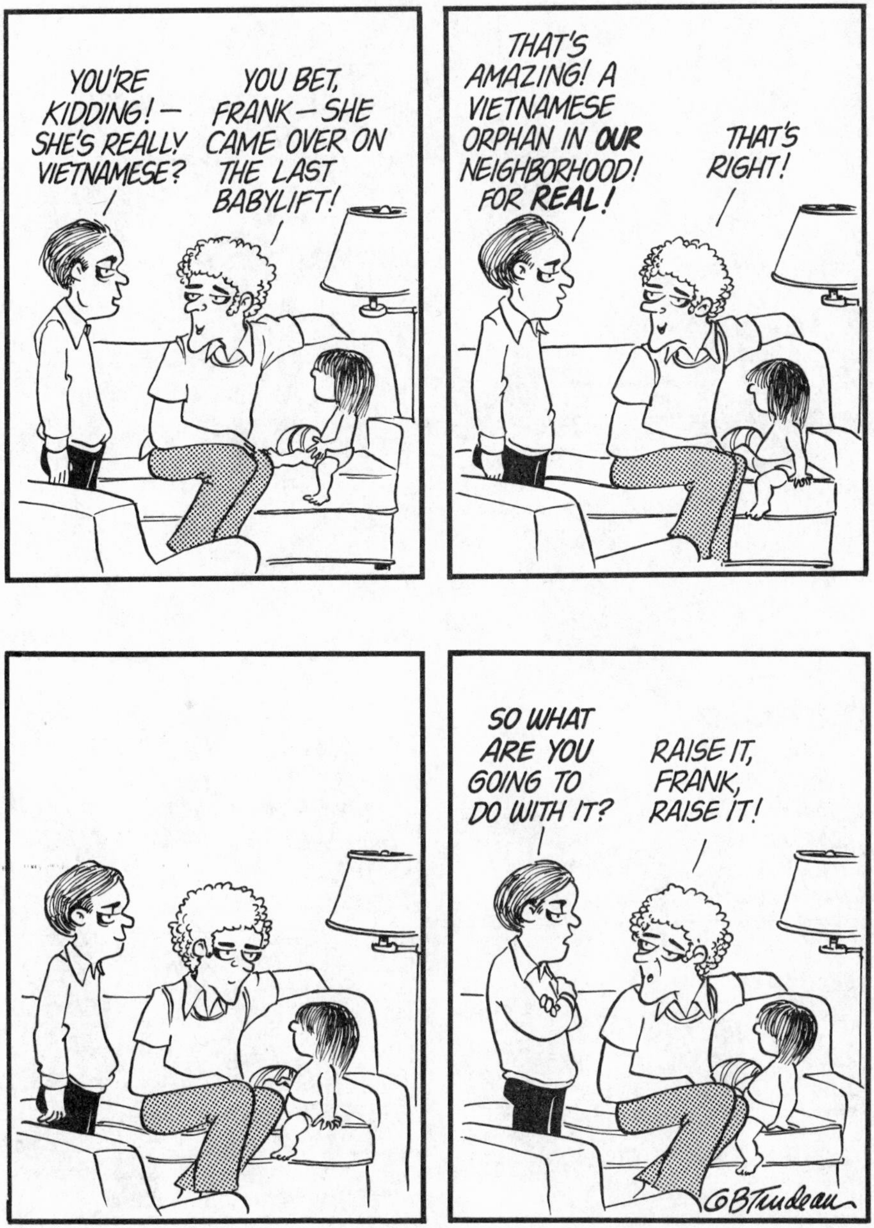
YOU'RE KIDDING! — SHE'S REALLY VIETNAMESE?
YOU BET, FRANK — SHE CAME OVER ON THE LAST BABYLIFT!
THAT'S AMAZING! A VIETNAMESE ORPHAN IN **OUR** NEIGHBORHOOD! FOR **REAL**!
THAT'S RIGHT!
SO WHAT ARE YOU GOING TO DO WITH IT?
RAISE IT, FRANK, RAISE IT!
©BTrudeau

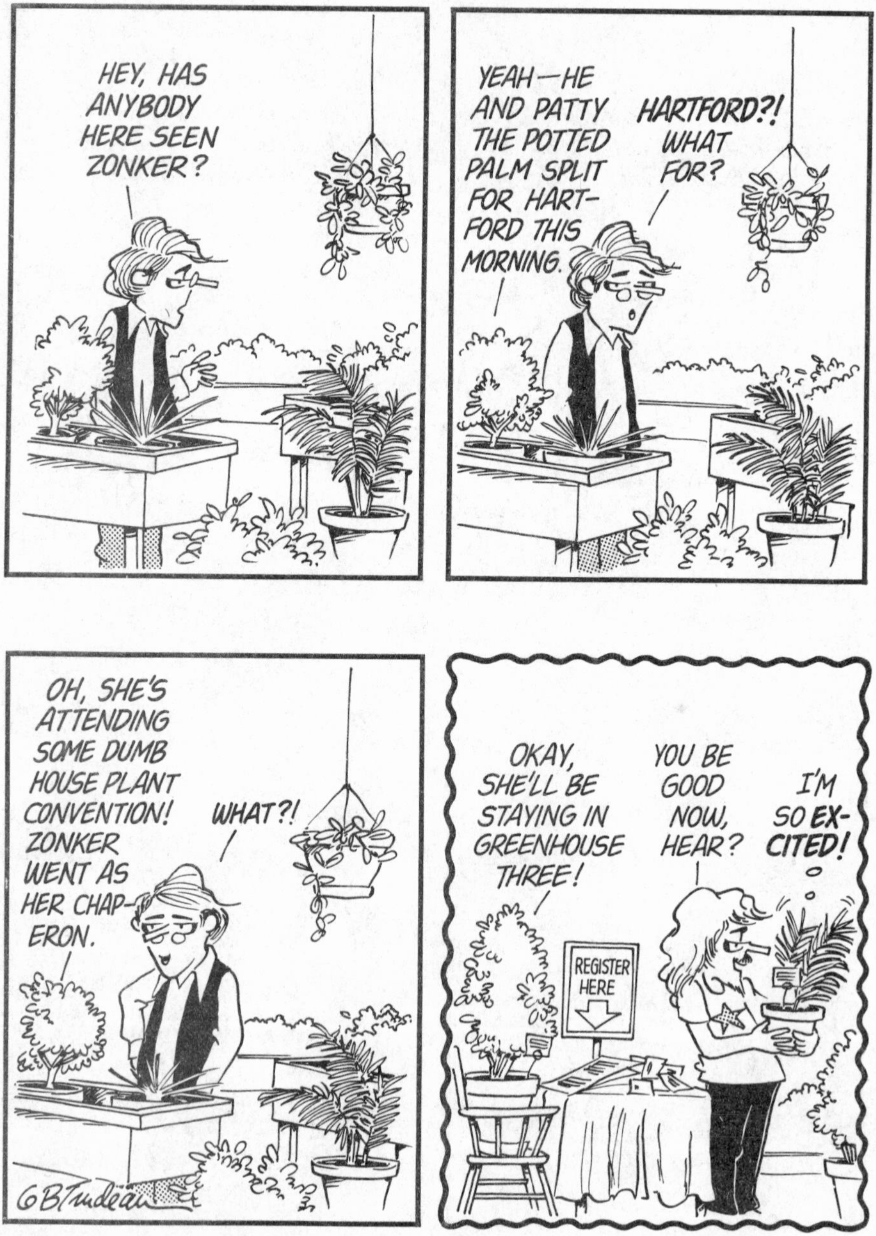
HEY, HAS ANYBODY HERE SEEN ZONKER?
YEAH—HE AND PATTY THE POTTED PALM SPLIT FOR HART-FORD THIS MORNING.
HARTFORD?! WHAT FOR?
OH, SHE'S ATTENDING SOME DUMB HOUSE PLANT CONVENTION! ZONKER WENT AS HER CHAP-ERON.
WHAT?!
G B Trudeau
OKAY, SHE'LL BE STAYING IN GREENHOUSE THREE!
REGISTER HERE
YOU BE GOOD NOW, HEAR?
I'M SO **EX-CITED**!

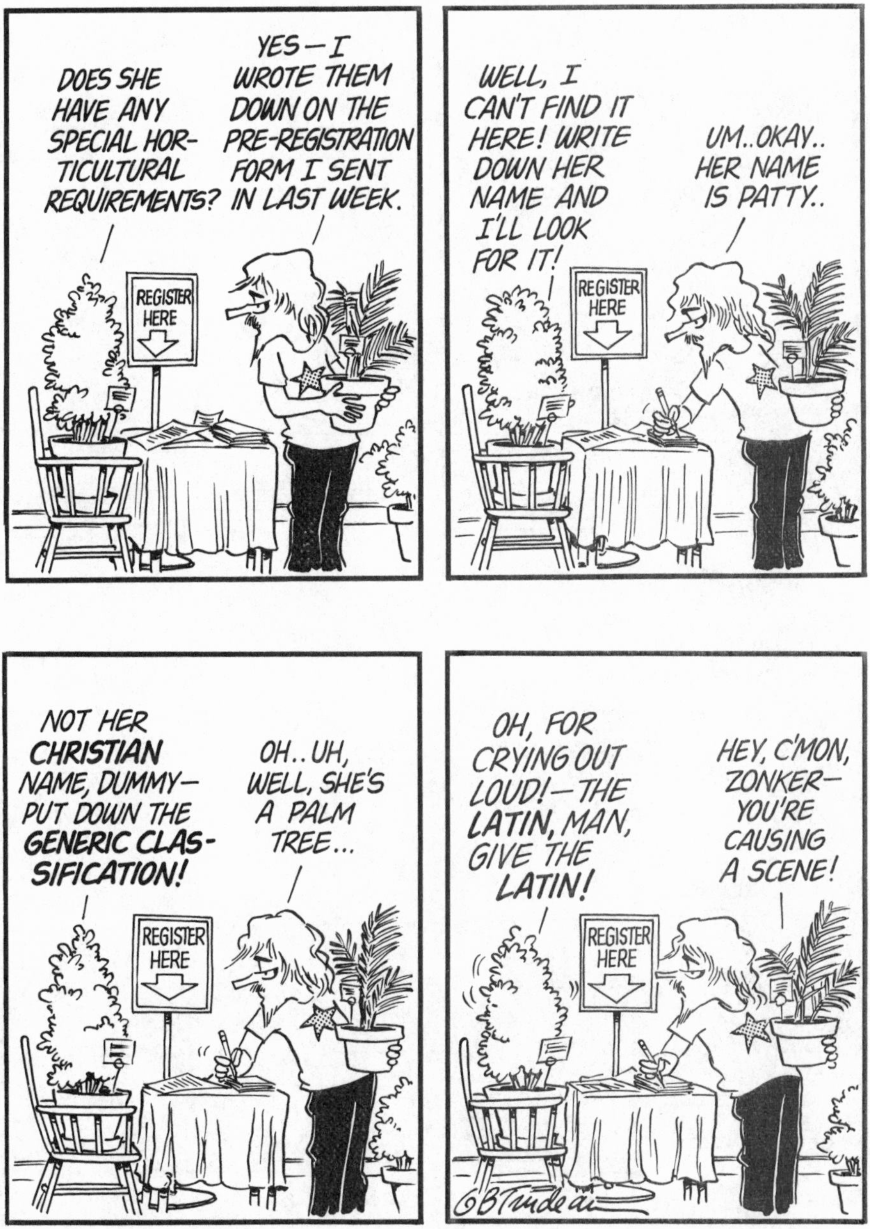
DOES SHE HAVE ANY SPECIAL HORTICULTURAL REQUIREMENTS?
YES—I WROTE THEM DOWN ON THE PRE-REGISTRATION FORM I SENT IN LAST WEEK.
REGISTER HERE
WELL, I CAN'T FIND IT HERE! WRITE DOWN HER NAME AND I'LL LOOK FOR IT!
UM..OKAY.. HER NAME IS PATTY..
REGISTER HERE
NOT HER **CHRISTIAN** NAME, DUMMY—PUT DOWN THE **GENERIC CLASSIFICATION!**
OH..UH, WELL, SHE'S A PALM TREE...
REGISTER HERE
OH, FOR CRYING OUT LOUD!—THE **LATIN,** MAN, GIVE THE **LATIN!**
HEY, C'MON, ZONKER—YOU'RE CAUSING A SCENE!
REGISTER HERE
©BTrudeau

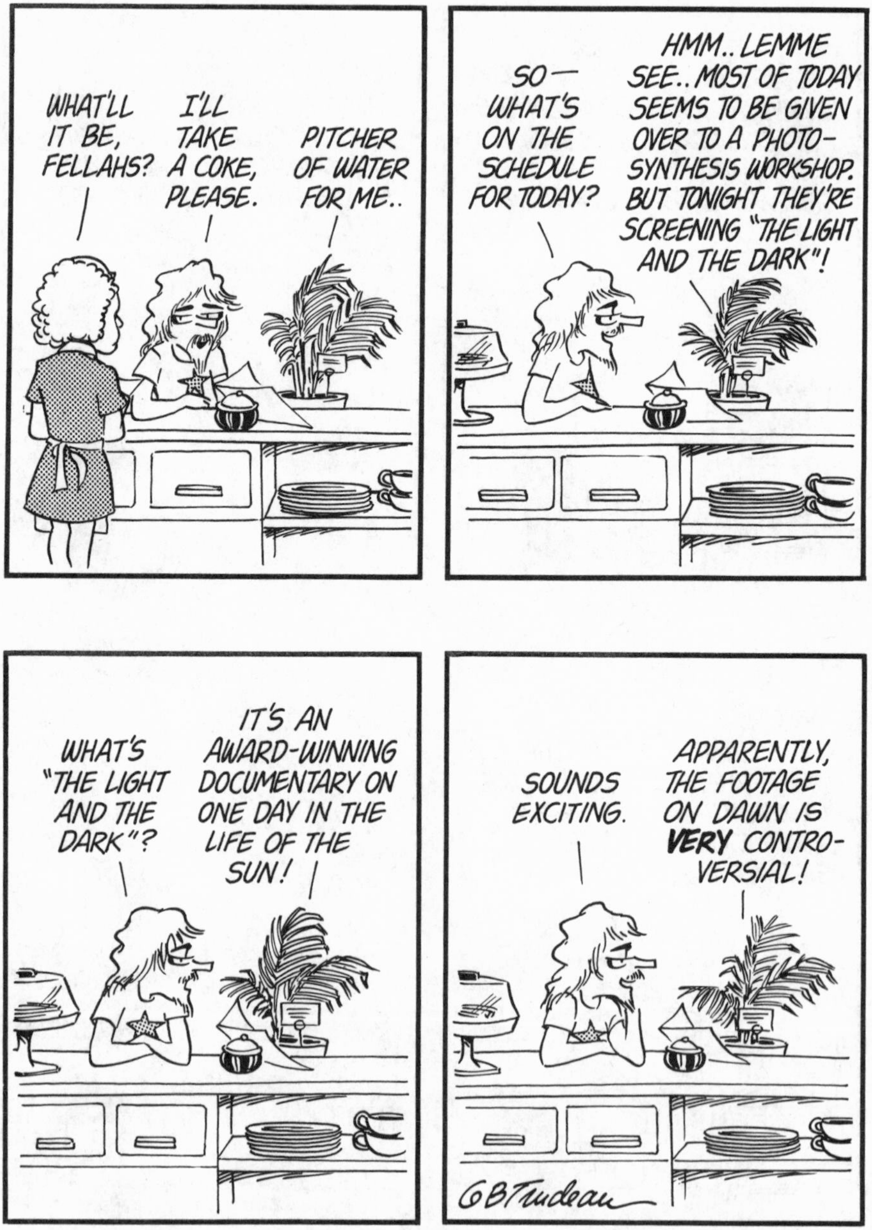
WHAT'LL IT BE, FELLAHS?
I'LL TAKE A COKE, PLEASE.
PITCHER OF WATER FOR ME..
SO— WHAT'S ON THE SCHEDULE FOR TODAY?
HMM.. LEMME SEE.. MOST OF TODAY SEEMS TO BE GIVEN OVER TO A PHOTO-SYNTHESIS WORKSHOP. BUT TONIGHT THEY'RE SCREENING "THE LIGHT AND THE DARK"!
WHAT'S "THE LIGHT AND THE DARK"?
IT'S AN AWARD-WINNING DOCUMENTARY ON ONE DAY IN THE LIFE OF THE SUN!
SOUNDS EXCITING.
APPARENTLY, THE FOOTAGE ON DAWN IS **VERY** CONTRO-VERSIAL!
GBTrudeau

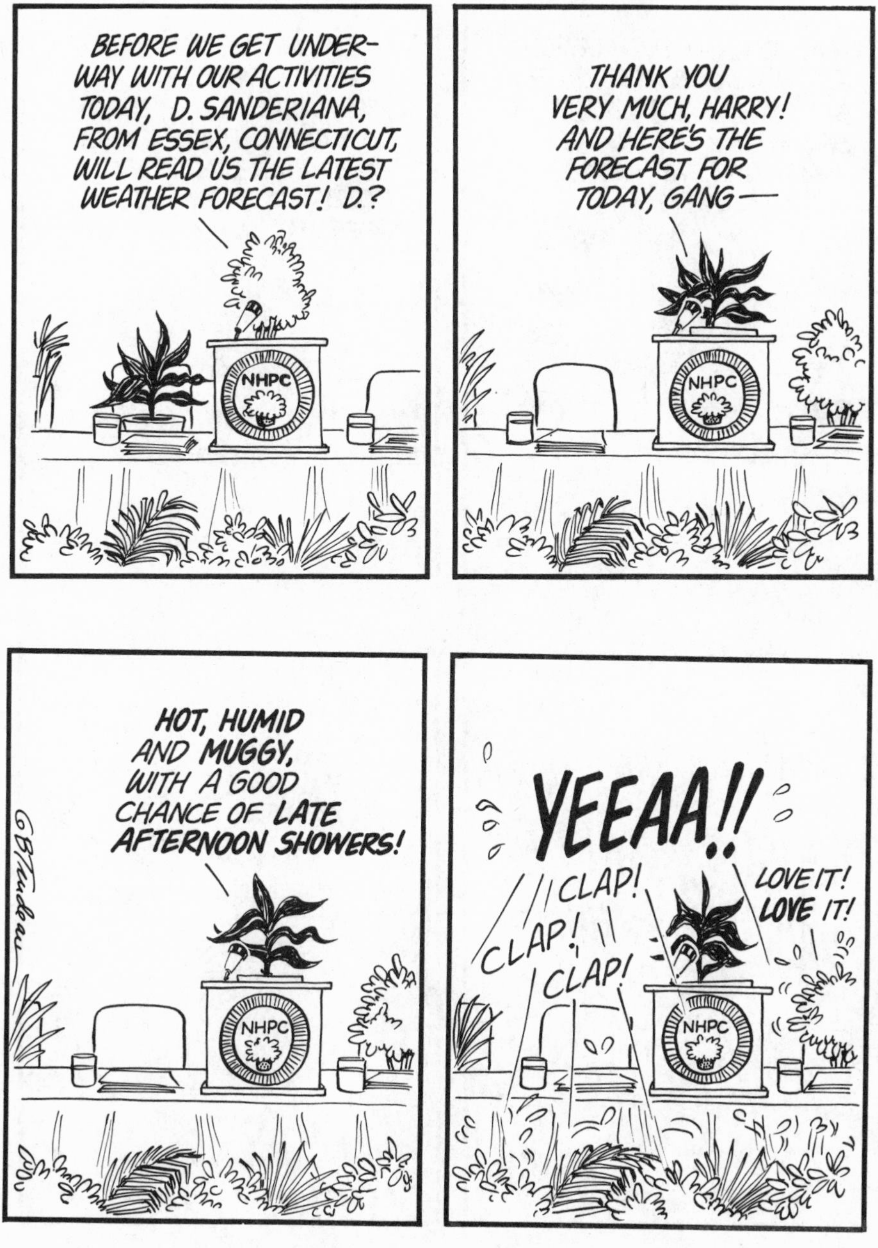
BEFORE WE GET UNDER-WAY WITH OUR ACTIVITIES TODAY, D. SANDERIANA, FROM ESSEX, CONNECTICUT, WILL READ US THE LATEST WEATHER FORECAST! D.?
NHPC
THANK YOU VERY MUCH, HARRY! AND HERE'S THE FORECAST FOR TODAY, GANG—
NHPC
HOT, HUMID AND MUGGY, WITH A GOOD CHANCE OF LATE AFTERNOON SHOWERS!
©GBTrudeau
NHPC
YEEAA!!
CLAP!
CLAP!
CLAP!
LOVE IT! LOVE IT!
NHPC

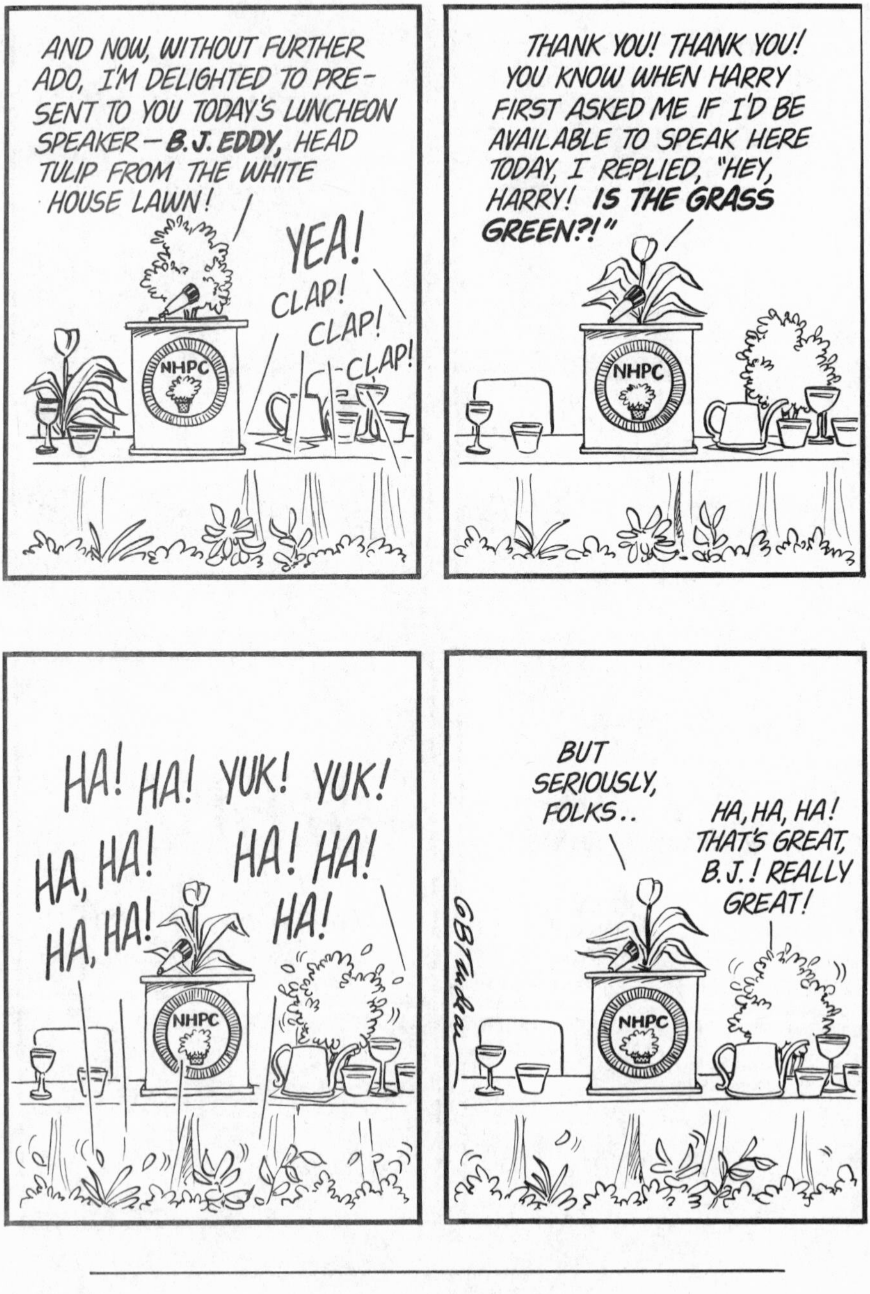
AND NOW, WITHOUT FURTHER ADO, I'M DELIGHTED TO PRESENT TO YOU TODAY'S LUNCHEON SPEAKER—B. J. EDDY, HEAD TULIP FROM THE WHITE HOUSE LAWN!
YEA!
CLAP! CLAP! CLAP!
NHPC
THANK YOU! THANK YOU! YOU KNOW WHEN HARRY FIRST ASKED ME IF I'D BE AVAILABLE TO SPEAK HERE TODAY, I REPLIED, "HEY, HARRY! IS THE GRASS GREEN?!"
NHPC
HA! HA! YUK! YUK!
HA, HA! HA, HA!
HA! HA! HA!
NHPC
BUT SERIOUSLY, FOLKS..
HA, HA, HA! THAT'S GREAT, B.J.! REALLY GREAT!
NHPC
GBTrudeau

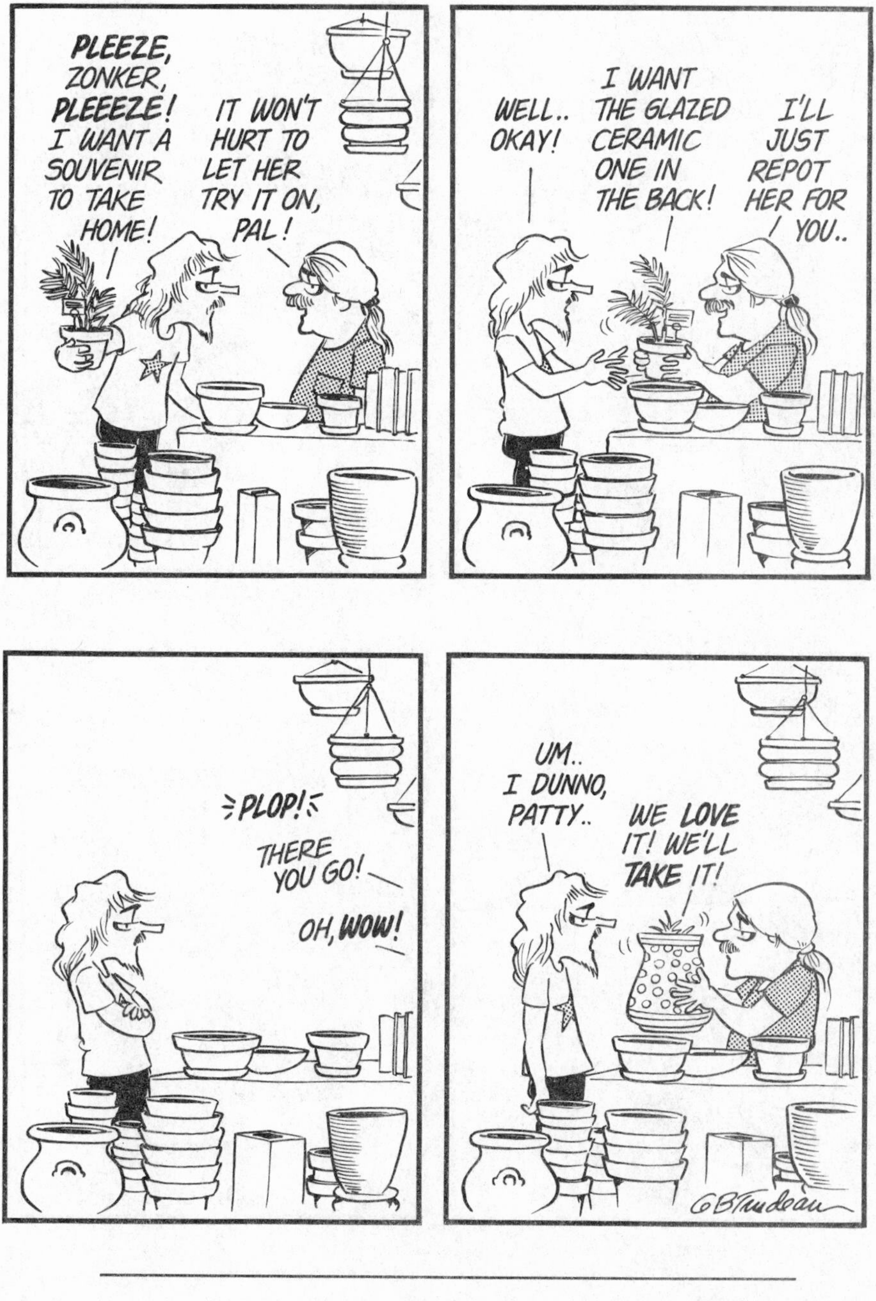
PLEEZE, ZONKER, PLEEEZE! I WANT A SOUVENIR TO TAKE HOME!
IT WON'T HURT TO LET HER TRY IT ON, PAL!
WELL.. OKAY!
I WANT THE GLAZED CERAMIC ONE IN THE BACK!
I'LL JUST REPOT HER FOR YOU..
PLOP!
THERE YOU GO!
OH, WOW!
UM.. I DUNNO, PATTY..
WE LOVE IT! WE'LL TAKE IT!
GBTrudeau

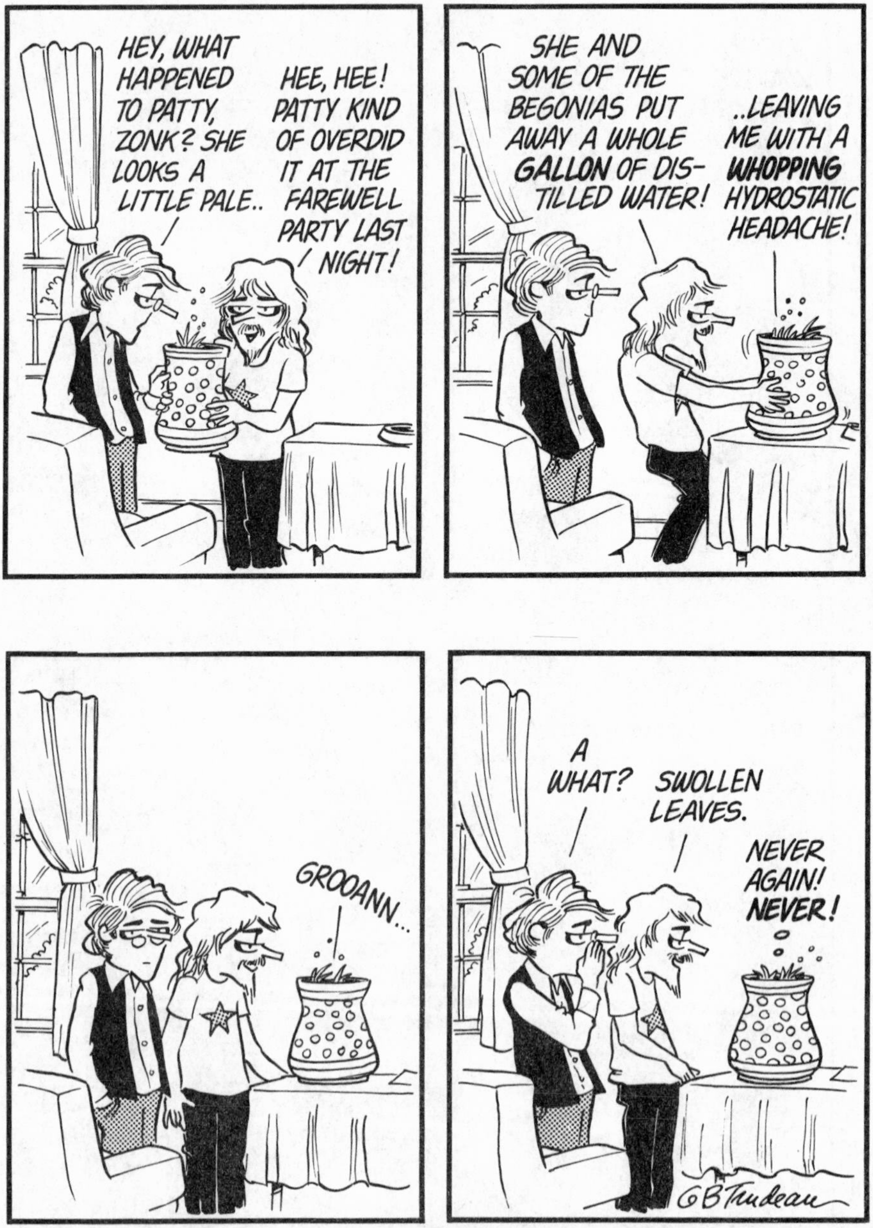
HEY, WHAT HAPPENED TO PATTY, ZONK? SHE LOOKS A LITTLE PALE..
HEE, HEE! PATTY KIND OF OVERDID IT AT THE FAREWELL PARTY LAST NIGHT!
SHE AND SOME OF THE BEGONIAS PUT AWAY A WHOLE **GALLON** OF DIS-TILLED WATER!
..LEAVING ME WITH A **WHOPPING** HYDROSTATIC HEADACHE!
GROOANN...
A WHAT?
SWOLLEN LEAVES.
NEVER AGAIN! **NEVER!**
GB Trudeau

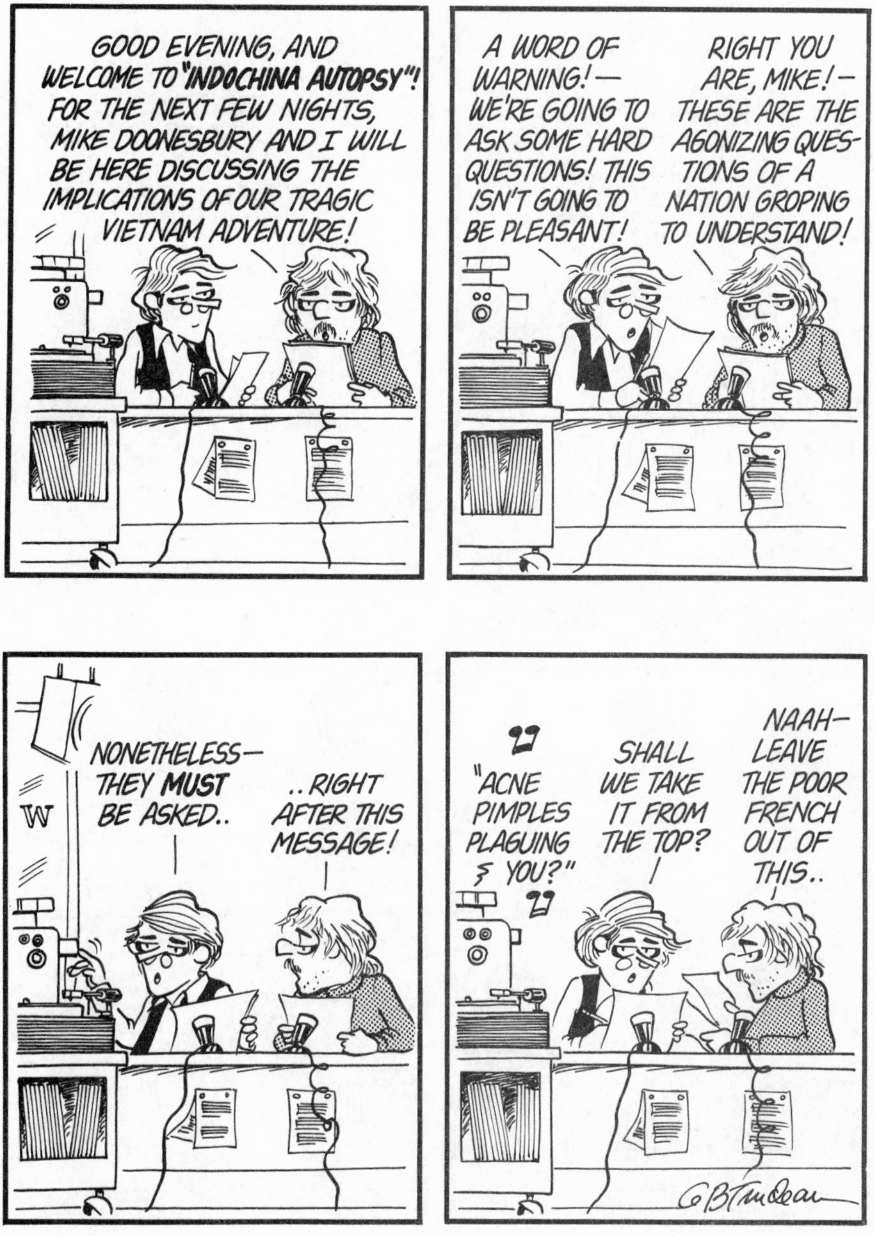
GOOD EVENING, AND WELCOME TO "INDOCHINA AUTOPSY"! FOR THE NEXT FEW NIGHTS, MIKE DOONESBURY AND I WILL BE HERE DISCUSSING THE IMPLICATIONS OF OUR TRAGIC VIETNAM ADVENTURE!
A WORD OF WARNING! — WE'RE GOING TO ASK SOME HARD QUESTIONS! THIS ISN'T GOING TO BE PLEASANT!
RIGHT YOU ARE, MIKE! — THESE ARE THE AGONIZING QUESTIONS OF A NATION GROPING TO UNDERSTAND!
W
NONETHELESS — THEY MUST BE ASKED..
..RIGHT AFTER THIS MESSAGE!
"ACNE PIMPLES PLAGUING YOU?"
SHALL WE TAKE IT FROM THE TOP?
NAAH — LEAVE THE POOR FRENCH OUT OF THIS..
GBTrudeau

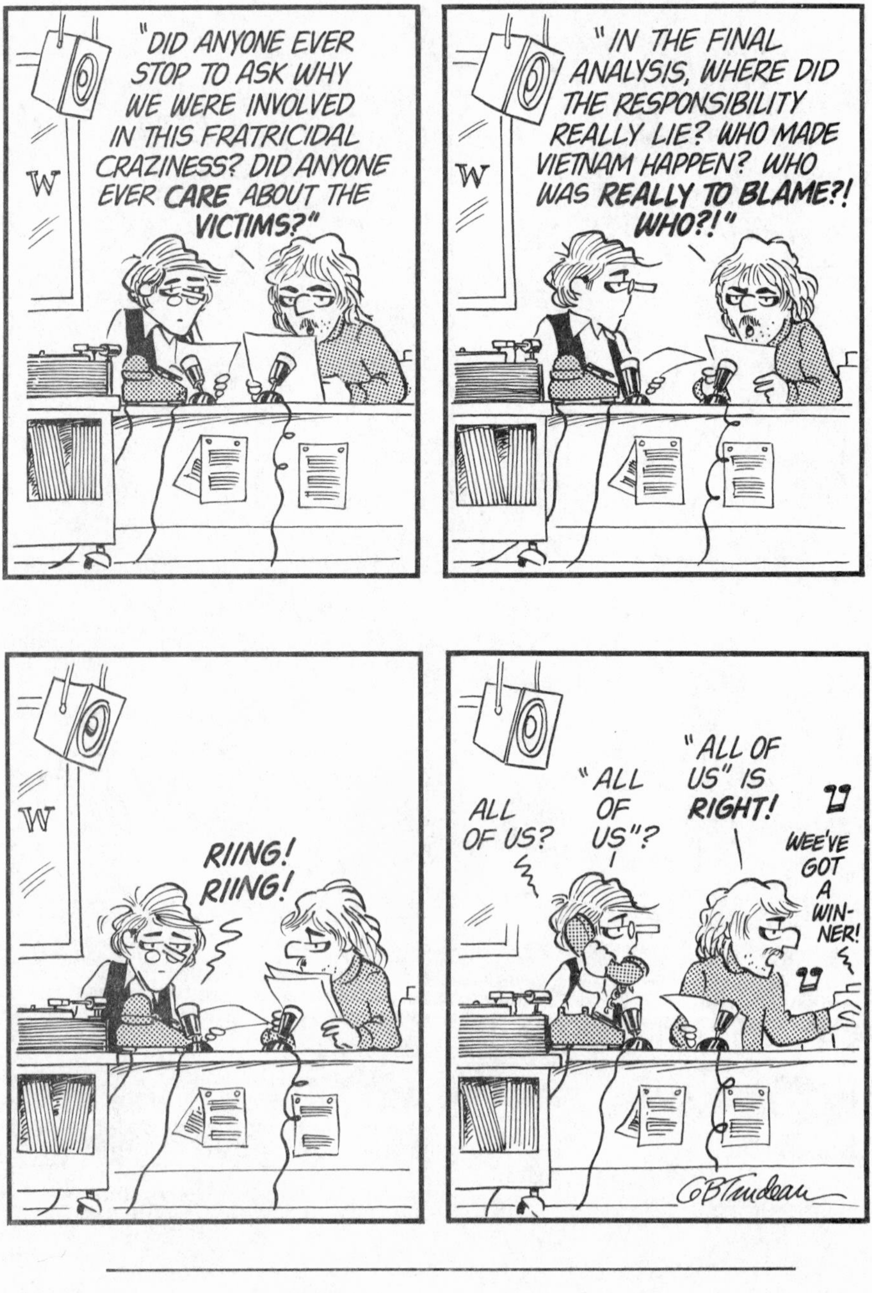
"DID ANYONE EVER STOP TO ASK WHY WE WERE INVOLVED IN THIS FRATRICIDAL CRAZINESS? DID ANYONE EVER CARE ABOUT THE VICTIMS?"
"IN THE FINAL ANALYSIS, WHERE DID THE RESPONSIBILITY REALLY LIE? WHO MADE VIETNAM HAPPEN? WHO WAS REALLY TO BLAME?! WHO?!"
RIING! RIING!
ALL OF US?
"ALL OF US"?
"ALL OF US" IS RIGHT!
WEE'VE GOT A WIN-NER!
GBTrudeau

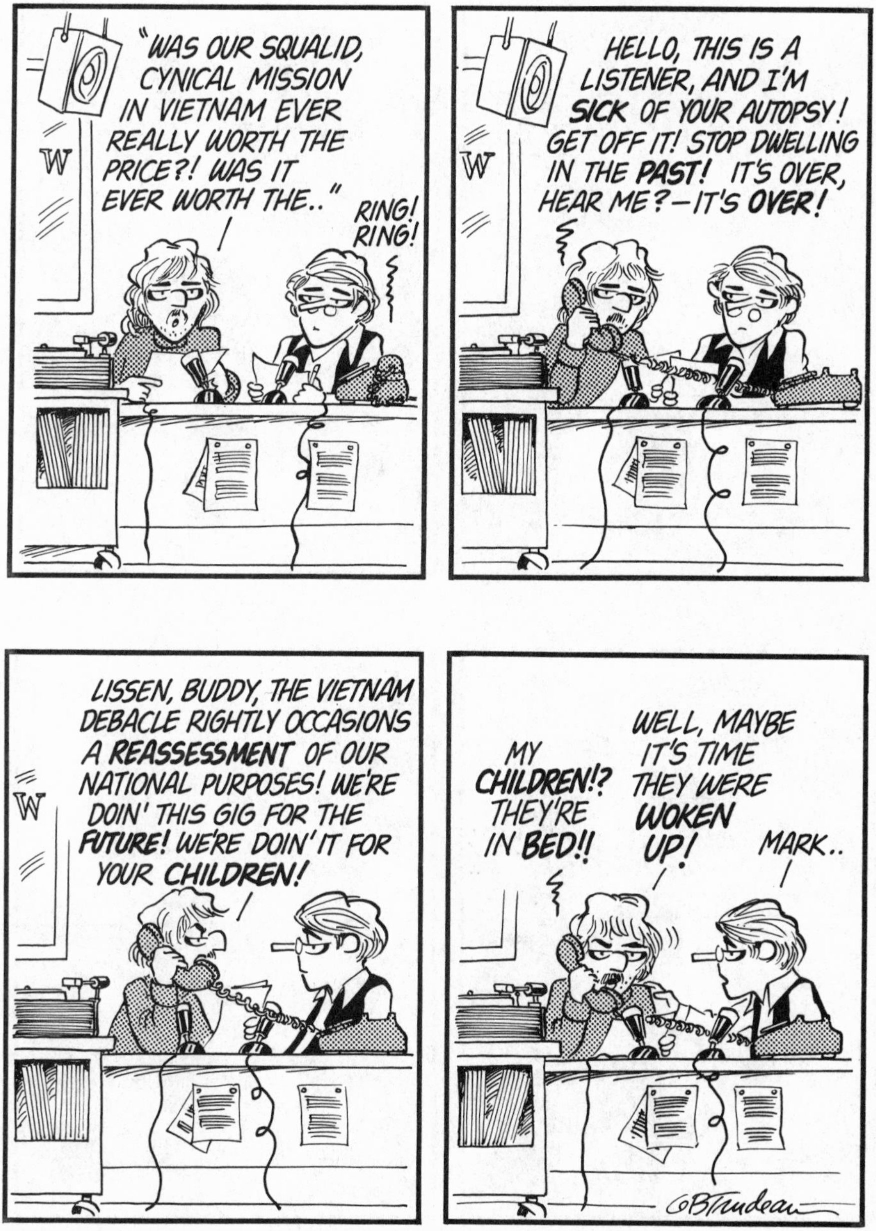
"WAS OUR SQUALID, CYNICAL MISSION IN VIETNAM EVER REALLY WORTH THE PRICE?! WAS IT EVER WORTH THE.."
RING! RING!
HELLO, THIS IS A LISTENER, AND I'M **SICK** OF YOUR AUTOPSY! GET OFF IT! STOP DWELLING IN THE **PAST!** IT'S OVER, HEAR ME?—IT'S **OVER!**
LISSEN, BUDDY, THE VIETNAM DEBACLE RIGHTLY OCCASIONS A **REASSESSMENT** OF OUR NATIONAL PURPOSES! WE'RE DOIN' THIS GIG FOR THE **FUTURE!** WE'RE DOIN' IT FOR YOUR **CHILDREN!**
MY **CHILDREN!?** THEY'RE IN **BED!!**
WELL, MAYBE IT'S TIME THEY WERE **WOKEN UP!**
MARK..
GBTrudeau

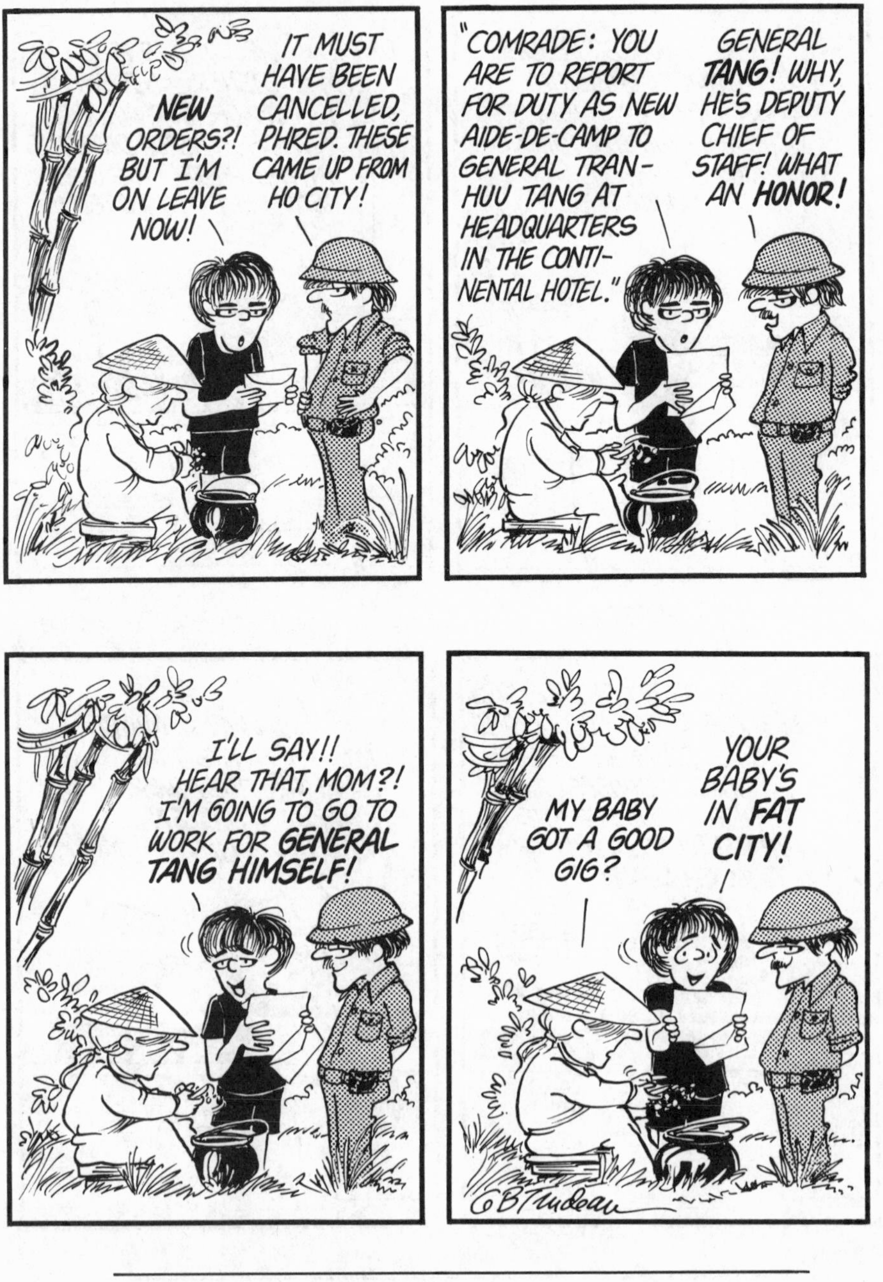
NEW ORDERS?! BUT I'M ON LEAVE NOW!
IT MUST HAVE BEEN CANCELLED, PHRED. THESE CAME UP FROM HO CITY!
"COMRADE: YOU ARE TO REPORT FOR DUTY AS NEW AIDE-DE-CAMP TO GENERAL TRAN-HUU TANG AT HEADQUARTERS IN THE CONTI-NENTAL HOTEL."
GENERAL TANG! WHY, HE'S DEPUTY CHIEF OF STAFF! WHAT AN HONOR!
I'LL SAY!! HEAR THAT, MOM?! I'M GOING TO GO TO WORK FOR GENERAL TANG HIMSELF!
MY BABY GOT A GOOD GIG?
YOUR BABY'S IN FAT CITY!
GBTrudeau

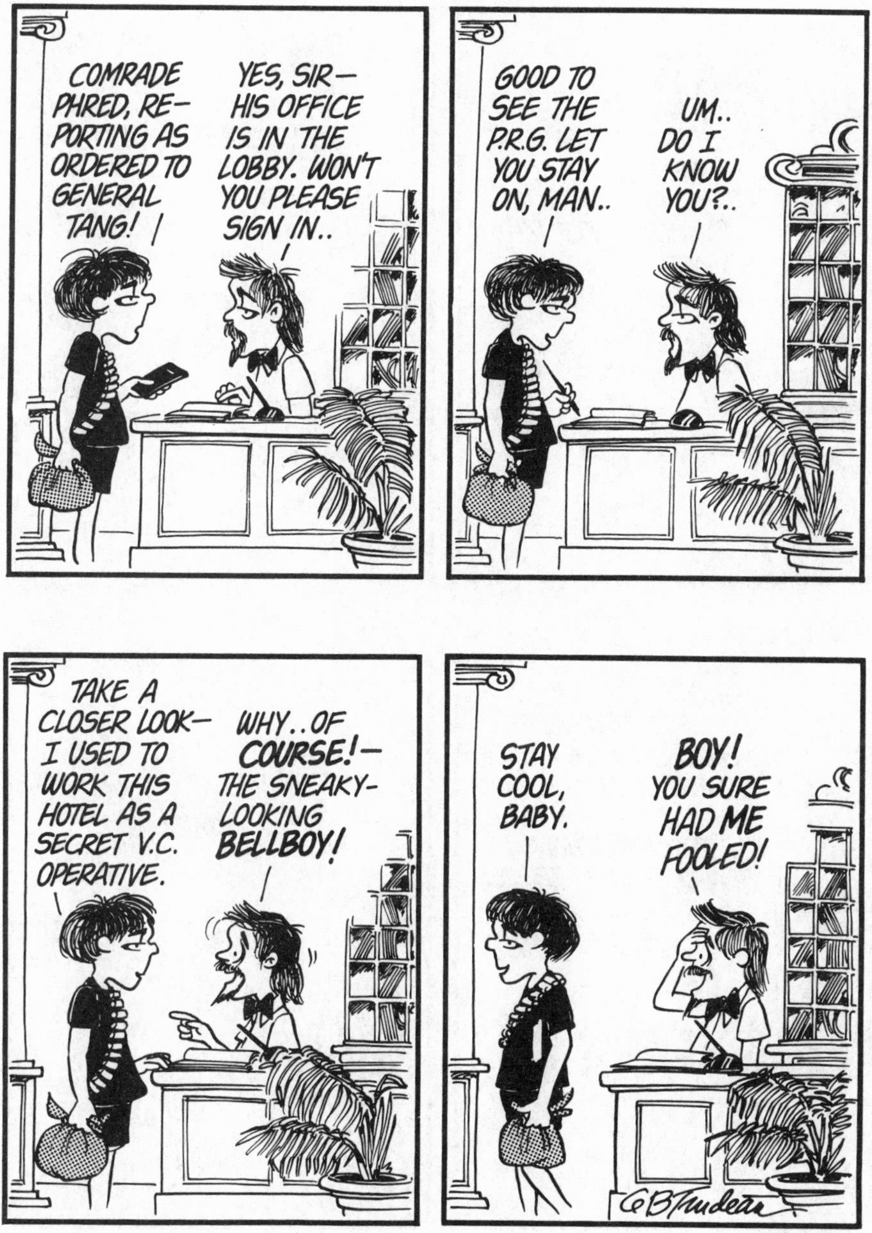
COMRADE PHRED, REPORTING AS ORDERED TO GENERAL TANG!
YES, SIR— HIS OFFICE IS IN THE LOBBY. WON'T YOU PLEASE SIGN IN..
GOOD TO SEE THE P.R.G. LET YOU STAY ON, MAN..
UM.. DO I KNOW YOU?..
TAKE A CLOSER LOOK— I USED TO WORK THIS HOTEL AS A SECRET V.C. OPERATIVE.
WHY..OF COURSE!— THE SNEAKY-LOOKING BELLBOY!
STAY COOL, BABY.
BOY! YOU SURE HAD ME FOOLED!
GB Trudeau

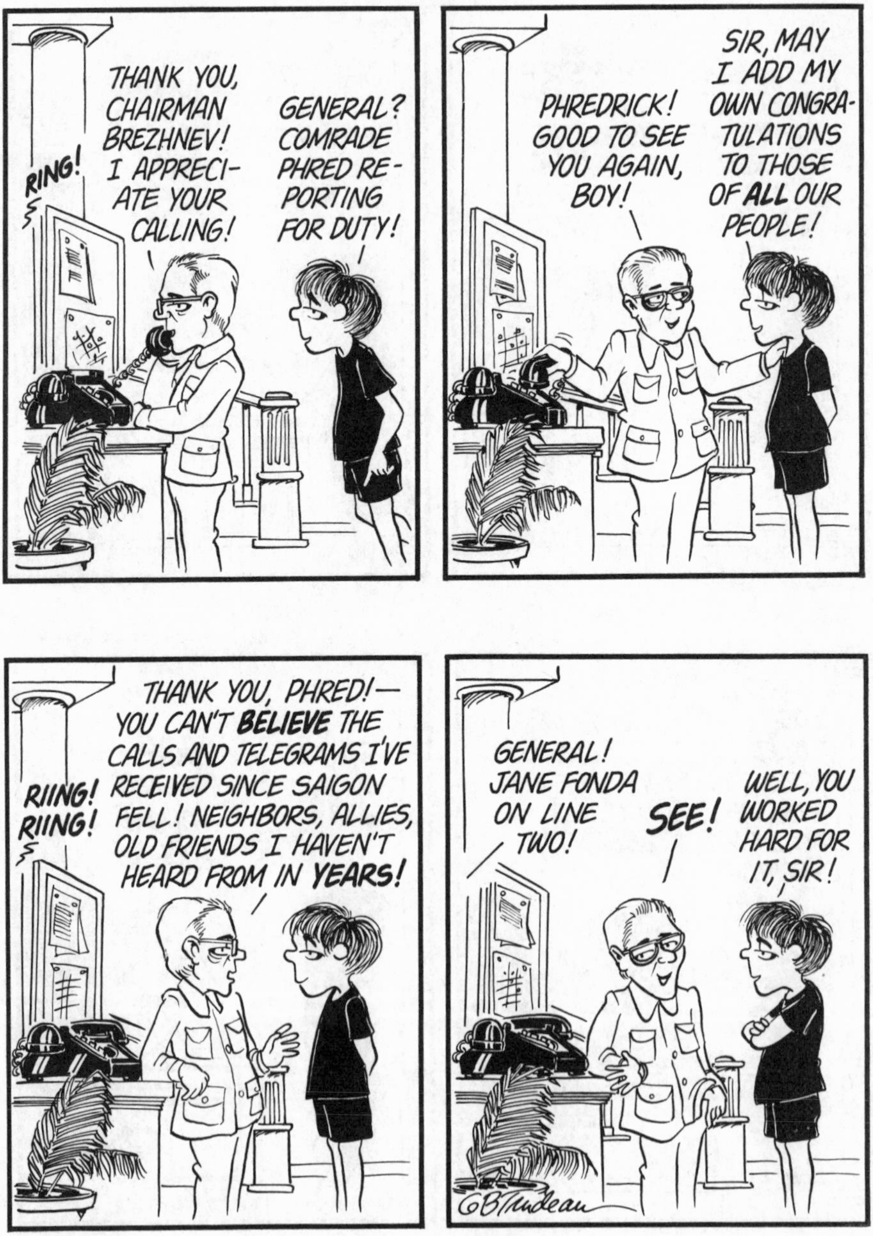
RING!
THANK YOU, CHAIRMAN BREZHNEV! I APPRECIATE YOUR CALLING!
GENERAL? COMRADE PHRED REPORTING FOR DUTY!
PHREDRICK! GOOD TO SEE YOU AGAIN, BOY!
SIR, MAY I ADD MY OWN CONGRATULATIONS TO THOSE OF **ALL** OUR PEOPLE!
RIING! RIING!
THANK YOU, PHRED!— YOU CAN'T **BELIEVE** THE CALLS AND TELEGRAMS I'VE RECEIVED SINCE SAIGON FELL! NEIGHBORS, ALLIES, OLD FRIENDS I HAVEN'T HEARD FROM IN **YEARS**!
GENERAL! JANE FONDA ON LINE TWO!
**SEE**!
WELL, YOU WORKED HARD FOR IT, SIR!
GBTrudeau

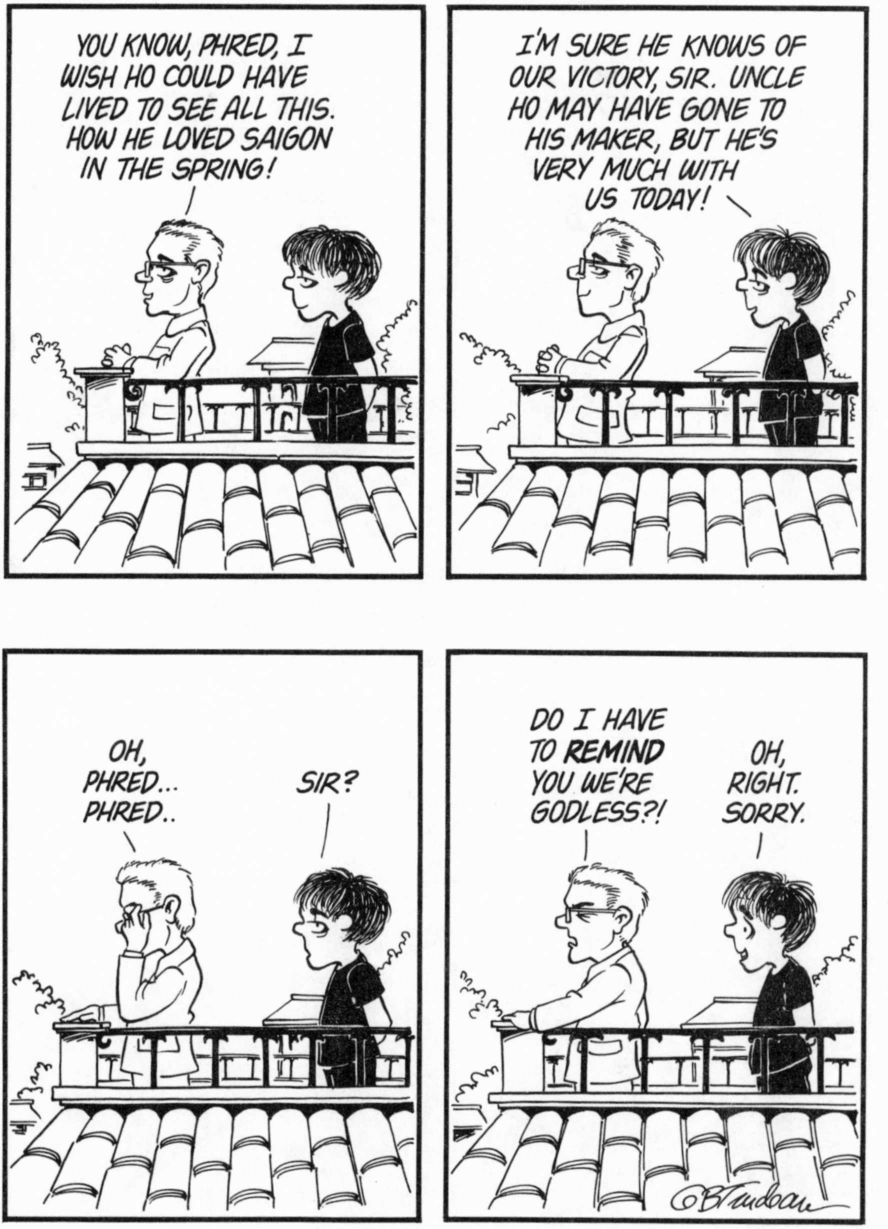
YOU KNOW, PHRED, I WISH HO COULD HAVE LIVED TO SEE ALL THIS. HOW HE LOVED SAIGON IN THE SPRING!
I'M SURE HE KNOWS OF OUR VICTORY, SIR. UNCLE HO MAY HAVE GONE TO HIS MAKER, BUT HE'S VERY MUCH WITH US TODAY!
OH, PHRED... PHRED..
SIR?
DO I HAVE TO **REMIND** YOU WE'RE GODLESS?!
OH, RIGHT. SORRY.
©BTrudeau

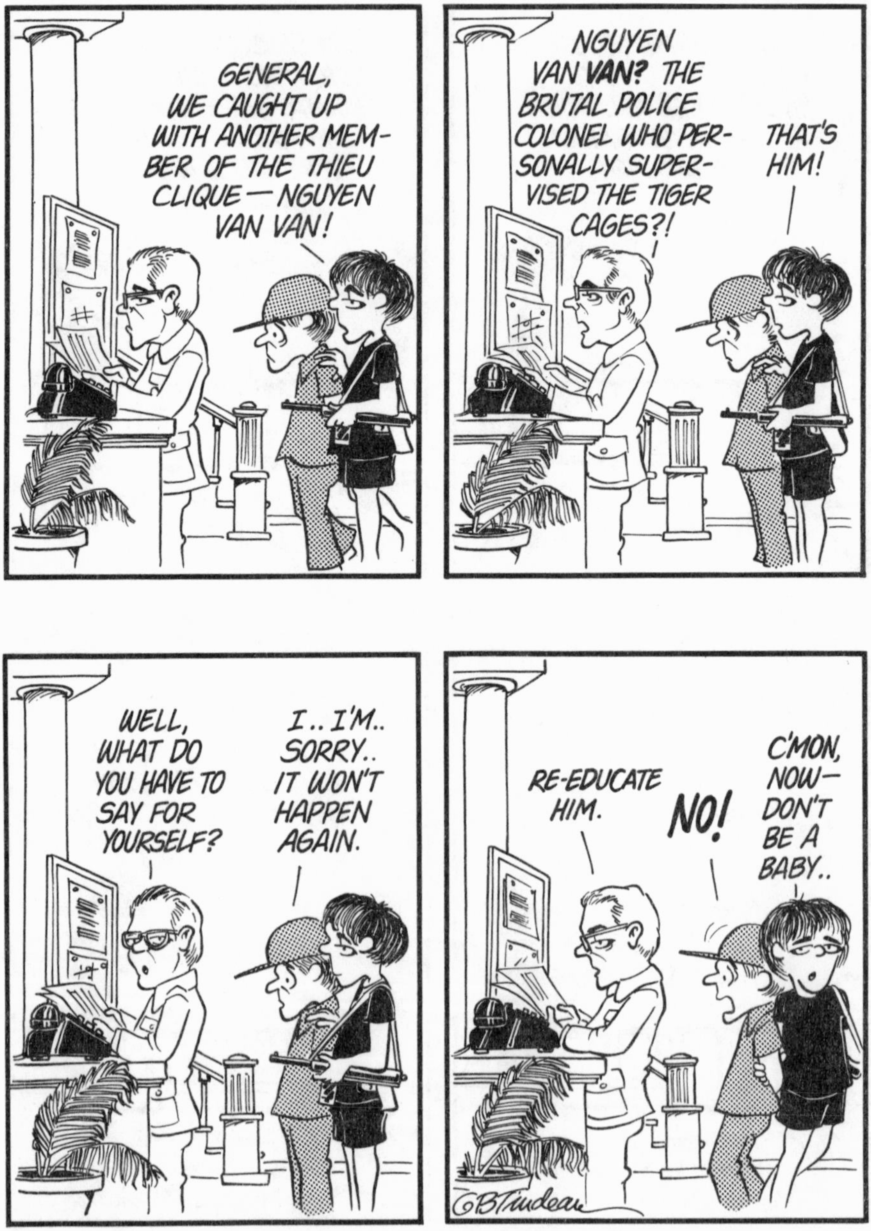
GENERAL, WE CAUGHT UP WITH ANOTHER MEMBER OF THE THIEU CLIQUE — NGUYEN VAN VAN!
NGUYEN VAN **VAN?** THE BRUTAL POLICE COLONEL WHO PERSONALLY SUPERVISED THE TIGER CAGES?!
THAT'S HIM!
WELL, WHAT DO YOU HAVE TO SAY FOR YOURSELF?
I.. I'M.. SORRY.. IT WON'T HAPPEN AGAIN.
RE-EDUCATE HIM.
NO!
C'MON, NOW— DON'T BE A BABY..
GBTrudeau

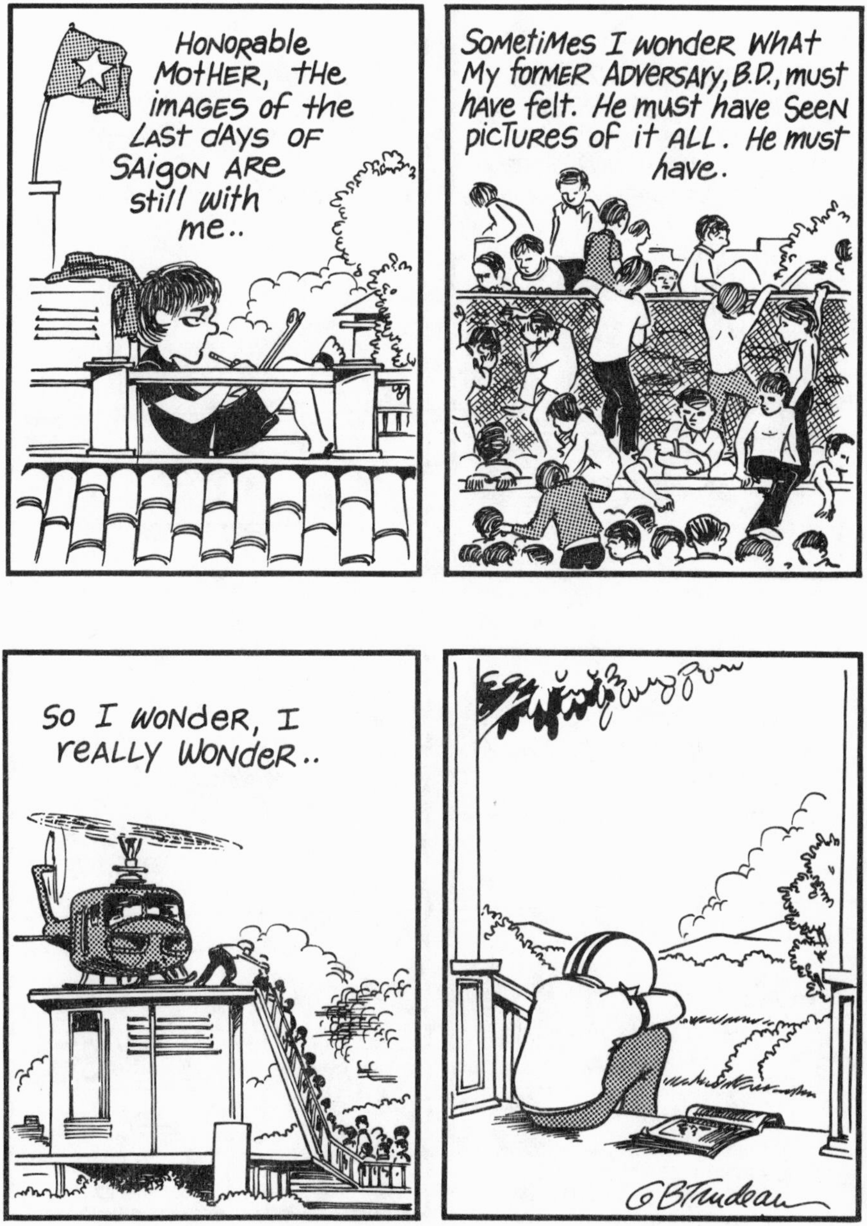
HONORABLE MOTHER, THE IMAGES OF THE LAST DAYS OF SAIGON ARE STILL WITH ME..
SOMETIMES I WONDER WHAT MY FORMER ADVERSARY, B.D., MUST HAVE FELT. HE MUST HAVE SEEN PICTURES OF IT ALL. HE MUST HAVE.
SO I WONDER, I REALLY WONDER..
©GBTrudeau

YOU KNOW, IT'S BAD ENOUGH THOSE PEOPLE LET THEMSELVES GET BEAT — NOW WE GOT TO FIND HOMES FOR OVER 100,000 OF THEM!
WE OUGHTA SEND THEM PACKIN'! THAT'S WHAT WE OUGHTA DO!
NO, NO, B.D.—YOU CAN'T MEAN THAT...
WE LED THE VIETNAMESE ON FOR TEN YEARS—THE VERY **LEAST** WE OWE THEM IS ONE REAL SHOT AT MAKING NEW LIVES FOR THEMSELVES!
GBTrudeau
PLEASE, SIR—I'M YEARNING TO BE FREE.
I CAN DIG IT. EMPTY YOUR POCKETS.

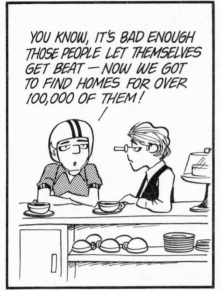

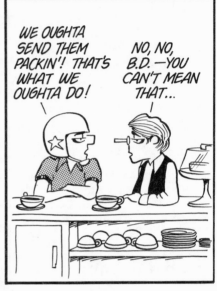

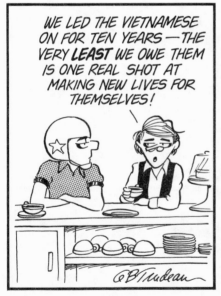

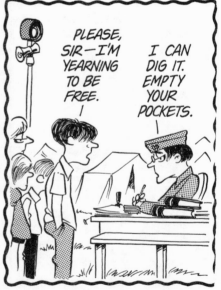

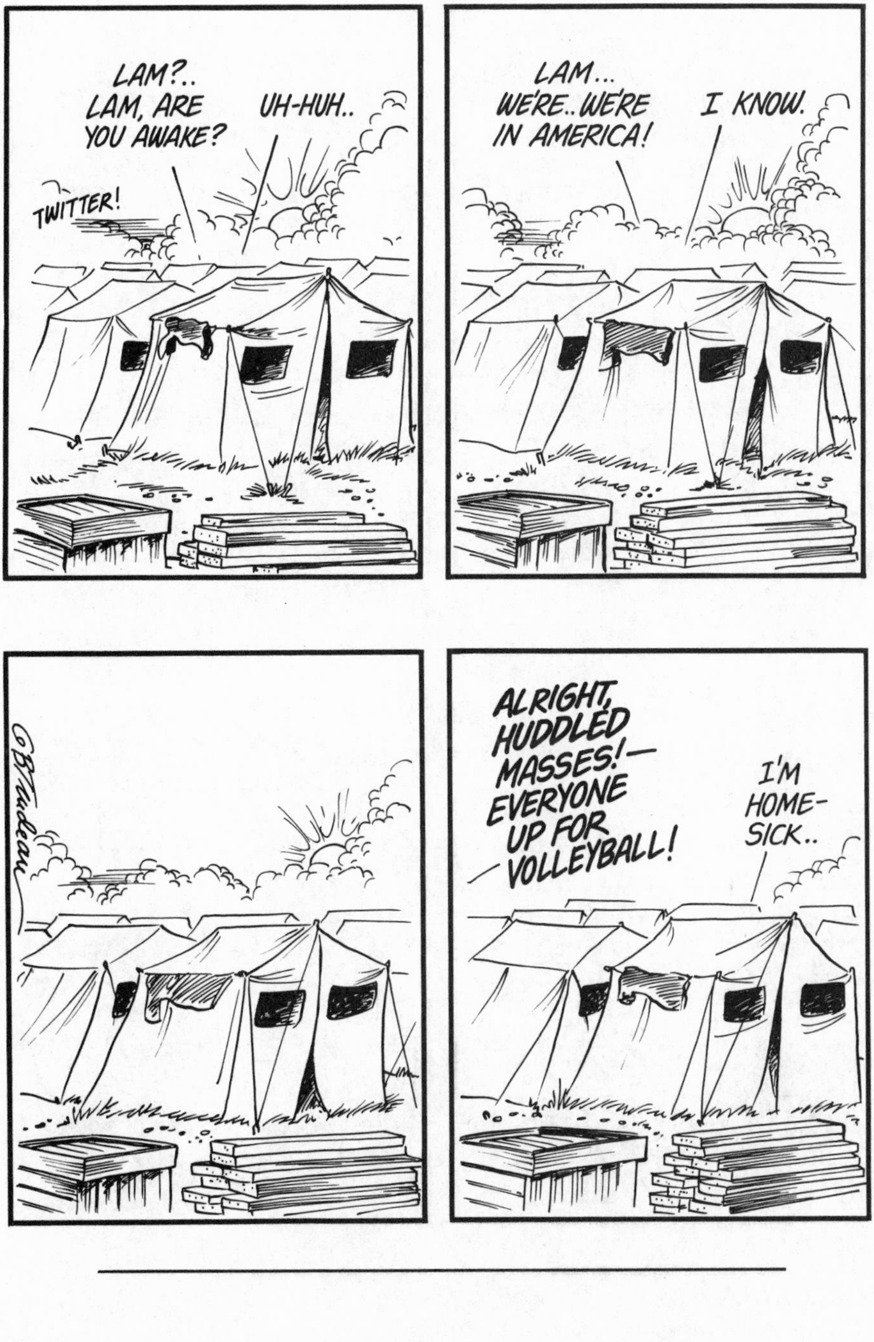
TWITTER!
LAM?.. LAM, ARE YOU AWAKE?
UH-HUH..
LAM... WE'RE..WE'RE IN AMERICA!
I KNOW.
©GBTrudeau
ALRIGHT, HUDDLED MASSES!— EVERYONE UP FOR VOLLEYBALL!
I'M HOME-SICK..

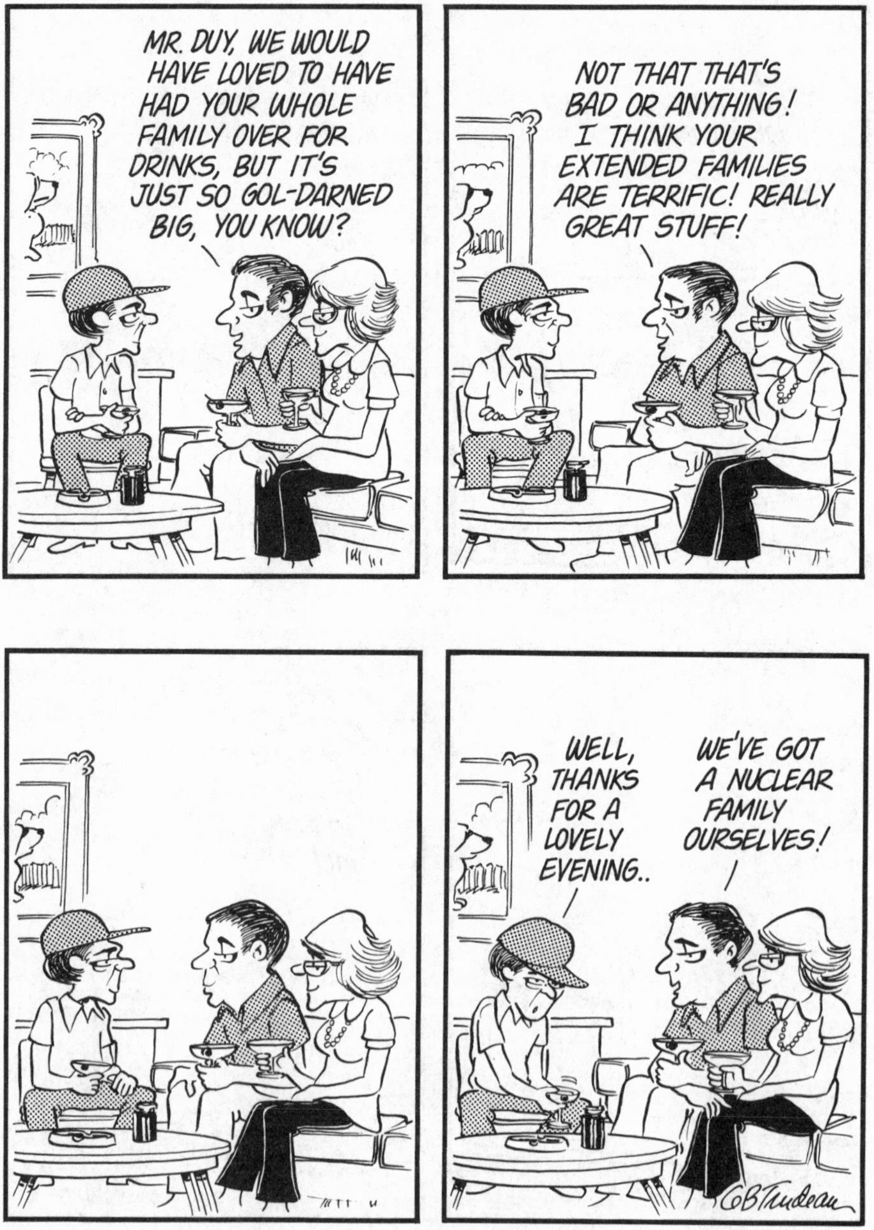
MR. DUY, WE WOULD HAVE LOVED TO HAVE HAD YOUR WHOLE FAMILY OVER FOR DRINKS, BUT IT'S JUST SO GOL-DARNED BIG, YOU KNOW?
NOT THAT THAT'S BAD OR ANYTHING! I THINK YOUR EXTENDED FAMILIES ARE TERRIFIC! REALLY GREAT STUFF!
WELL, THANKS FOR A LOVELY EVENING..
WE'VE GOT A NUCLEAR FAMILY OURSELVES!
GBTrudeau

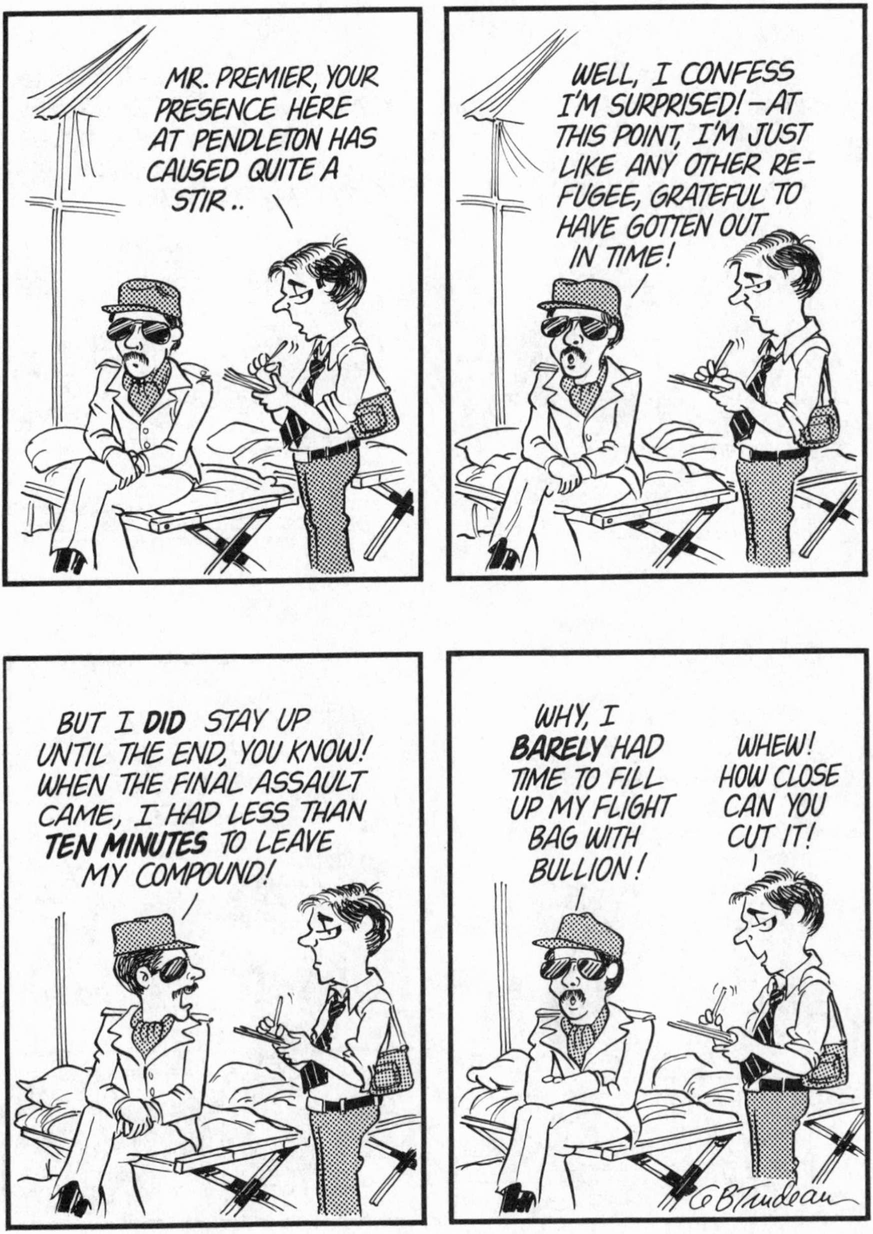
MR. PREMIER, YOUR PRESENCE HERE AT PENDLETON HAS CAUSED QUITE A STIR..
WELL, I CONFESS I'M SURPRISED!—AT THIS POINT, I'M JUST LIKE ANY OTHER REFUGEE, GRATEFUL TO HAVE GOTTEN OUT IN TIME!
BUT I **DID** STAY UP UNTIL THE END, YOU KNOW! WHEN THE FINAL ASSAULT CAME, I HAD LESS THAN **TEN MINUTES** TO LEAVE MY COMPOUND!
WHY, I **BARELY** HAD TIME TO FILL UP MY FLIGHT BAG WITH BULLION!
WHEW! HOW CLOSE CAN YOU CUT IT!
GBTrudeau

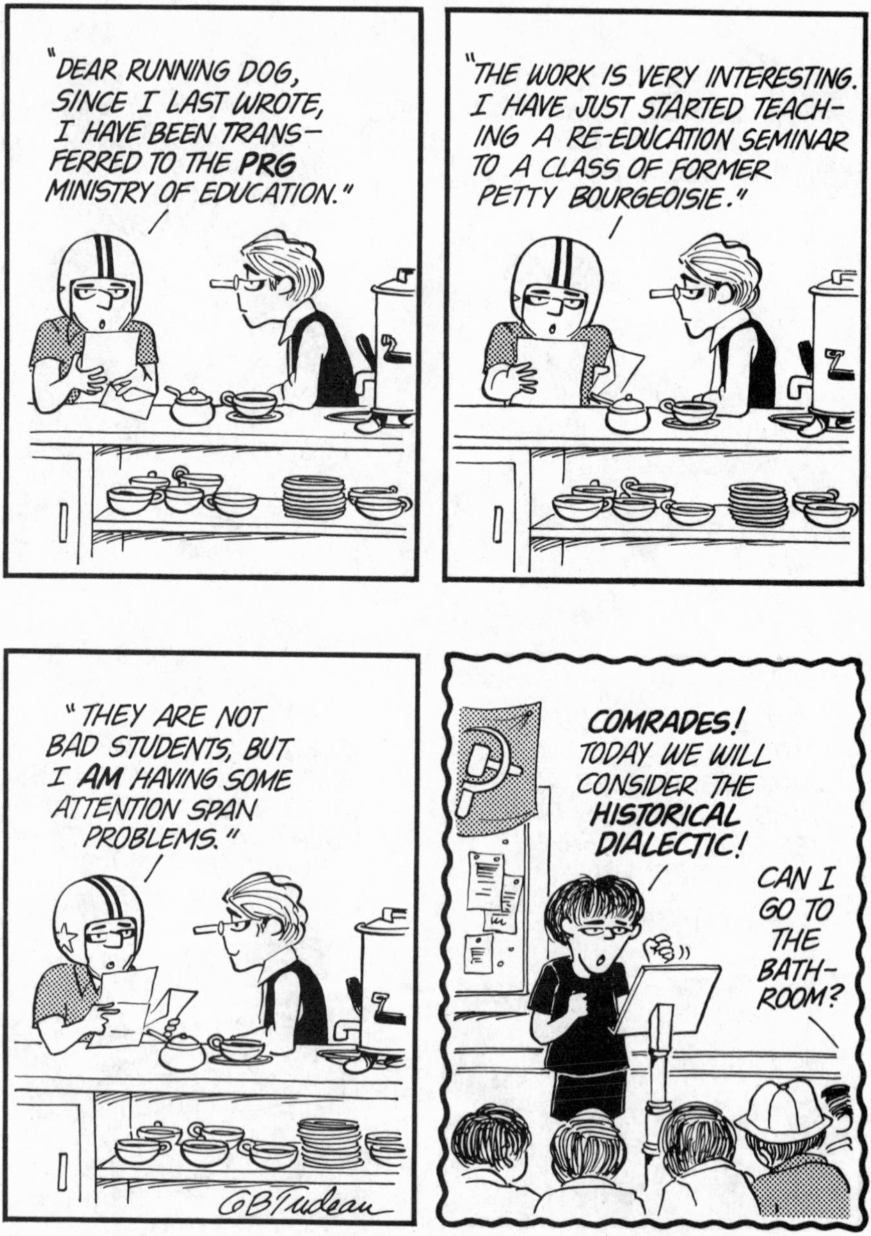
"DEAR RUNNING DOG, SINCE I LAST WROTE, I HAVE BEEN TRANS-FERRED TO THE **PRG** MINISTRY OF EDUCATION."
"THE WORK IS VERY INTERESTING. I HAVE JUST STARTED TEACH-ING A RE-EDUCATION SEMINAR TO A CLASS OF FORMER PETTY BOURGEOISIE."
"THEY ARE NOT BAD STUDENTS, BUT I **AM** HAVING SOME ATTENTION SPAN PROBLEMS."
GBTrudeau
**COMRADES!** TODAY WE WILL CONSIDER THE **HISTORICAL DIALECTIC!**
CAN I GO TO THE BATH-ROOM?

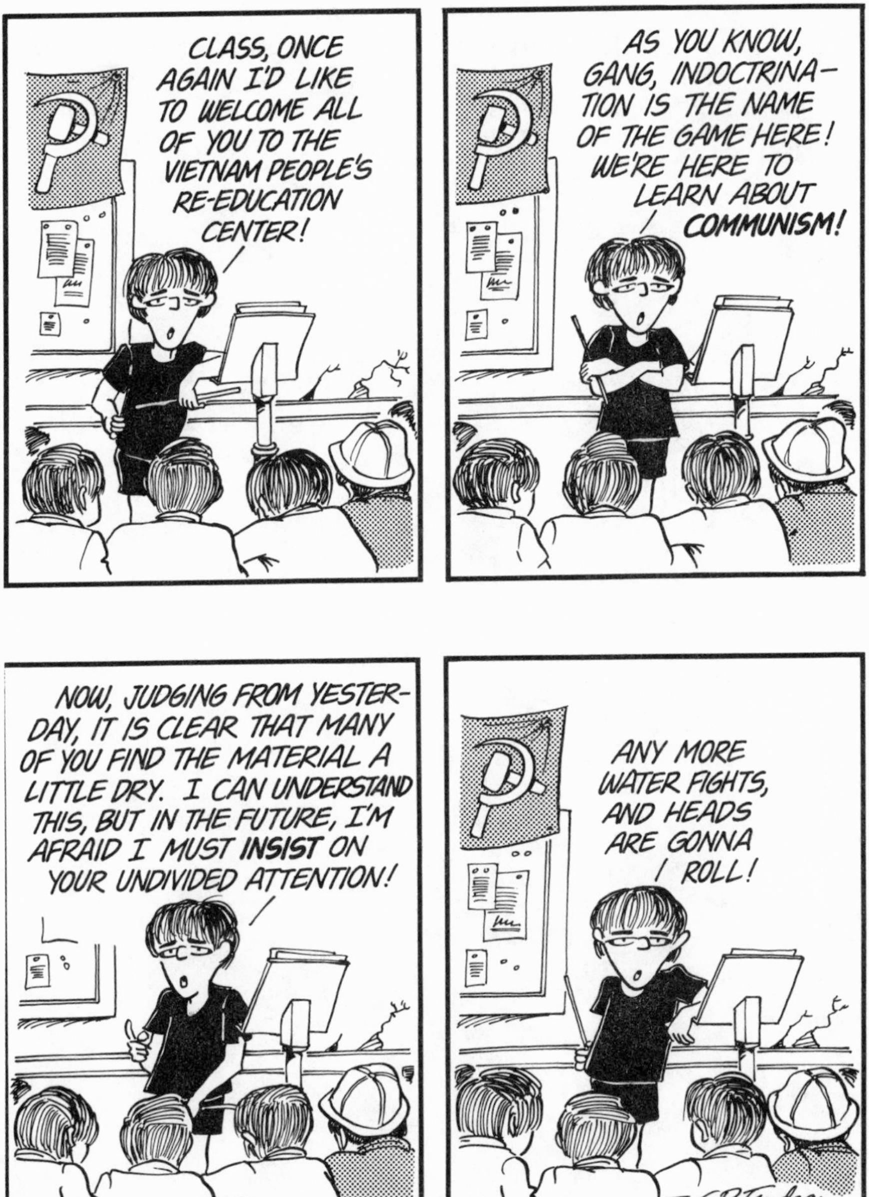

CLASS, ONCE AGAIN I'D LIKE TO WELCOME ALL OF YOU TO THE VIETNAM PEOPLE'S RE-EDUCATION CENTER!
AS YOU KNOW, GANG, INDOCTRINATION IS THE NAME OF THE GAME HERE! WE'RE HERE TO LEARN ABOUT **COMMUNISM!**
NOW, JUDGING FROM YESTERDAY, IT IS CLEAR THAT MANY OF YOU FIND THE MATERIAL A LITTLE DRY. I CAN UNDERSTAND THIS, BUT IN THE FUTURE, I'M AFRAID I MUST **INSIST** ON YOUR UNDIVIDED ATTENTION!
ANY MORE WATER FIGHTS, AND HEADS ARE GONNA ROLL!
©GBTrudeau

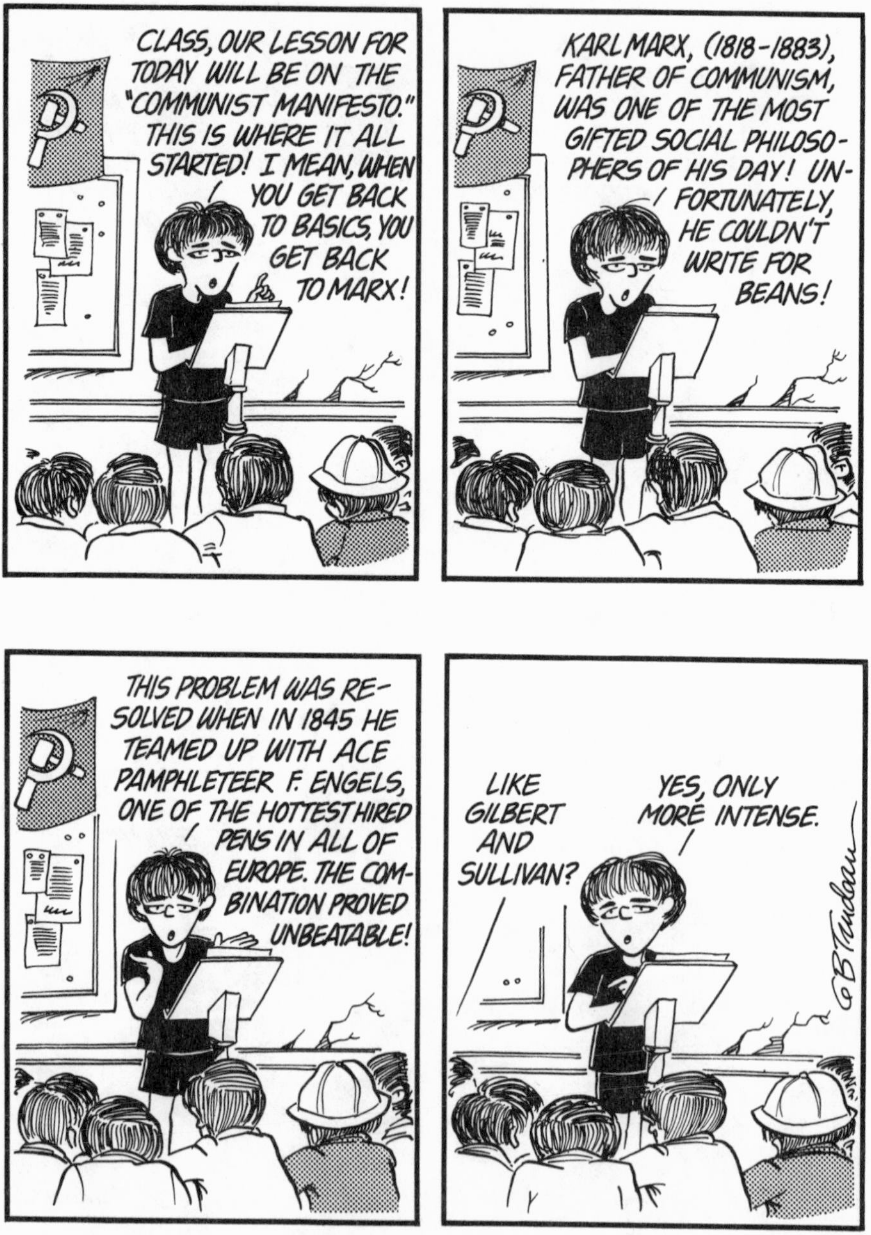
CLASS, OUR LESSON FOR TODAY WILL BE ON THE "COMMUNIST MANIFESTO." THIS IS WHERE IT ALL STARTED! I MEAN, WHEN YOU GET BACK TO BASICS, YOU GET BACK TO MARX!
KARL MARX, (1818-1883), FATHER OF COMMUNISM, WAS ONE OF THE MOST GIFTED SOCIAL PHILOSOPHERS OF HIS DAY! UNFORTUNATELY, HE COULDN'T WRITE FOR BEANS!
THIS PROBLEM WAS RESOLVED WHEN IN 1845 HE TEAMED UP WITH ACE PAMPHLETEER F. ENGELS, ONE OF THE HOTTEST HIRED PENS IN ALL OF EUROPE. THE COMBINATION PROVED UNBEATABLE!
LIKE GILBERT AND SULLIVAN?
YES, ONLY MORE INTENSE.
© B Trudeau

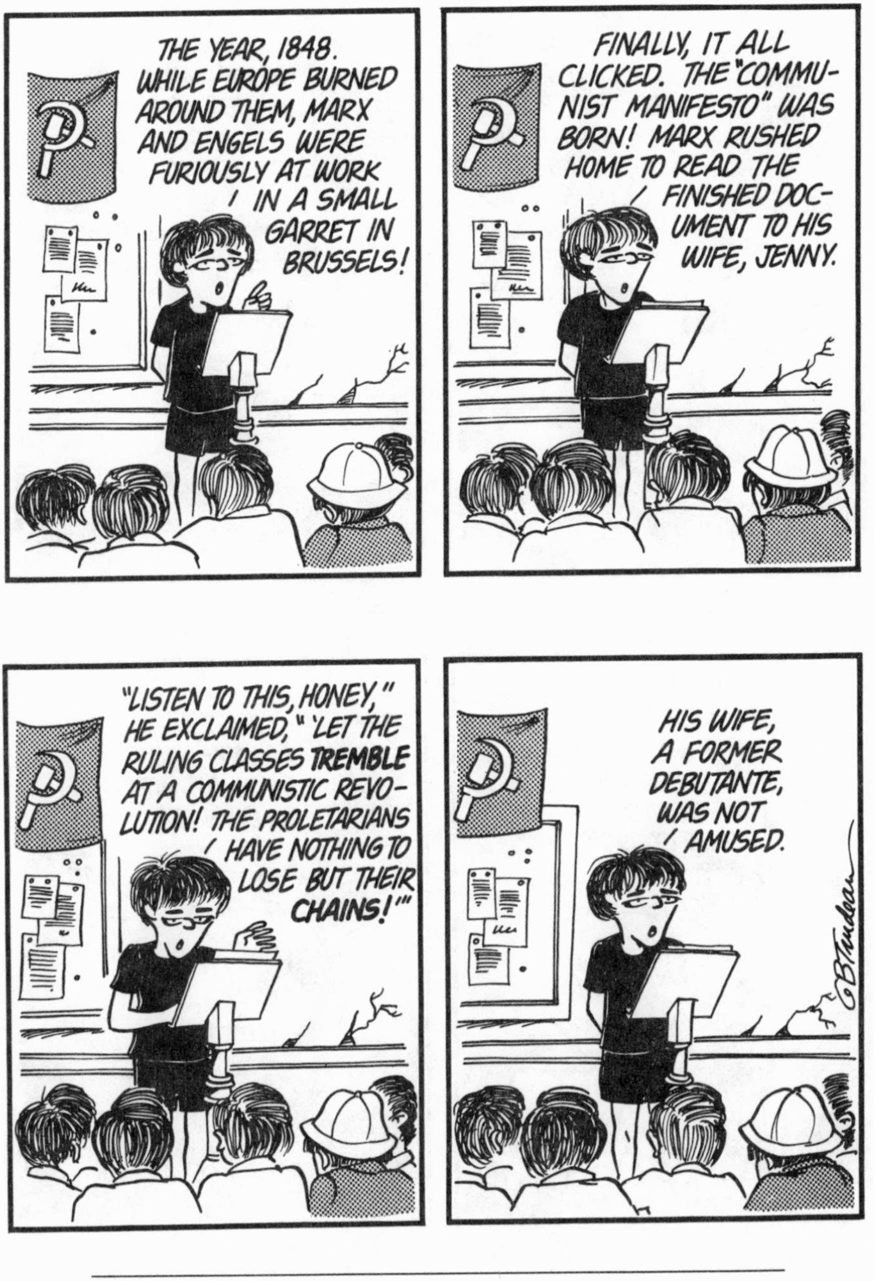
THE YEAR, 1848. WHILE EUROPE BURNED AROUND THEM, MARX AND ENGELS WERE FURIOUSLY AT WORK IN A SMALL GARRET IN BRUSSELS!
FINALLY, IT ALL CLICKED. THE "COMMUNIST MANIFESTO" WAS BORN! MARX RUSHED HOME TO READ THE FINISHED DOCUMENT TO HIS WIFE, JENNY.
"LISTEN TO THIS, HONEY," HE EXCLAIMED, "'LET THE RULING CLASSES TREMBLE AT A COMMUNISTIC REVOLUTION! THE PROLETARIANS HAVE NOTHING TO LOSE BUT THEIR CHAINS!'"
HIS WIFE, A FORMER DEBUTANTE, WAS NOT AMUSED.
©BTrudeau

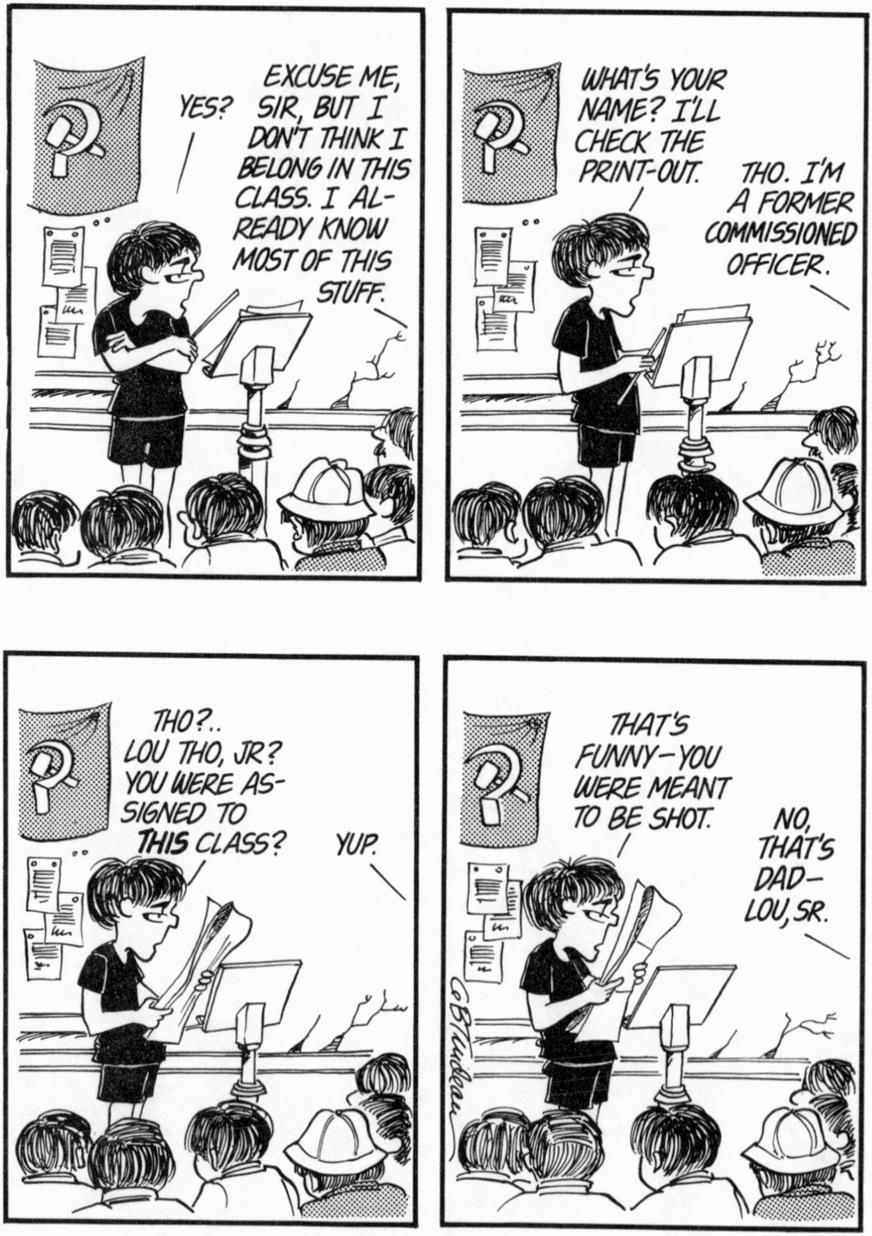
EXCUSE ME, SIR, BUT I DON'T THINK I BELONG IN THIS CLASS. I AL-READY KNOW MOST OF THIS STUFF.
YES?
WHAT'S YOUR NAME? I'LL CHECK THE PRINT-OUT.
THO. I'M A FORMER COMMISSIONED OFFICER.
THO?.. LOU THO, JR? YOU WERE AS-SIGNED TO THIS CLASS?
YUP.
THAT'S FUNNY—YOU WERE MEANT TO BE SHOT.
NO, THAT'S DAD—LOU, SR.

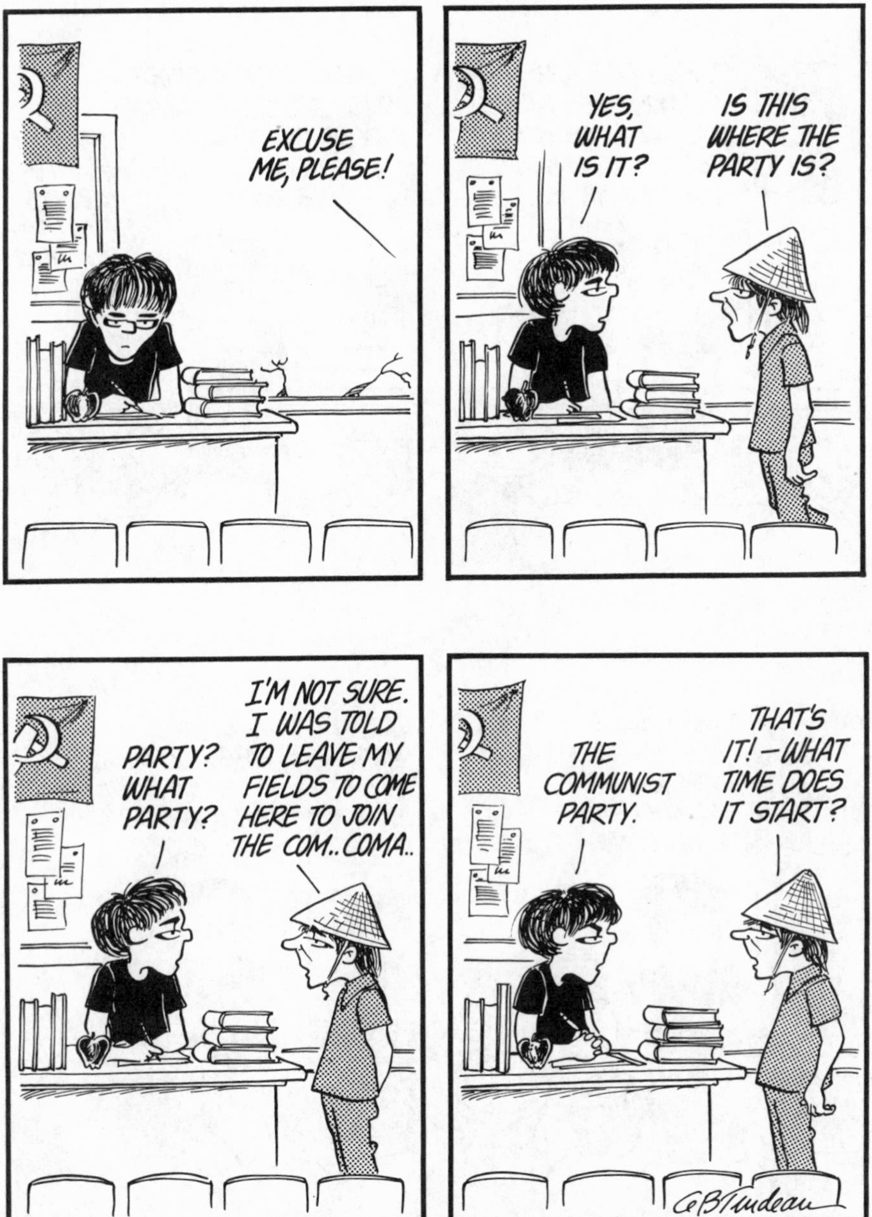

EXCUSE ME, PLEASE!
YES, WHAT IS IT?
IS THIS WHERE THE PARTY IS?
PARTY? WHAT PARTY?
I'M NOT SURE. I WAS TOLD TO LEAVE MY FIELDS TO COME HERE TO JOIN THE COM..COMA..
THE COMMUNIST PARTY.
THAT'S IT!—WHAT TIME DOES IT START?
GBTrudeau

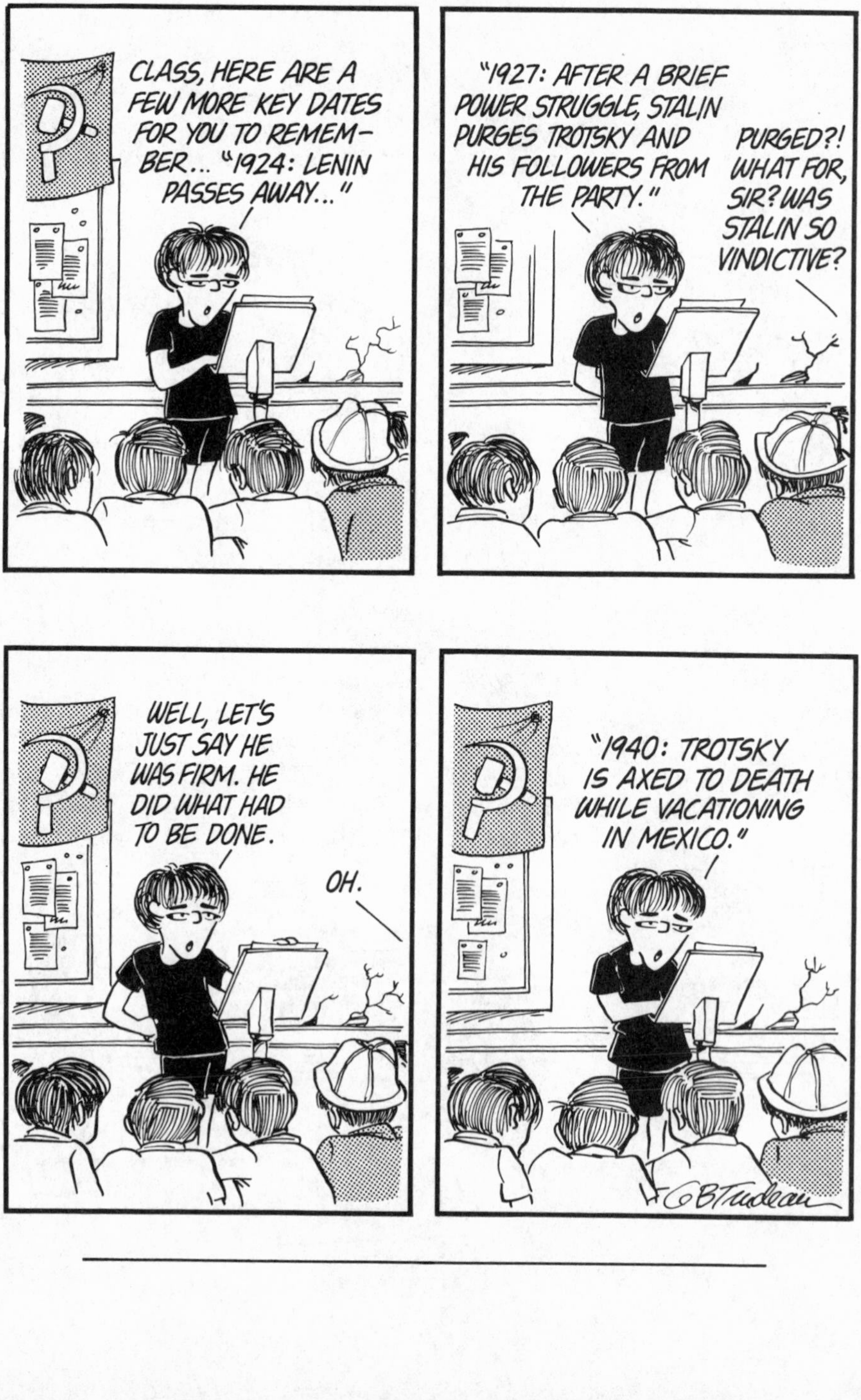
CLASS, HERE ARE A FEW MORE KEY DATES FOR YOU TO REMEMBER... "1924: LENIN PASSES AWAY..."
"1927: AFTER A BRIEF POWER STRUGGLE, STALIN PURGES TROTSKY AND HIS FOLLOWERS FROM THE PARTY."
PURGED?! WHAT FOR, SIR? WAS STALIN SO VINDICTIVE?
WELL, LET'S JUST SAY HE WAS FIRM. HE DID WHAT HAD TO BE DONE.
OH.
"1940: TROTSKY IS AXED TO DEATH WHILE VACATIONING IN MEXICO."
GBTrudeau

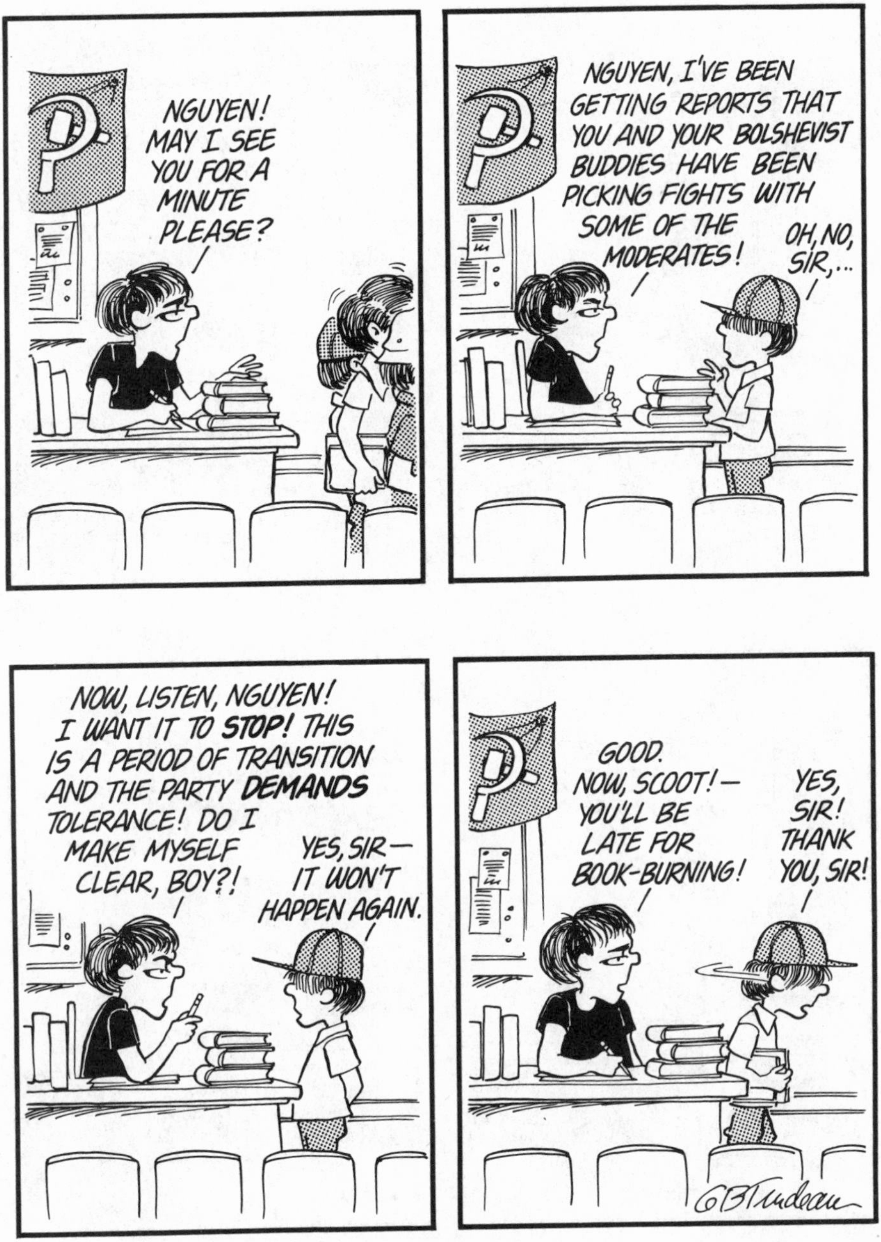
NGUYEN! MAY I SEE YOU FOR A MINUTE PLEASE?
NGUYEN, I'VE BEEN GETTING REPORTS THAT YOU AND YOUR BOLSHEVIST BUDDIES HAVE BEEN PICKING FIGHTS WITH SOME OF THE MODERATES!
OH, NO, SIR, ...
NOW, LISTEN, NGUYEN! I WANT IT TO **STOP!** THIS IS A PERIOD OF TRANSITION AND THE PARTY **DEMANDS** TOLERANCE! DO I MAKE MYSELF CLEAR, BOY?!
YES, SIR— IT WON'T HAPPEN AGAIN.
GOOD. NOW, SCOOT!— YOU'LL BE LATE FOR BOOK-BURNING!
YES, SIR! THANK YOU, SIR!
GBTrudeau

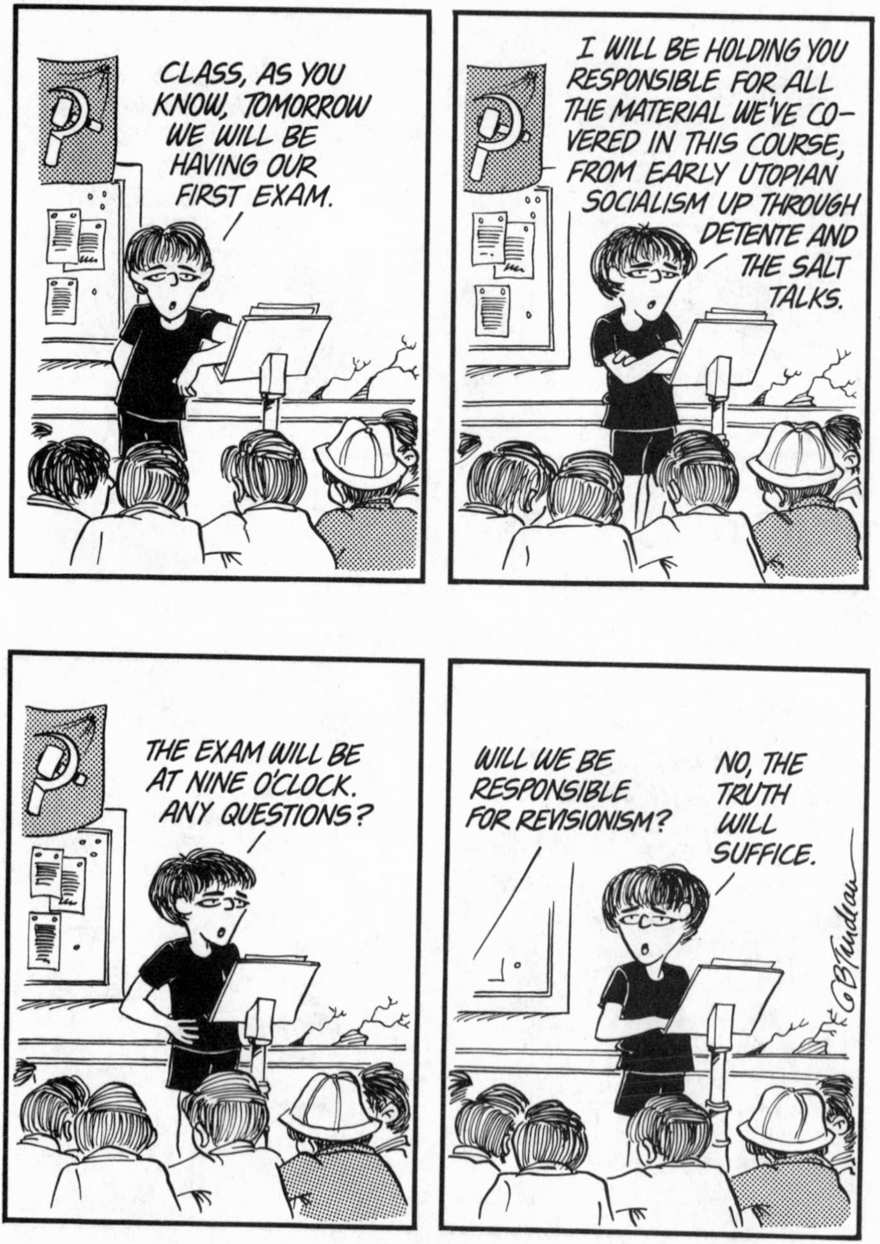

CLASS, AS YOU KNOW, TOMORROW WE WILL BE HAVING OUR FIRST EXAM.
I WILL BE HOLDING YOU RESPONSIBLE FOR ALL THE MATERIAL WE'VE COVERED IN THIS COURSE, FROM EARLY UTOPIAN SOCIALISM UP THROUGH DETENTE AND THE SALT TALKS.
THE EXAM WILL BE AT NINE O'CLOCK. ANY QUESTIONS?
WILL WE BE RESPONSIBLE FOR REVISIONISM?
NO, THE TRUTH WILL SUFFICE.
GBTrudeau

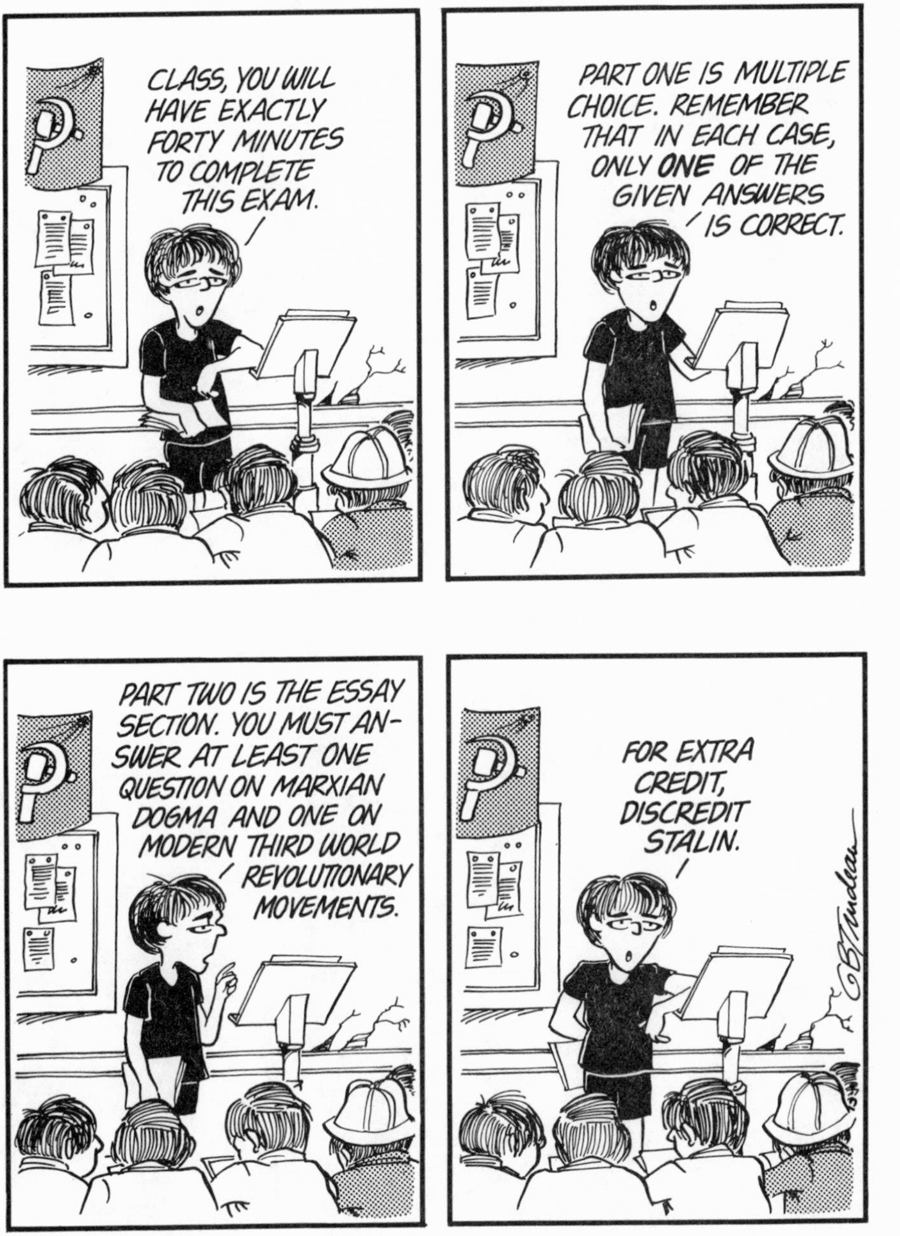
CLASS, YOU WILL HAVE EXACTLY FORTY MINUTES TO COMPLETE THIS EXAM.
PART ONE IS MULTIPLE CHOICE. REMEMBER THAT IN EACH CASE, ONLY ONE OF THE GIVEN ANSWERS IS CORRECT.
PART TWO IS THE ESSAY SECTION. YOU MUST ANSWER AT LEAST ONE QUESTION ON MARXIAN DOGMA AND ONE ON MODERN THIRD WORLD REVOLUTIONARY MOVEMENTS.
FOR EXTRA CREDIT, DISCREDIT STALIN.
GBTrudeau

COMRADE LIN, WOULD YOU PLEASE COME UP HERE AND PASS OUT THE CORRECTED EXAMS?
THO, A+... MINH, B.. LINHO, B+.. LAM, A...
AS YOU CAN SEE, MOST OF YOU DID QUITE WELL ON THE EXAM!
..THAM, F...
YOU WILL NOTE, HOWEVER, THAT ONE OF YOUR COMRADES FAILED. THE CENTRAL AUTHORITIES WERE NOT PLEASED!
UH.. THAM?.. THAM?
LET THIS BE A LESSON TO ALL OF US.
GBTrudeau

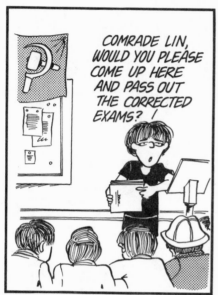

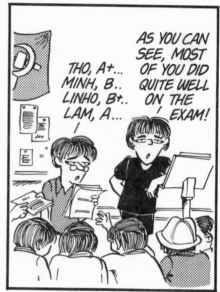

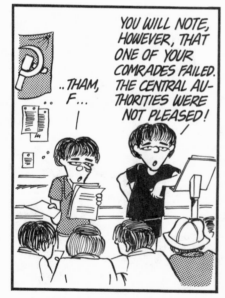

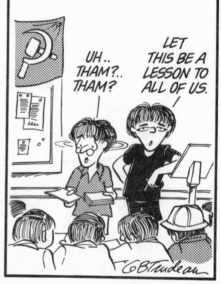

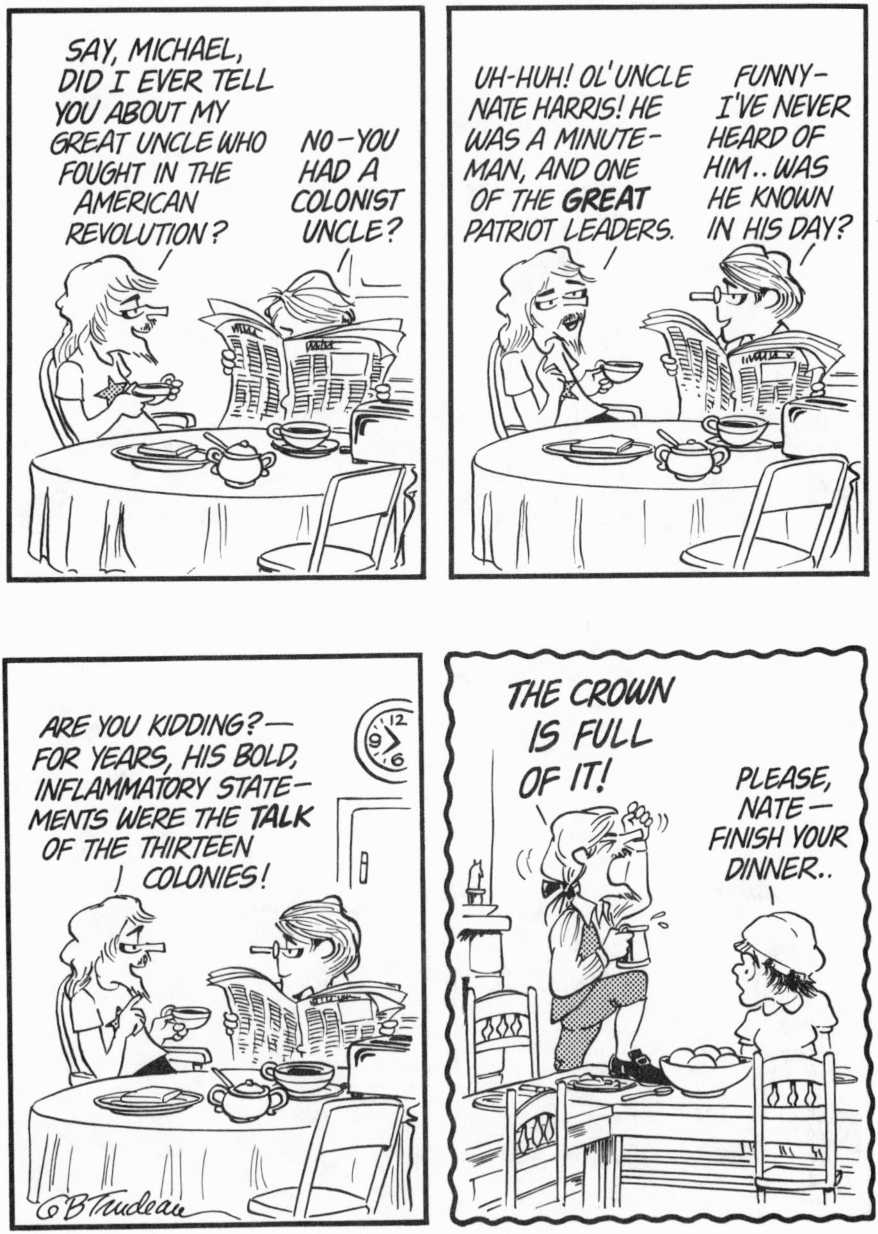
SAY, MICHAEL, DID I EVER TELL YOU ABOUT MY GREAT UNCLE WHO FOUGHT IN THE AMERICAN REVOLUTION?
NO—YOU HAD A COLONIST UNCLE?
UH-HUH! OL' UNCLE NATE HARRIS! HE WAS A MINUTE-MAN, AND ONE OF THE GREAT PATRIOT LEADERS.
FUNNY-I'VE NEVER HEARD OF HIM.. WAS HE KNOWN IN HIS DAY?
ARE YOU KIDDING?—FOR YEARS, HIS BOLD, INFLAMMATORY STATE-MENTS WERE THE TALK OF THE THIRTEEN COLONIES!
GB Trudeau
THE CROWN IS FULL OF IT!
PLEASE, NATE—FINISH YOUR DINNER..

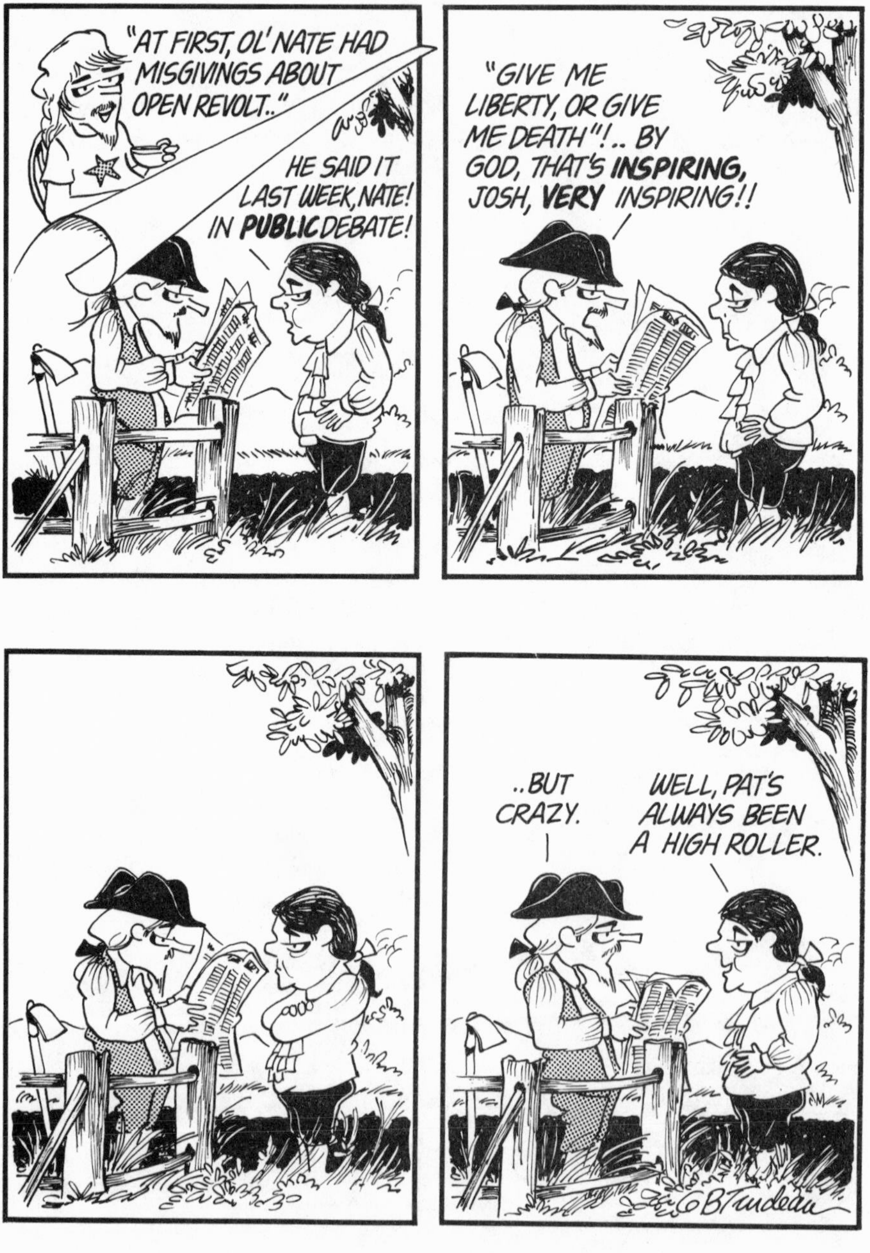
"AT FIRST, OL' NATE HAD MISGIVINGS ABOUT OPEN REVOLT.."
HE SAID IT LAST WEEK, NATE! IN **PUBLIC** DEBATE!
"GIVE ME LIBERTY, OR GIVE ME DEATH"!.. BY GOD, THAT'S **INSPIRING,** JOSH, **VERY** INSPIRING!!
..BUT CRAZY.
WELL, PAT'S ALWAYS BEEN A HIGH ROLLER.
G B Trudeau

AMY, I HAVE MADE A DECISION! I AM RESOLVED TO JOIN THE MINUTEMEN!
THE MINUTE-MEN?!
AYE— I AM A PATRIOT AND I MUST GO!
I REALIZE IT WON'T BE EASY, BUT I BELIEVE THIS IS THE RIGHT DECISION! AMY, I **BELONG** IN THE MINUTEMEN!
WELL, YOU'VE ALWAYS BEEN A FAST DRESSER..
SURE, AND I LOVE FIREARMS!
GB Trudeau

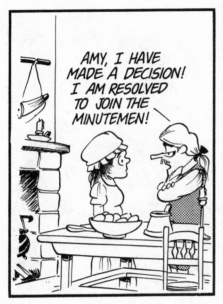

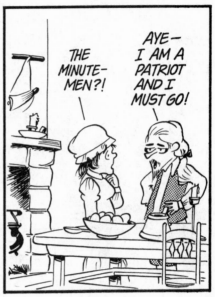

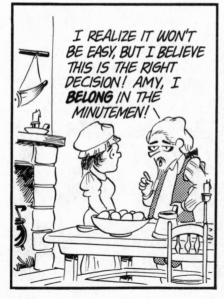

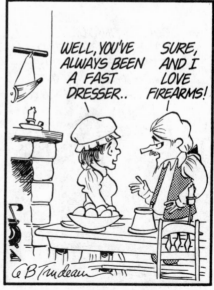

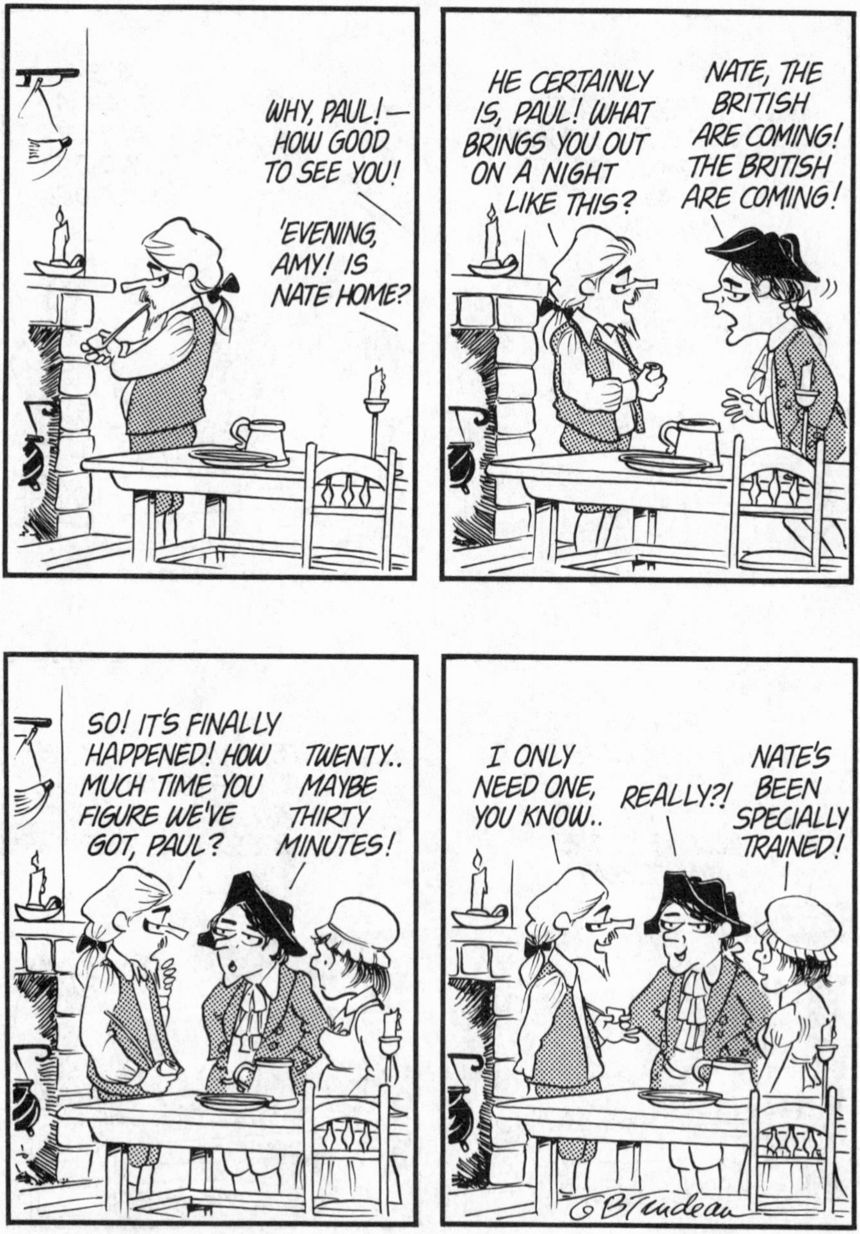
WHY, PAUL!— HOW GOOD TO SEE YOU!
'EVENING, AMY! IS NATE HOME?
HE CERTAINLY IS, PAUL! WHAT BRINGS YOU OUT ON A NIGHT LIKE THIS?
NATE, THE BRITISH ARE COMING! THE BRITISH ARE COMING!
SO! IT'S FINALLY HAPPENED! HOW MUCH TIME YOU FIGURE WE'VE GOT, PAUL?
TWENTY.. MAYBE THIRTY MINUTES!
I ONLY NEED ONE, YOU KNOW..
REALLY?!
NATE'S BEEN SPECIALLY TRAINED!
GBTrudeau

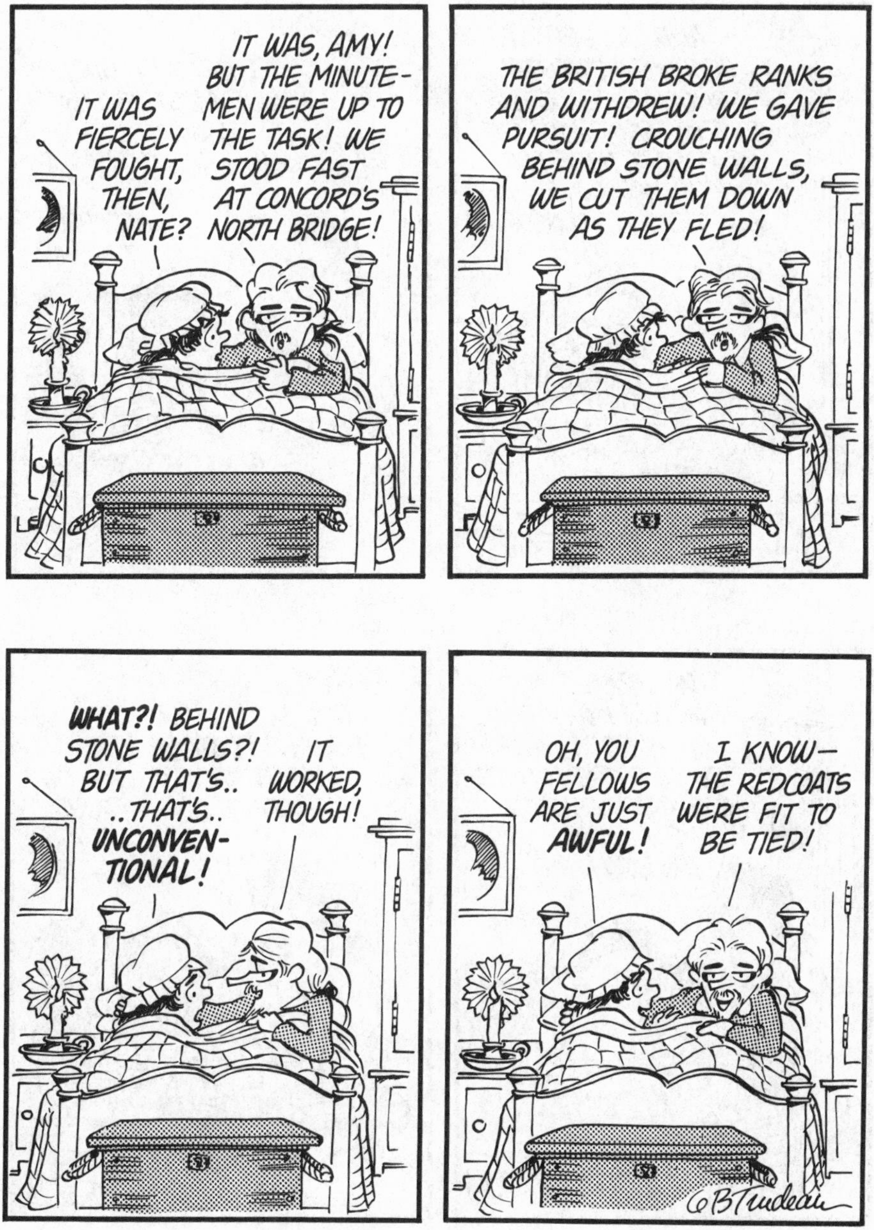
IT WAS FIERCELY FOUGHT, THEN, NATE?
IT WAS, AMY! BUT THE MINUTE-MEN WERE UP TO THE TASK! WE STOOD FAST AT CONCORD'S NORTH BRIDGE!
THE BRITISH BROKE RANKS AND WITHDREW! WE GAVE PURSUIT! CROUCHING BEHIND STONE WALLS, WE CUT THEM DOWN AS THEY FLED!
WHAT?! BEHIND STONE WALLS?! BUT THAT'S.. ..THAT'S.. UNCONVEN-TIONAL!
IT WORKED, THOUGH!
OH, YOU FELLOWS ARE JUST AWFUL!
I KNOW— THE REDCOATS WERE FIT TO BE TIED!
GBTrudeau

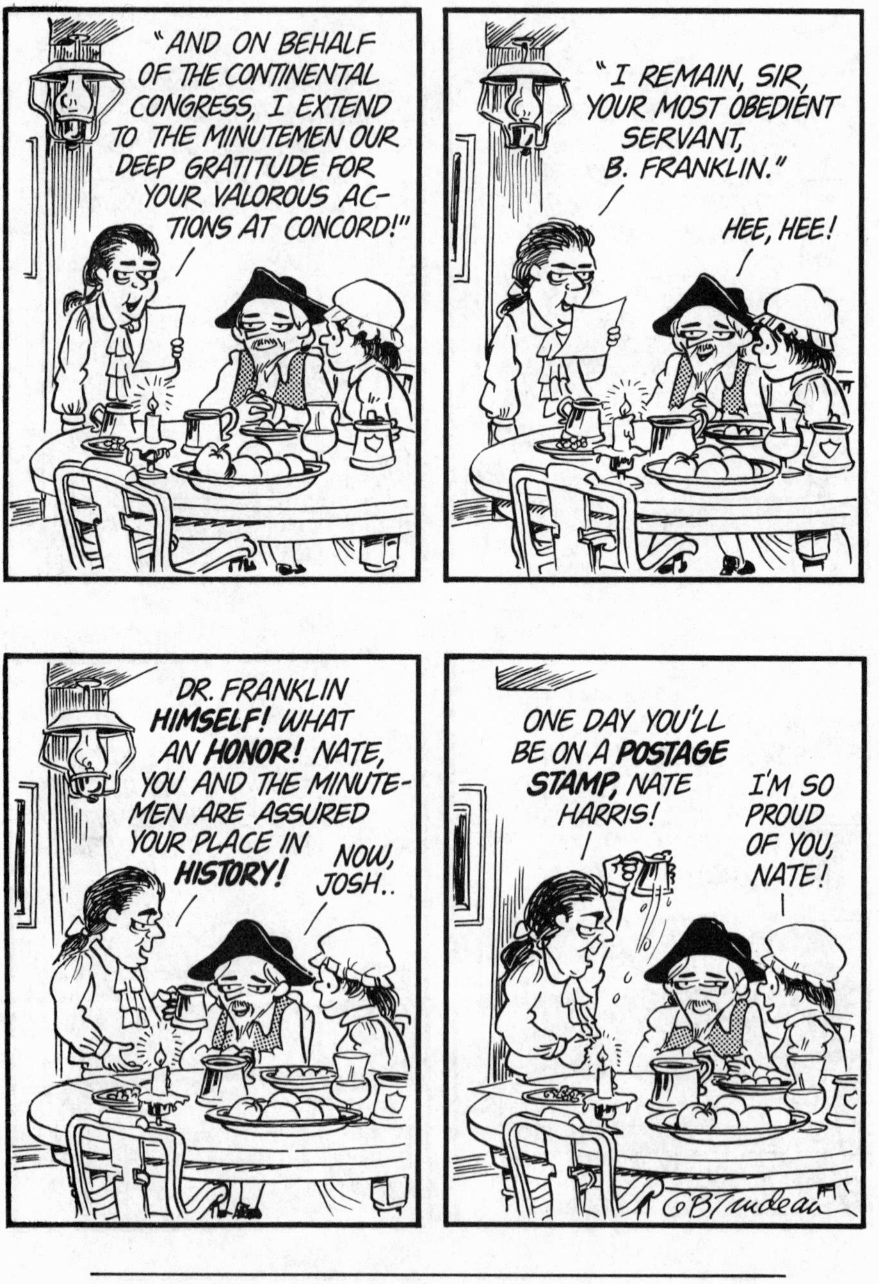
"AND ON BEHALF OF THE CONTINENTAL CONGRESS, I EXTEND TO THE MINUTEMEN OUR DEEP GRATITUDE FOR YOUR VALOROUS ACTIONS AT CONCORD!"
"I REMAIN, SIR, YOUR MOST OBEDIENT SERVANT, B. FRANKLIN."
HEE, HEE!
DR. FRANKLIN HIMSELF! WHAT AN HONOR! NATE, YOU AND THE MINUTEMEN ARE ASSURED YOUR PLACE IN HISTORY!
NOW, JOSH..
ONE DAY YOU'LL BE ON A POSTAGE STAMP, NATE HARRIS!
I'M SO PROUD OF YOU, NATE!
GBTrudeau

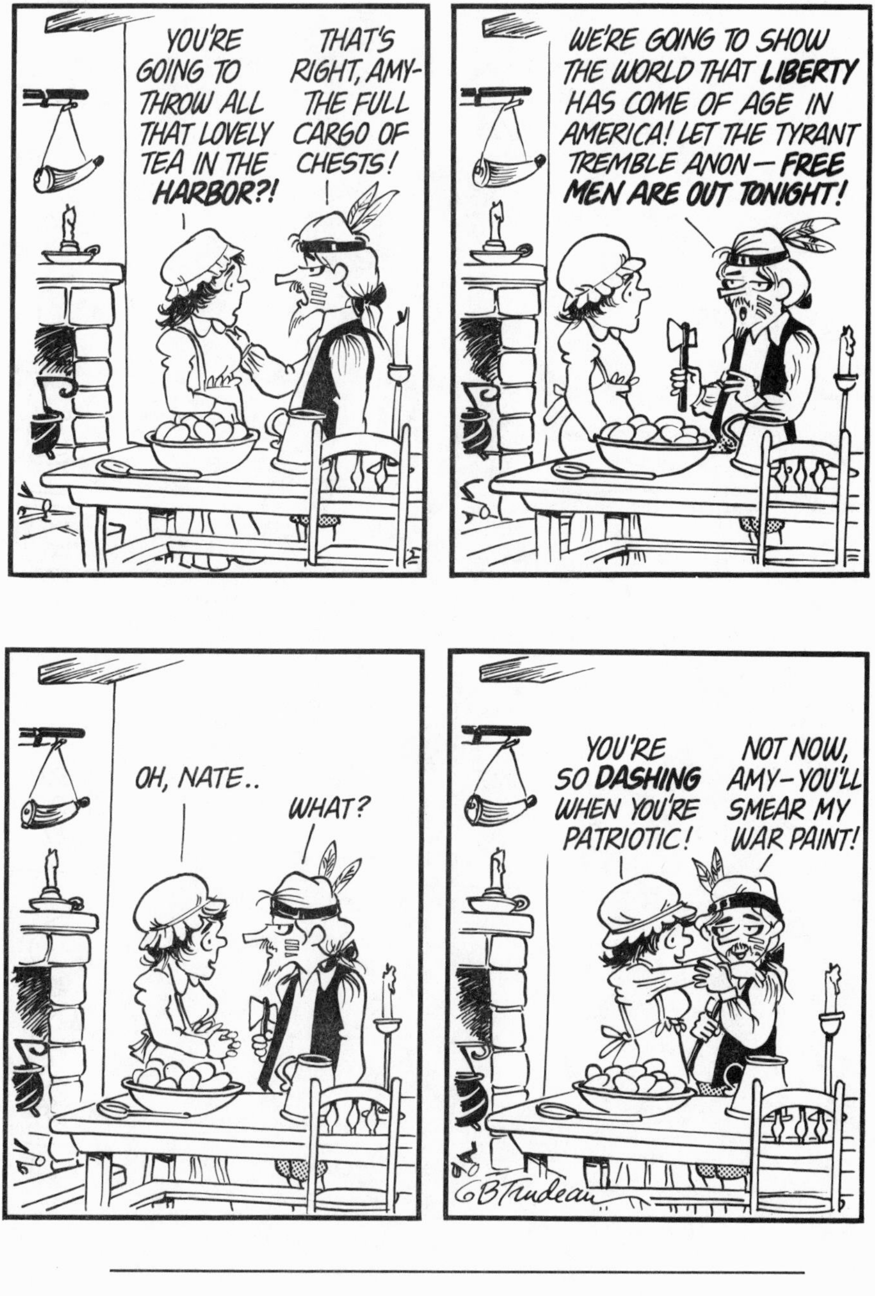
YOU'RE GOING TO THROW ALL THAT LOVELY TEA IN THE **HARBOR?!**
THAT'S RIGHT, AMY- THE FULL CARGO OF CHESTS!
WE'RE GOING TO SHOW THE WORLD THAT **LIBERTY** HAS COME OF AGE IN AMERICA! LET THE TYRANT TREMBLE ANON- **FREE MEN ARE OUT TONIGHT!**
OH, NATE..
WHAT?
YOU'RE SO **DASHING** WHEN YOU'RE PATRIOTIC!
NOT NOW, AMY- YOU'LL SMEAR MY WAR PAINT!
GBTrudeau

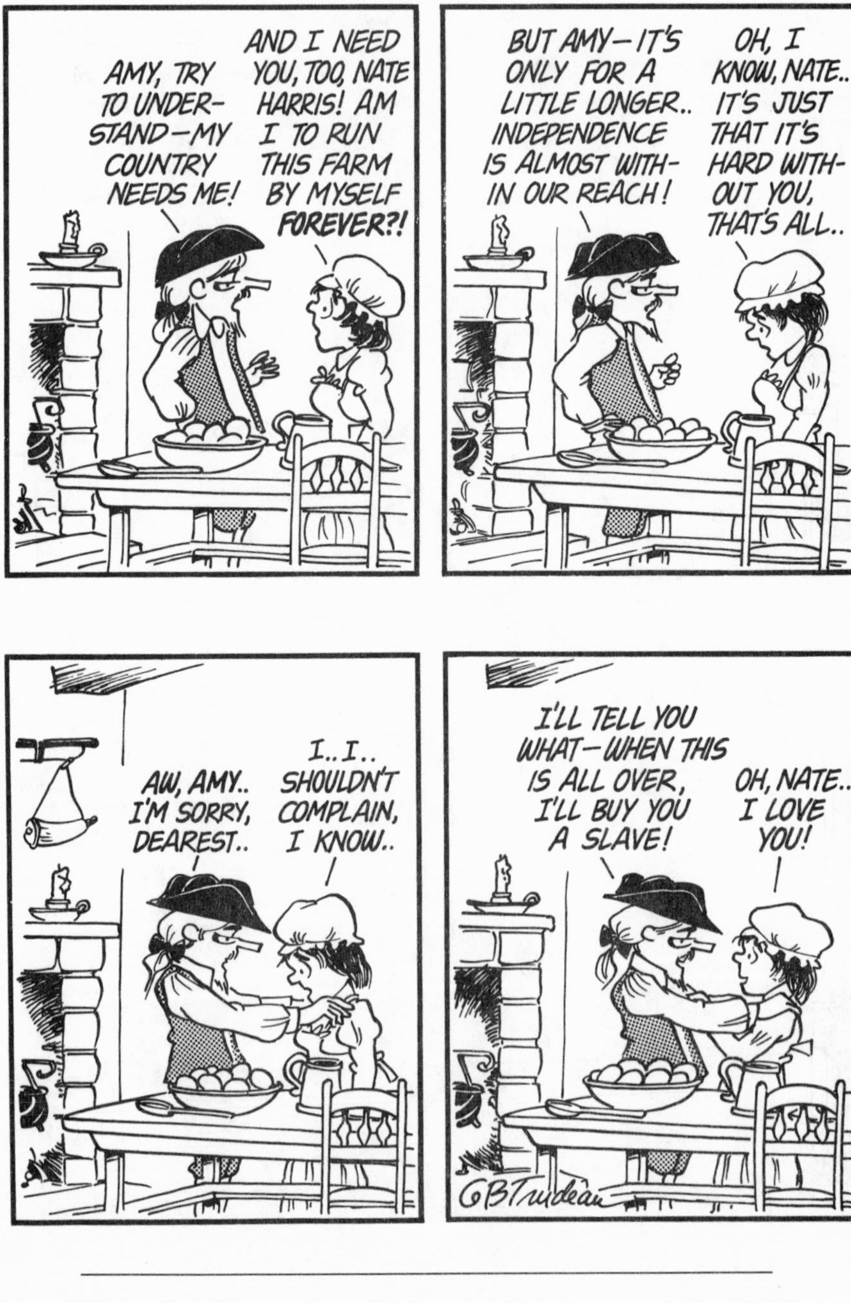

AMY, TRY TO UNDER-STAND—MY COUNTRY NEEDS ME!
AND I NEED YOU, TOO, NATE HARRIS! AM I TO RUN THIS FARM BY MYSELF FOREVER?!
BUT AMY—IT'S ONLY FOR A LITTLE LONGER.. INDEPENDENCE IS ALMOST WITH-IN OUR REACH!
OH, I KNOW, NATE.. IT'S JUST THAT IT'S HARD WITH-OUT YOU, THAT'S ALL..
AW, AMY.. I'M SORRY, DEAREST..
I..I.. SHOULDN'T COMPLAIN, I KNOW..
I'LL TELL YOU WHAT—WHEN THIS IS ALL OVER, I'LL BUY YOU A SLAVE!
OH, NATE.. I LOVE YOU!
GBTrudeau

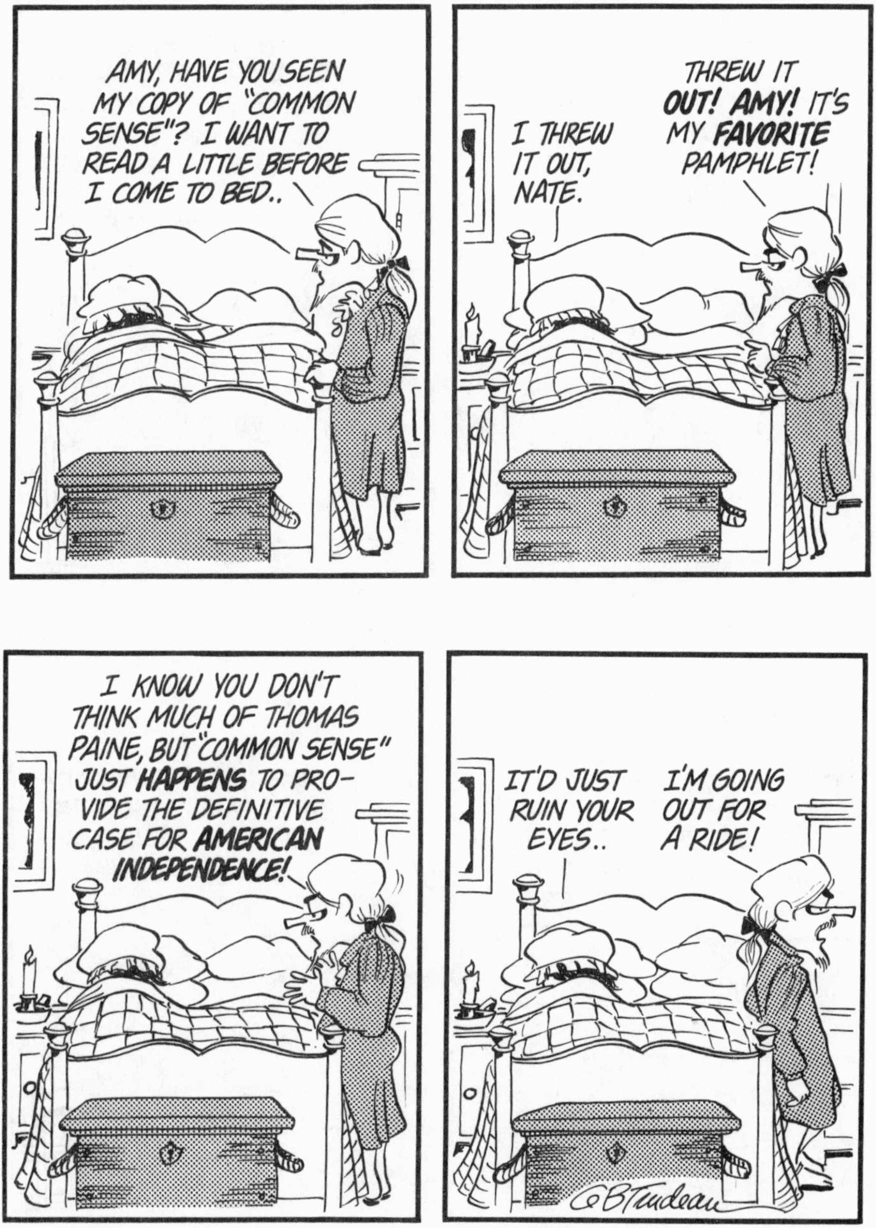
AMY, HAVE YOU SEEN MY COPY OF "COMMON SENSE"? I WANT TO READ A LITTLE BEFORE I COME TO BED..
I THREW IT OUT, NATE.
THREW IT OUT! AMY! IT'S MY FAVORITE PAMPHLET!
I KNOW YOU DON'T THINK MUCH OF THOMAS PAINE, BUT "COMMON SENSE" JUST HAPPENS TO PROVIDE THE DEFINITIVE CASE FOR AMERICAN INDEPENDENCE!
IT'D JUST RUIN YOUR EYES..
I'M GOING OUT FOR A RIDE!
GBTrudeau

WELL, AMY—IT WOULD SEEM THAT WORK ON THE DE-CLARATION IS PROCEEDING APACE!
JOHN ADAMS HAS PROMISED A STIRRING DOCUMENT! HE SAYS THAT THE RIGHTS AND PRIVILEGES OF **ALL** MEN WILL BE SECURED AND GUARANTEED!
OH, YES? WELL, WHAT DOES THE GREAT JOHN ADAMS HAVE TO SAY ABOUT THE RIGHTS OF THE OTHER HALF OF AMERICA—THE **WOMEN**!
ON THAT POINT, HE IS RESOLUTELY SILENT.
WELL, **ABIGAIL** ISN'T! SHE SAYS..
SAY, AMY—HOW'S THAT NEW QUILT COMING ALONG?
GBTrudeau

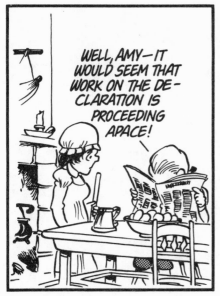

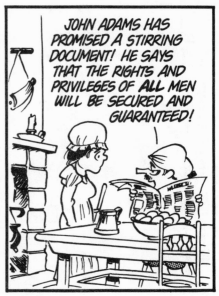

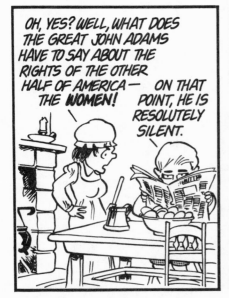

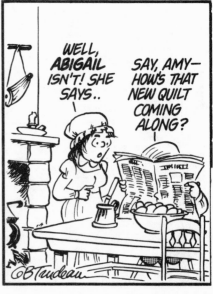

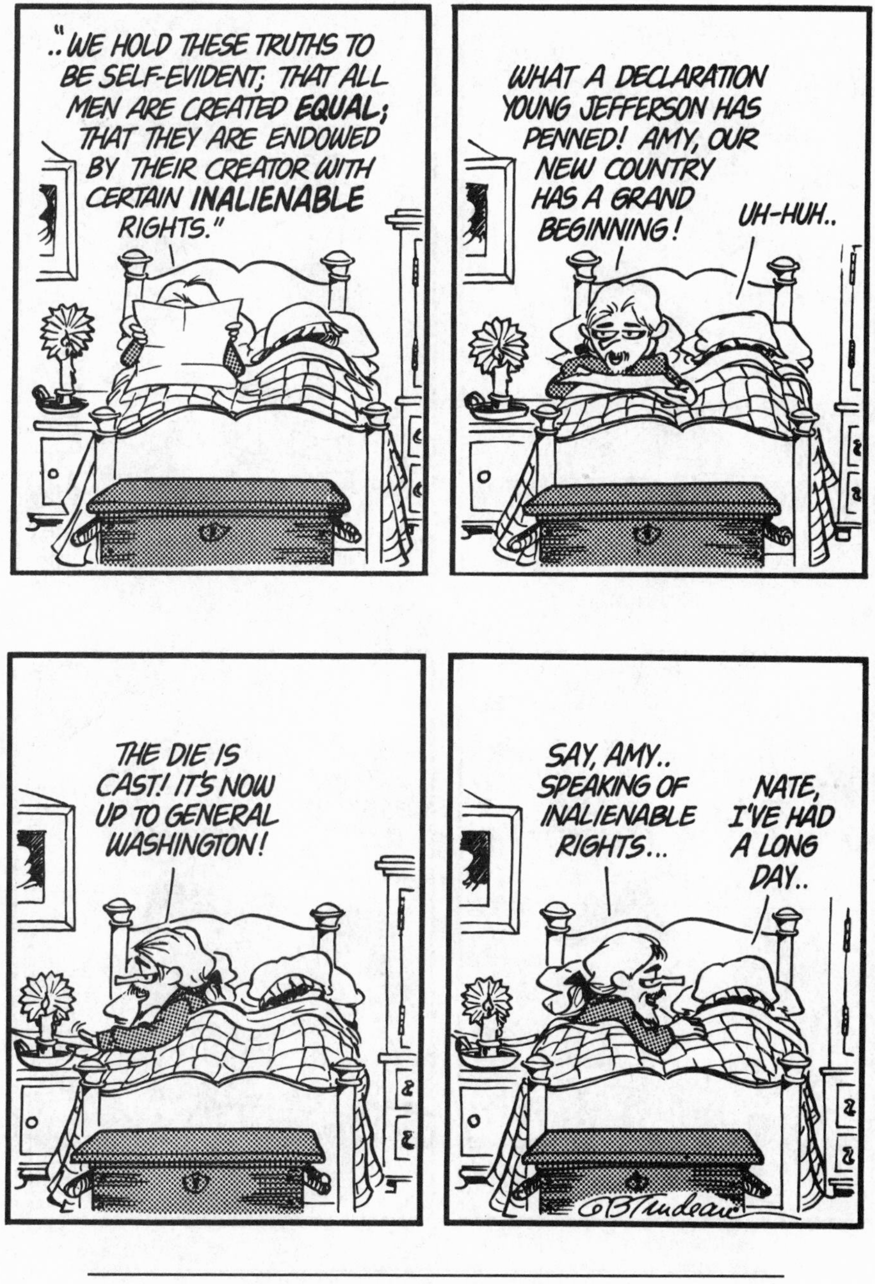

.."WE HOLD THESE TRUTHS TO BE SELF-EVIDENT; THAT ALL MEN ARE CREATED EQUAL; THAT THEY ARE ENDOWED BY THEIR CREATOR WITH CERTAIN INALIENABLE RIGHTS."
WHAT A DECLARATION YOUNG JEFFERSON HAS PENNED! AMY, OUR NEW COUNTRY HAS A GRAND BEGINNING!
UH-HUH..
THE DIE IS CAST! IT'S NOW UP TO GENERAL WASHINGTON!
SAY, AMY.. SPEAKING OF INALIENABLE RIGHTS...
NATE, I'VE HAD A LONG DAY..
©BTrudeau

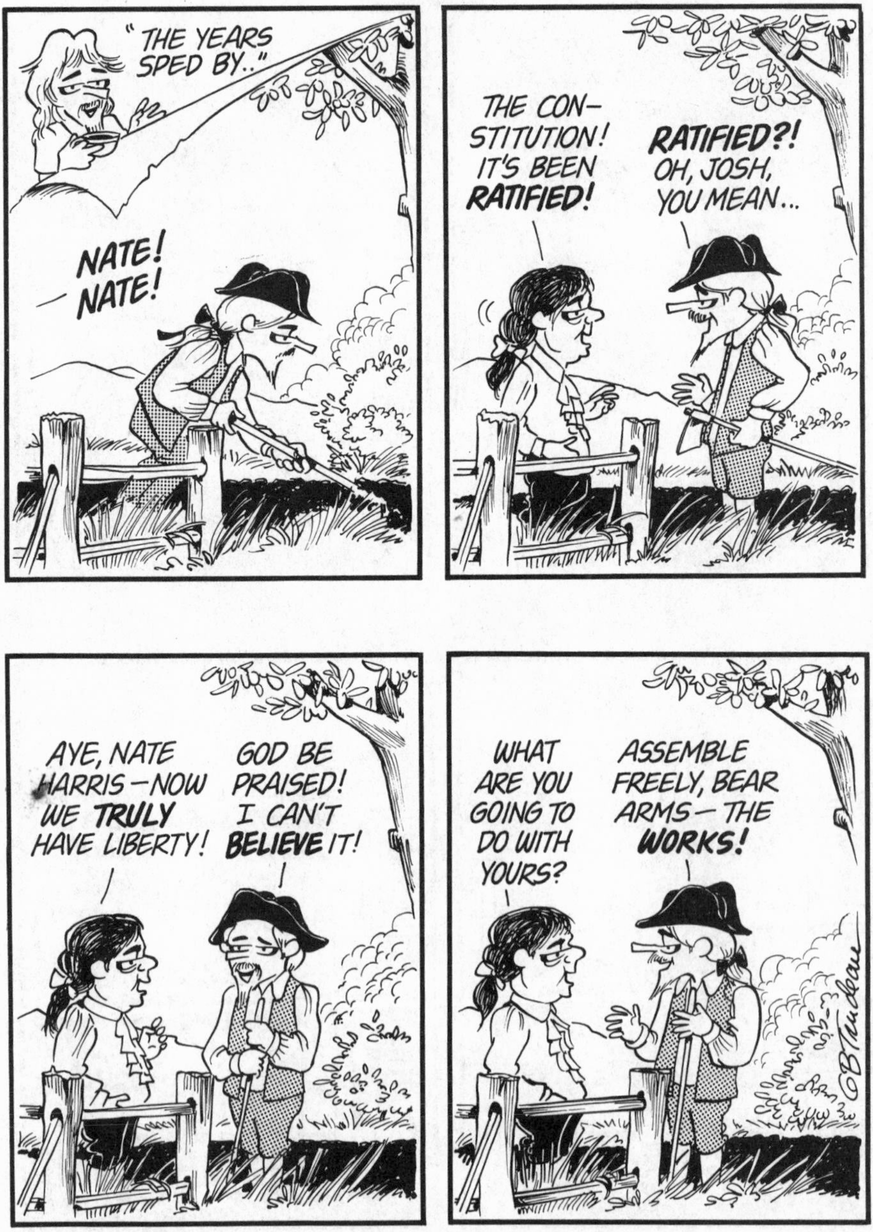
"THE YEARS SPED BY.."
NATE! NATE!
THE CON-STITUTION! IT'S BEEN RATIFIED!
RATIFIED?! OH, JOSH, YOU MEAN...
AYE, NATE HARRIS—NOW WE TRULY HAVE LIBERTY!
GOD BE PRAISED! I CAN'T BELIEVE IT!
WHAT ARE YOU GOING TO DO WITH YOURS?
ASSEMBLE FREELY, BEAR ARMS—THE WORKS!
©BTrudeau